Developmental and Educational Psychology

Developmental and Educational Psychology

Zack Wilson

CLANRYE INTERNATIONAL
www.clanryeinternational.com

Clanrye International,
750 Third Avenue, 9th Floor,
New York, NY 10017, USA

ISBN: 978-1-64726-111-5

Cataloging-in-Publication Data

Developmental and educational psychology / Zack Wilson.
p. cm.
Includes bibliographical references and index.
ISBN 978-1-64726-111-5
1. Developmental psychology. 2. Educational psychology. 3. Psychology.
4. Child psychology. I. Wilson, Zack.
BF713 .D48 2021
155--dc23

For information on all Clanrye International publications
visit our website at www.clanryeinternational.com

CLANRYE
INTERNATIONAL

Contents

Preface

The branch of psychology which focuses on human learning is known as educational psychology. It is associated with the study of memory, conceptual processes and differences between individuals for the purpose of formulating new strategies for learning processes in humans. Educational psychology relies heavily on another branch of psychology known as developmental psychology. This discipline studies how the feelings, behavior and thinking of an individual change throughout the life. Developmental psychology defines human cognitive development over different periods of development. Therefore, the developmental sequence of a student can provide information about the level and kind of knowledge which can be absorbed by them. This in turn can be useful in deciding the subject matter to be taught to them. This book is a valuable compilation of topics, ranging from the basic to the most complex advancements in the field of educational and developmental psychology. It provides significant information of this discipline to help develop a good understanding of this field and related fields. Those in search of information to further their knowledge will be greatly assisted by this book.

To facilitate a deeper understanding of the contents of this book a short introduction of every chapter is written below:

Chapter 1- The branch of psychology which seeks to study why and how human beings change over their life is referred to as developmental psychology. There are numerous important themes within this discipline such as nature and nurture, continuity and discontinuity and stability vs. change. This is an introductory chapter which will introduce briefly all these significant aspects of developmental psychology.

Chapter 2- The domain of psychology which deals with the scientific study of human learning is termed as educational psychology. Some of the important theories within this field are Piaget's theory of moral development, Lewin's field theory of learning and Tolman's sign theory of learning. This chapter has been carefully written to provide an easy understanding of these theories within educational psychology.

Chapter 3- The development of a child's muscles, bones as well as the ability to move around is termed as motor development. The different motor skills which fall under this field are broadly divided into gross motor skills and fine motor skills. The chapter closely examines these key motor skills as well as their principles of development to provide an extensive understanding of the subject.

Chapter 4- The branch of psychology which seeks to understand how children think, explore and figure things out is termed as cognitive development. There are a number of important theories within this field of study such as Jean Piaget theory, Lev Vygotsky theory and dual coding theory. This chapter discusses in detail these theories related to cognitive development.

Chapter 5- The mental quality through which human beings are able to learn from experience as well as adapt to new situations is termed as intelligence. There are a number of theories which deal with the conceptions of intelligence such as Sternberg's Triarchic theory intelligence, Spearman theory and Gardner's frames of mind. This chapter discusses in detail these theories and concepts related to intelligence.

Chapter 6- The activities which are aimed at improving awareness and identity, build human capital, and develop talents and potential are known as personal development. There are renowned philosophers who have developed theories related to this field such as Sigmund Freud and Erik Erikson. The topics elaborated in this chapter will help in gaining a better perspective about personal and social development as well as the theories related to it.

Chapter 7- The entirety of all biological processes through which particular characteristics are transmitted from parents to their offspring is called heredity, or inheritance. The topics elaborated in this chapter will help in gaining a better perspective about heredity as well as the factors which affect growth and development in children.

I would like to share the credit of this book with my editorial team who worked tirelessly on this book. I owe the completion of this book to the never-ending support of my family, who supported me throughout the project.

Zack Wilson

1

Developmental Psychology

The branch of psychology which seeks to study why and how human beings change over their life is referred to as developmental psychology. There are numerous important themes within this discipline such as nature and nurture, continuity and discontinuity and stability vs. change. This is an introductory chapter which will introduce briefly all these significant aspects of developmental psychology.

People go through many changes over the course of their lives. Development describes the growth of humans throughout their lifespan, from conception to death. Psychologists strive to understand and explain how and why people change throughout life. While many of these changes are normal and expected, they can still pose challenges that people sometimes need extra assistance to manage.

By understanding the process of normative development, professionals are better able to spot potential problems and provide early interventions that can result in better outcomes. Developmental psychologists can work with people of all ages to treat issues and support growth, although some choose to specialize in a specific area such as childhood, adulthood, or old age.

Developmental psychology is the branch of psychology that focuses on how people grow and change over the course of a lifetime. Those who specialize in this field are not just concerned with the physical changes that occur as people grow; they also look at the social, emotional, and cognitive development that occurs throughout life.

Some of the many issues that developmental psychologists may help patients deal with include:

- Motor skill development.
- Language acquisition.
- Emotional development.
- The emergence of self-awareness and self-concept.
- Cognitive development during childhood and throughout life.
- Social and cultural influences on child development.
- Personality development
- Moral reasoning.
- Developmental challenges and learning disabilities.

These professionals spend a great deal of time investigating and observing how these processes occur under normal circumstances, but they are also interested in learning about things that can disrupt developmental processes.

By better understanding how and why people change and grow, developmental psychologists can help people live up to their full potential. Understanding the course of normal human development and recognizing potential problems early on is important, because untreated developmental problems may lead to difficulties with depression, low self-esteem, frustration, and low achievement in school.

Developmental Psychology Theories

Developmental psychologists often utilize a number of theories to think about different aspects of human development. For example, a psychologist assessing intellectual development in a child might consider Piaget's theory of cognitive development, which outlined the key stages that children go through as they learn. A psychologist working with a child might also want to consider how the child's relationships with care givers influences his or her behavior and so turn to Bowlby's theory of attachment.

Psychologists are also interested in looking at how social relationships influence the development of both children and adults. Erikson's theory of psychosocial development and Vygotsky's theory of sociocultural development are two popular theoretical frameworks that address the social influences on the developmental process. Each approach tends to stress different aspects of development such as mental, social, or parental influences on how children grow and progress.

While development tends to follow a fairly predictable pattern, there are times when things might go off course. Parents often focus on what are known as developmental milestones, which represent abilities that most children tend to display by a certain point in development. These typically focus on one of four different areas: physical, cognitive, social/emotional, and communication. For example, walking is one physical milestone that most children achieve sometime between the ages of 9 and 15 months. If a child is not walking or attempting to walk by 16 to 18 months, parents might consider consulting with their family physician to determine if a developmental issue might be present.

While all children develop at different rates, when a child fails to meet certain milestones by a certain age, there may be cause for concern. By being aware of these milestones, parents can seek assistance and healthcare professionals can offer interventions that can help kids overcome developmental delays.

These professionals often evaluate children to determine if a developmental delay might be present, or they might work with elderly patients who are facing health concerns associated with old age such as cognitive declines, physical struggles, emotional difficulties, or degenerative brain disorders.

Developmental psychologists can provide support to individuals at all points of life who may be facing developmental issues or problems related to aging.

Concerns at Different Stages of Development

As you might imagine, developmental psychologists often break down development according to various phases of life. Each of these periods of development represents a time when different milestones are typically achieved. People may face particular challenges at each point, and developmental psychologists can often help people who might be struggling with problems to get back on track.

1. Prenatal: The prenatal period is of interest to developmental psychologists who seek to understand how the earliest influences on development can impact later growth during childhood. Psychologists may look at how primary reflexes emerge before birth, how fetuses respond to stimuli in the womb, and the sensations and perceptions that fetuses are capable of detecting prior to birth. Developmental psychologists may also look at potential problems such as Down syndrome, maternal drug use, and inherited diseases that might have an impact on the course of future development.

2. Early Childhood: The period from infancy through early childhood is a time of remarkable growth and change. Developmental psychologists look at things such as the physical, cognitive, and emotional growth that takes place during this critical period of development. In addition to providing interventions for potential developmental problems at this point, psychologists are also focused on helping kids achieve their full potential. Parents and healthcare experts are often on the lookout to ensure that kids are growing properly, receiving adequate nutrition, and achieving cognitive milestones appropriate for their age.

3. Middle Childhood: This period of development is marked by both physical maturation and increased importance of social influences as children make their way through elementary school. Kids begin to make their mark on the world as they form friendships, gain competency through schoolwork, and continue to build their unique sense of self. Parents may seek the assistance of a developmental psychologist to help kids deal with potential problems that might arise at this age including social, emotional, and mental health issues.

4. Adolescence: The teenage years are often the subject of considerable interest as children experience the psychological turmoil and transition that often accompanies this period of development. Psychologists such as Erik Erikson were especially interested in looking at how navigating this period leads to identity formation. At this age, kids often test limits and explore new identities as they explore the question of who they are and who they want to be. Developmental psychologists can help support teens as they deal with some of the challenging issues unique to the adolescent period including puberty, emotional turmoil, and social pressure.

5. Early Adulthood: This period of life is often marked by forming and maintaining relationships. Forming bonds, intimacy, close friendships, and starting a family are often critical milestones during early adulthood. Those who can build and sustain such relationships tend to experience connectedness and social support while those who struggle with such relationships may be left feeling alienated and lonely. People facing such issues might seek the assistance of a developmental psychologist in order to build healthier relationships and combat emotional difficulties.

6. Middle Adulthood: This stage of life tends to center on developing a sense of purpose and contributing to society. Erikson described this as the conflict between generativity and stagnation. Those who engage in the world contribute things that will outlast them, and leave a mark on the next generation emerge with a sense of purpose. Activities such as

careers, families, group memberships, and community involvement are all things that can contribute to this feeling of generativity.

7. Old Age: The senior years are often viewed as a period of poor health, yet many older adults are capable of remaining active and busy well into their 80s and 90s. Increased health concerns mark this period of development, and some individuals may experience mental declines related to dementia. Erikson also viewed the elder years as a time of reflection back on life. Those who are able to look back and see a life well lived emerge with a sense of wisdom and readiness to face the end of their lives, while those who look back with regret may be left with feelings of bitterness and despair. Developmental psychologists may work with elderly patients to help them cope with issues related to the aging process.

Diagnosis of a Developmental Issue

To determine if a developmental problem is present, a psychologist or other highly trained professional may administer either a developmental screening or evaluation. For children, such an evaluation typically involves interviews with parents and other caregivers to learn about behaviors they may have observed, a review of a child's medical history, and standardized testing to measure functioning in terms of communication, social/emotional skills, physical/motor development, and cognitive skills. If a problem is found to be present, the patient may then be referred to a specialist such as a speech-language pathologist, physical therapist, or occupational therapist.

Receiving a diagnosis of a developmental issue can often feel both confusing and frightening, particularly when it is your child who is affected. Once you or your loved one has received a diagnosis of a developmental issue, spend some time learning as much as you can about the diagnosis and available treatments. Prepare a list of questions and concerns you may have and discuss these issues with your doctor, developmental psychologist, and other healthcare professionals who may be part of the treatment team. By taking an active role in the process, you will feel better informed and equipped to tackle the next steps in the treatment process.

Themes in Developmental Psychology

Nature and Nurture

The nature versus nurture debate involves the extent to which particular aspects of behavior are a product of either inherited (i.e., genetic) or acquired (i.e., learned) influences.

Nature is what we think of as pre-wiring and is influenced by genetic inheritance and other biological factors. Nurture is generally taken as the influence of external factors after conception, e.g., the product of exposure, life experiences and learning on an individual. The nature-nurture debate is concerned with the relative contribution that both influences make to human behavior such as personality, cognitive traits, temperament and psychopathology.

It has long been known that certain physical characteristics are biologically determined by genetic inheritance. Color of eyes, straight or curly hair, pigmentation of the skin and certain diseases (such as Huntingdon's chorea) are all a function of the genes we inherit.

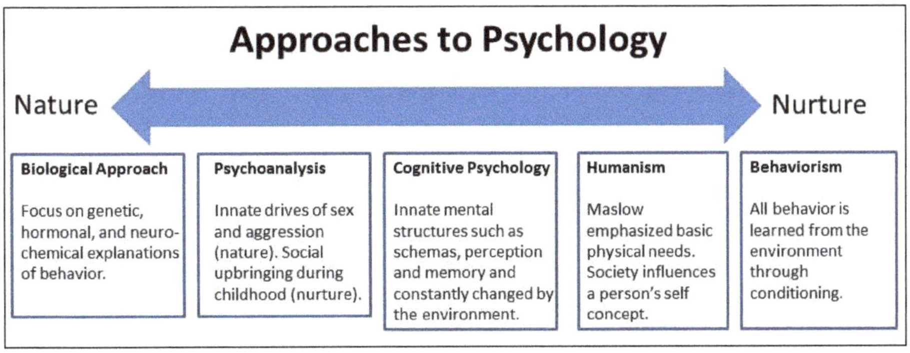

These facts have led many to speculate as to whether psychological characteristics such as behavioral tendencies, personality attributes, and mental abilities are also "wired in" before we are even born.

Those who adopt an extreme hereditary position are known as nativists. Their basic assumption is that the characteristics of the human species as a whole are a product of evolution and that individual difference are due to each person's unique genetic code. In general, the earlier a particular ability appears, the more likely it is to be under the influence of genetic factors. Estimates of genetic influence are called heritability.

Examples of an extreme nature positions in psychology include Chomsky, who proposed language is gained through the use of an innate language acquisition device. Another example of nature is Freud's theory of aggression as being an innate drive (called Thanatos).

Characteristics and differences that are not observable at birth, but which emerge later in life, are regarded as the product of maturation. That is to say, we all have an inner "biological clock" which switches on (or off) types of behavior in a pre-programmed way.

The classic example of the way this affects our physical development are the bodily changes that occur in early adolescence at puberty. However, nativists also argue that maturation governs the emergence of attachment in infancy, language acquisition and even cognitive development as a whole.

In practice, hardly anyone today accepts either of the extreme positions. There are simply too many "facts" on both sides of the argument which are inconsistent with an "all or nothing" view.

So instead of asking whether psychological traits are influenced by nature or nurture the question has been reformulated as "How much?" That is to say, given that heredity and environment both influence the person we become, which is the more important? This question was first framed by Francis Galton in the late 19th century. Galton (himself a relative of Charles Darwin) was convinced that intellectual ability was largely inherited and that the tendency for "genius" to run in families was the outcome of a natural superiority.

This view has cropped up time and again in the history of psychology and has stimulated much of the research into intelligence testing. A modern proponent is the American psychologist Arthur Jenson. Finding that the average I.Q. scores of black Americans were significantly lower than whites he went on to argue that genetic factors were mainly responsible – even going so far as to suggest that intelligence is 80% inherited.

The storm of controversy that developed around Jenson's claims was not mainly due to logical and empirical weaknesses in his argument. It was more to do with the social and political implications that are often drawn from research that claims to demonstrate natural inequalities between social groups.

Galton himself in 1883 suggested that human society could be improved by "better breeding." In the 1920's the American Eugenics Society campaigned for the sterilization of men and women in psychiatric hospitals. Today in Britain many believe that the immigration policies are designed to discriminate against Black and Asian ethnic groups.

For many environmentalists there is a barely disguised right-wing agenda behind the work of the behavioral geneticists. In their view, part of the difference in the I.Q. scores of different ethnic groups are due to inbuilt biases in the methods of testing.

More fundamentally, they believe that differences in intellectual ability are a product of social inequalities in access to material resources and opportunities. To put it simply children brought up in the ghetto tend to score lower on tests because they are denied the same life chances as more privileged members of society.

Now we can see why the nature-nurture debate has become such a hotly contested issue. What begins as an attempt to understand the causes of behavioral differences often develops into a politically motivated dispute about distributive justice and power in society.

What's more, this doesn't only apply to the debate over I.Q. It is equally relevant to the psychology of sex and gender, where the question of how much of the (alleged) differences in male and female behavior is due to biology and how much to culture is just as controversial.

Empiricism (Extreme Nurture Position)

At the other end of the spectrum are the environmentalists – also known as empiricists. Their basic assumption is that at birth the human mind is a tabula rasa (a blank slate) and that this is gradually "filled" as a result of experience (e.g., behaviorism).

From this point of view, psychological characteristics and behavioral differences that emerge through infancy and childhood are the results of learning. It is how you are brought up (nurture) that governs the psychologically significant aspects of child development and the concept of maturation applies only to the biological.

For example, Bandura's social learning theory states that aggression is learned from the environment through observation and imitation. This is seen in his famous Bobo doll experiment. Also, Skinner believed that language is learnt from other people via behavior shaping techniques.

Freud stated that events in our childhood have a great influence on our adult lives, shaping our personality. He thought that parenting is of primary importance to a child's development, and the family as the most importance feature of nurture was a common theme throughout twentieth century psychology (which was dominated by environmentalists' theories).

Behavioral Genetics

Researchers in the field of behavioral genetics study variation in behavior as it is affected by genes, which are the units of heredity passed down from parents to offspring.

"We now know that DNA differences are the major systematic source of psychological differences between us. Environmental effects are important but what we have learned in recent years is that they are mostly random – unsystematic and unstable – which means that we cannot do much about them.

Behavioral genetics has enabled psychology to quantify the relative contribution of nature and nurture with regard to specific psychological traits. One way to do this is to study relatives who share the same genes (nature) but a different environment (nurture). Adoption acts as a natural experiment which allows researchers to do this.

Empirical studies have consistently showed that adoptive children show greater resemblance to their biological parents, rather than their adoptive, or environmental parents.

Another way of studying heredity is by comparing the behavior of twins, who can either be identical (sharing the same genes) or non-identical (sharing 50% of genes). Like adoption studies, twin studies support the first rule of behavior genetics; that psychological traits are extremely heritable, about 50% on average.

The Twins in Early Development Study (TEDS) revealed correlations between twins on a range of behavioral traits, such as personality (empathy and hyperactivity) and components of reading such as phonetics.

Polygenic Inheritance

Rather than the presence or absence of single genes being the determining factor that accounts for psychological traits, behavioral genetics has demonstrated that multiple genes – often thousands, collectively contribute to specific behaviours.

Thus, psychological traits follow a polygenic mode of inheritance (as opposed to being determined by a single gene). Depression is a good example of a polygenic trait, which is thought to be influenced by around 1000 genes.

This means a person with a lower number of these genes (under 500) would have a lower risk of experiencing depression than someone with a higher number.

The Nature of Nurture

Nurture assumes that correlations between environmental factors and psychological outcomes are caused environmentally. For example, how much parents read with their children and how well children learn to read appear to be related. Other examples include environmental stress and its effect on depression.

However, behavioral genetics argues that what look like environmental effects are to a large extent really a reflection of genetic differences. People select, modify and create environments correlated with their genetic disposition. This means that what sometimes appears to be an environmental influence (nurture) is a genetic influence (nature).

So, children that are genetically predisposed to be competent readers will be happy to listen to their parents read them stories, and be more likely to encourage this interaction.

Interaction Effects

However, in recent years there has been a growing realization that the question of "how much" behavior is due to heredity and "how much" to the environment may itself be the wrong question. Take intelligence as an example. Like almost all types of human behavior, it is a complex, many-sided phenomenon which reveals itself (or not) in a great variety of ways.

The "how much" question assumes that psychological traits can all be expressed numerically and that the issue can be resolved in a quantitative manner. Heritability statistics revealed by behavioral genetic studies have been criticized as meaningless, mainly because biologists have established that genes cannot influence development independently of environmental factors; genetic and nongenetic factors always cooperate to build traits. The reality is that nature and culture interact in a host of qualitatively different ways.

Instead of defending extreme nativist or nurturist views, most psychological researchers are now interested in investigating how nature and nurture interact. For example, in psychopathology, this means that both a genetic predisposition and an appropriate environmental trigger are required for a mental disorder to develop.

Therefore, it makes more sense to say that the difference between two people's behavior is mostly due to hereditary factors or mostly due to environmental factors. This realization is especially important given the recent advances in genetics, such as polygenic testing. The Human Genome Project, for example, has stimulated enormous interest in tracing types of behavior to particular strands of DNA located on specific chromosomes.

If these advances are not to be abused, then there will need to be a more general understanding of the fact that biology interacts with both the cultural context and the personal choices that people make about how they want to live their lives. There is no neat and simple way of unraveling these qualitatively different and reciprocal influences on human behavior.

Continuity and Discontinuity

The description and explanation of intra-individual change involves the concepts of developmental continuity and discontinuity, whereas the description and explanation of inter-individual differences in intra-individual change involves the concepts of stability and instability.

In regard to continuity and discontinuity, descriptions or explanations of development can involve quantitative or qualitative changes. Descriptively, quantitative changes involve differences in how much (or how many) of something exists. For example, in adolescence, quantitative changes occur in such areas as height and weight since there is an adolescent growth spurt, and these changes are often interpreted as resulting from quantitative increases in the production of growth-stimulating hormones.

In turn, descriptive qualitative changes involve differences in what exists, in what sort of phenomenon is present. The emergence in adolescence of a drive state never before present in life—that is, a reproductively mature sexual drive—and the emergence in adolescence of new and abstract thought capabilities not present in younger people—that is, in Jean Piaget's terms, formal operations—are instances of changes interpreted as arising from qualitative alterations in the person. It is believed that the person is not just "more of the same"; rather, the person is seen as having a new quality or characteristic.

Explanations of development also can vary in regard to whether one accounts for change by positing quantitative changes (e.g., increases in the amounts of growth hormone present in the bloodstream) or by positing a new reason for behavior (e.g., an infant's interactions in his or her social world are predicated on the need to establish a sense of basic trust in the world, whereas an adolescent's social interactions involve the need to establish a sense of identity, or a self-definition). In other words, it is possible to offer an explanatory discontinuous interpretation of development involving either quantitative or qualitative change.

For instance, when particular types of explanatory discontinuous qualitative changes are said to be involved in development, the critical period hypothesis is often raised, as in Erik Erikson's work. The point is that on the basis of adherence to a particular theory of development (e.g., what has been termed, in the scholarship of Gilbert Gottlieb, a predetermined epigenetic, or natural one), qualitative changes are believed to characterize ontogeny, and because of this, discontinuous explanations of change are needed.

Thus, virtually any statement about the character of intra-individual development involves, explicitly or implicitly, taking a position in regard to three dimensions of change: (1) descriptive continuity-discontinuity, (2) explanatory continuity-discontinuity, and (3) the quantitative versus the qualitative character of one's descriptions and explanations—that is, the quantitative-qualitative dimension pertains to both description and explanation. In essence, then, one may have descriptive quantitative discontinuity coupled with explanatory qualitative continuity, or descriptive qualitative continuity coupled with explanatory quantitative discontinuity, and so forth.

For example, a feature of personality (e.g., a component of temperament, such as mood) may remain descriptively the same over time. It may be represented or depicted isomorphically at two different temporal points (e.g., positive mood may be represented by the percentage of facial expressions per unit time that are scored as indicative of smiling). Such cases therefore may be an instance of descriptive, qualitative continuity. However, more of this qualitatively invariant phenomenon may exist at time 2 (e.g., there may be more smiles per unit time), and thus descriptive quantitative discontinuity may be coupled with descriptive qualitative continuity.

Moreover, both descriptive quantitative discontinuity and descriptive qualitative continuity may be explained by the same ideas, such as by continuous explanatory principles. For example, smiling may be assumed to be released across life by biogenetically based physiological mechanisms. Alternatively, descriptive continuity or descriptive discontinuity may be explained by different ideas, such as by discontinuous explanatory principles. For instance, smiling may be assumed to be biogenetically released in early infancy and mediated by cognitively and socially textured processes across subsequent developmental periods. Indeed, if different explanations are, in fact, invoked, they may involve statements that constitute either quantitatively or qualitatively altered processes.

In short, the particular couplings that one posits as involved in human life will depend on the substantive domain of development one is studying (e.g., intelligence, motivation, personality, or peer group relations) and, as we shall see, primarily on one's theory of development. That is, any particular description or explanation of intra-individual change is the result of a particular theoretical view of development. This implies that commitment to a theory that focuses only on certain variables or processes will restrict one's view of the variety of changes that may characterize development. Indeed, theory, not data, is the major lens through which one "observes" continuity or discontinuity in development.

The Contributions of Heinz Werner

Heinz Werner believed that considerable confusion existed among human develop mentalists over the continuity-discontinuity issue and that at the crux of this confusion was a lack of understanding about two different aspects of change (i.e., quantitative and qualitative). He argued that these two aspects of change must always be considered in discussions of descriptive and explanatory continuity-discontinuity. However, Werner explained the superordinate conceptual importance of the qualitative-quantitative dimension of change.

Quantitative Change

In regard to the quantitative aspect of development, we have noted that there is change in a feature of development in regard to how much of something exists. Quantitative change is an alteration in the amount, frequency, magnitude, or amplitude of a developmental variable or process. For example, imagine that a person's weight has been measured at the same time during each of his 8th through 13th years. He weighed 125 pounds when he was measured at 8, 9, 10, 11, and 12; but he weighed 150 pounds when he was measured at 13. Thus, a quantitative change occurred in how much weight existed between the times of measurement occurring at ages 12 and 13 years.

Alternatively, the child's change in weight could have been gradual. By gaining 5 pounds per year, the child gradually goes from 125 to 150 pounds between his 8th and 13th years. With gradual quantitative changes, the rate of change stays the same—is continuous— from one measurement time to the next. This is quantitative continuity.

Thus, quantitative change may be abrupt. There are no intermediate steps by which the person's weight gradually moved from one level (amount) to the next. In measuring this change, there is a gap between one point in the measurement curve and another; that is, a curve representing the different measurements is not smooth but has an abrupt change in its direction. There is a "gappiness" in the curve—a lack of an intermediate stage between the earlier and later levels of a variable. The occurrence of an abrupt change is quantitative discontinuity.

Qualitative Change

The second aspect of change that Werner specifies is the qualitative one. Here we are primarily concerned not with how much of something exists but with what exists what kind or type of thing exists. Thus, we are concerned with whether or not a new quality has come to characterize an organism, whether something new has emerged in development. When we are considering qualitative change we are dealing with epigenesis, or emergence.

In distinguishing between quantitative and qualitative aspects of change, Werner highlights a core conception of the organismic position. Some of the types of changes that comprise development are emergent changes. These are changes in what exists rather than in how much of something exists. Something new comes about in development, and because it is new— because it is qualitatively different from what went before—it cannot be reduced to what went before. Hence, if at time 1 we can be represented by 10 oranges and at time 2 we can be represented by a motorcycle, we cannot reduce our time 2 motorcycle status to our time 1 orange status.

To take another example, before puberty a person may be characterized as being (in part) composed of several drives—for example, a hunger drive, a thirst drive, a drive to avoid pain, and perhaps a curiosity drive. With puberty, however, a new drive emerges (or, at least, emerges in a mature form)—the sex drive. With this emergence the adolescent begins to have new feelings, new thoughts, and even new behaviors which, according to Anna Freud, may be interpreted as being a consequence of this new drive. The emergence of this new drive is an instance of qualitative discontinuity. The sex drive cannot be reduced to hunger and thirst drives, for instance.

Hence, qualitative changes are by their very nature discontinuous. A qualitative, emergent, epigenetic change is always an instance of discontinuity. Moreover, not only is an emergent change an irreducible change, but it is a change characterized by gappiness. As indicated above, developmental gappiness occurs when there is a lack of an intermediate level between earlier and later levels of development. It should be clear that gappiness must also be a part of an emergent change. The presence of an intermediate step between what exists at time 1 and the new quality that emerges at time 2 would suggest that the new quality at time 2 could be reduced through reference to the intermediate step. Since we have just seen that an emergent change is defined in terms of its developmental irreducibility to what went before, it is clear that gappiness must also be a characteristic of any emergence.

Stability vs. Change

Stabilization and change addressing the existence of personality traits that existed among babies throughout the life cycle. The believers believe that personality will change through family interaction, school experience, and adaptation to culture.

Research on children often shows long-term stability of development, such as affection for the parents and personality. However, there is evidence of the opposite view that change is possible or under appropriate conditions.

Freud was one of the first psychologists to emphasize the important nature of our early development. He believes that how he resolves sexual and radical urges is strongly related to the character of adults. Psychologists believe that the character traits of the first five years of development can predict the character of adults.

Developmental psychologists will study which features are most stable and consistent and which features are more flexible and changeable. Certain aspects of temperament such as energy level and extroversion seem to be relatively stable, but the social attitude is likely to change.

For example, are outgoing and talkative babies maintaining such a life? Discussion about stability and change is one of the fundamental problems related to the development of psychology and nature and cultivation. Generally, cross-sectional studies and longitudinal studies are used in research on stability and variation.

Stability and change, freedom and discipline, stock and flow, nature and cultivation, efforts to make a choice between risk and safety. Most of the things that make life interesting are the tensions caused by these inconsistencies. Trying to solve these conflicts by choosing one or the other not only creates a simple appearance but also makes life more interesting at the same time by looking at richness, so it is reasonable and passionate. The reason is to observe the world around us, to apply the logical and experimental rules systematically and to conclude that others can follow. It often tries to abstract from details in order to draw out and protect general conclusions.

Human life depends on stability. Without it, there is no structure, organization or society. Without stability, confusion and confusion will occur. "Dictionary" defines stability as "resistance to change, movement, falling" or "consistency for personality and purpose". This word reminds me of a structure like a windy building. This also made me think about perseverance. Stability will last for a long time. Stable things will resist change, but you can maintain yourself through that. But in Aldous Huxley's novel "The Brave New World" stability is a way of life. The motto of the world is "community, identity, stability".

Intuitively and consciously, all of us are seeking stability. Nationally, we are fighting for stability; investigation of any company is constantly changing and lacking stability, it is the first project to worry about employees and make them very dissatisfied One of them. All of us want to maintain this fun future state with our income growing and expecting our own confidence in the future. Too many people want this - a major merchant who has acquired the authority, delicious pie, administrator at every level, they want to reduce the stress of life, keep their existing status, and what company Even ordinary employees. All changes are pain in the butt, so there is no necessary result, but the difficulty is imminent.

Creativity

Creativity has undoubtedly influenced cultural institutions throughout the world from the beginning of time. For instance, consider the power of the muses on ancient Greek religion and God-worship, the impact of the belief that art and musical talent was bestowed upon an individual by God, Ancient Rome's emphasis on the beautification of public spaces by artists and the creative inspiration Charles Darwin gleaned from his children's play that fueled his research into evolution. While history has solidified the importance of creativity, the impact creativity has on development throughout the lifespan and its importance in the psychological construction of the individual remains a hotly debated topic. Research thus far has yielded inconsistent findings and does not provide overwhelming evidence that activities associated with the use of creativity (such as pretend play, divergent thinking, and the use of art activities) significantly impact psychological development. Still, perhaps the effectiveness of creativity throughout the lifespan, especially in childhood when creative play and divergent thinking are most encouraged and practiced, cannot be completely measured by empirical research. However, the richness and importance of creativity in cognitive and social development can be examined in a psychological context through an analysis of the role creativity plays in various developmental theories. In order to understand how creativity plays a role in development, these theories must be thoroughly studied and understood. Although there are myriads of developmental theories, creativity is mostly reflected in the renowned developmental theories of Urie Bronfenbrenner, Sigmund Freud, Erik Erikson, Jean Piaget and Lev Vygotsky. While these theories have been difficult to test through empirical study, they have earned their place in psychological history by being both widely believed and serving as the basis for a variety of more contemporary theories related to human development. Creativity arguably plays an important role in the daily application of each stage of these developmental theories, creating a plausible answer to the difficult question of the importance of creativity.

Before creativity can be thoroughly discussed and examined, it is necessary to provide a definition of creativity. While creativity may be defined casually in a relatively simple fashion, the operational definition of creativity has been subject to much debate, especially in the scientific research community. Mihaly Csikszentmihalyi defined creativity as "Any act, idea, or product that changes an existing domain or that transforms an existing domain into a new one". While seemingly all inclusive, this explanation has been subject to criticism since it does not apply to the principal area where creativity is most commonly experienced: childhood. For example, Czikszentmihalyi's definition may appear less relevant to children, since a child playing house rarely transforms the domain of family life; a child who is finger-painting rarely transforms the domain of fine art. In a different opinion, Ellen Dissanayake's "What is Art for?" defined creativity simply as a survival mechanism used by ancestors to further the human race, asserting that humans would not have preserved the act of creative endeavors if these behaviors did not somehow further their survival. However, many individuals would argue that creativity does much more than aid survival; it can be used as a tool to promote social change, express emotion and celebrate the trials and triumphs of life. Dissanayake argue that creativity cannot be operationally defined, since an individual's creative capacity and cognition is influenced solely by his or her unique experiences. To this day, the universal definition of creativity is still unclear; however, in this chapter, creativity will be defined as any action or thought that encourages an individual to reach beyond the given objects or situations physically available. In addition, play may be used interchangeably with creativity while discussing the use of creativity in children before adolescence (under the age of ten). This is because play is one of the most widely used expressions of creativity in children and can be found in almost every culture.

Life Stages of Psychological Development

Prenatal Development

Prenatal development is a time of remarkable change that helps set the stage for future psychological development. The brain develops over the course of the prenatal period, but it will continue to go through more changes during the early years of childhood at the major stages and events that take place during the prenatal period of development. The process of prenatal development occurs in three main stages.

The first two weeks after conception are known as the germinal stage, the third through the eighth week is known as the embryonic period, and the time from the ninth week until birth is known as the fetal period.

Germinal Stage

The germinal stage begins at conception when the sperm and egg cell unite in one of the two fallopian tubes. The fertilized egg, known as a zygote, then moves toward the uterus, a journey that can take up to a week to complete. Cell division begins approximately 24 to 36 hours after conception.

Within just a few hours after conception, the single-celled zygote begins making a journey down the fallopian tube to the uterus where it will begin the process of cell division and growth. Through the process of mitosis, the zygote first divides into two cells, then into four, eight, sixteen, and so on. A significant number of zygotes never progress past this early part of cell division, with as many as half of all zygote's surviving less than two weeks.

Once the eight-cell point has been reached, the cells begin to differentiate and take on certain characteristics that will determine the type of cells they will eventually become.

As the cells multiply, they will also separate into two distinctive masses: the outer cells will eventually become the placenta while the inner cells will form the embryo.

Cell division continues at a rapid rate and the cells then develop into what is known as a blastocyst. The blastocyst is made up of three layers:

1. The ectoderm (which will become the skin and nervous system).
2. The endoderm (which will become the digestive and respiratory systems).
3. The mesoderm (which will become the muscle and skeletal systems).

Finally, the blastocyst arrives at the uterus and attached to the uterine wall, a process known as implantation. Implantation occurs when the cells nestle into the uterine lining and rupture tiny blood vessels. The connective web of blood vessels and membranes that form between them will provide nourishment for the developing being for the next nine months. Implantation is not always an automatic and sure-fire process.

Researcher estimate that approximately 60 percent of all natural conceptions never become properly implanted in the uterus, which results in the new life ending before the mother is ever aware she is pregnant.

When implantation is successful, hormonal changes halt a woman's normal menstrual cycle and cause a whole host of physical changes. For some women, activities they previously enjoyed such as smoking and drinking alcohol or coffee may become less palatable, possibly part of nature's way of protecting the growing life inside her.

Embryonic Stage

At this point, the mass of cells is now known as an embryo. The beginning of the third week after conception marks the start of the embryonic period, a time when the mass of cells becomes distinct as a human. The embryonic stage plays an important role in the development of the brain.

The embryo begins to divide into three layers each of which will become an important body system. Approximately four weeks after conception, the neural tube forms. This tube will later develop into the central nervous system including the spinal cord and brain.

The neural tube begins to form along an area known as the neural plate. The earliest signs of development of the neural tube are the emergence of two ridges that form along each side of the neural place. Over the next few days, more ridges form and fold inward until a hollow tube is formed. Once this tube is fully formed, the cells begin to form near the center. The tube begins to close and brain vesicles form. These vesicles will eventually develop into parts of the brain including the structures of the forebrain, midbrain, and hindbrain.

Around the fourth week, the head begins to form quickly followed by the eyes, nose, ears, and mouth. The cardiovascular system is where the earliest activity begins as the blood vessel that will become the heart start to pulse. During the fifth week, buds that will form the arms and legs appear.

By the time the eighth week of development has been reached, the embryo has all of the basic organs and parts except those of the sex organs. It even has knees and elbows! At this point, the embryo weighs just one gram and is about one inch in length.

By the end of the embryonic period, the basic structures of the brain and central nervous system have been established. At this point in development, the basic structure of the central and peripheral nervous system are also defined.

Research has shown that the production of neurons begins around day 42 after conception and is mostly complete sometime around the middle of pregnancy.

As neurons form, they migrate to different areas of the brain. Once they have reached the correct location, they begin to form connections with other neural cells, establishing rudimentary neural networks.

Fetal Stage

Once cell differentiation is mostly complete, the embryo enters the next stage and becomes known as a fetus. The fetal period of prenatal develop marks more important changes in the brain. This period of development begins during the ninth week and lasts until birth.

The early body systems and structures established in the embryonic stage continue to develop. It is at this point in prenatal development that the neural tube develops into the brain and spinal cord and neurons continue to form. Once these neurons have formed, they begin to migrate to their correct locations. Synapses, or the connections between neurons, also begin to develop.

It is during the period between the 9th and 12th week at the earliest reflexes begin to emerge and the fetus begins to make reflexive motions with his arms and legs.

This stage of prenatal development lasts the longest and is marked by amazing change and growth. During the third month of gestation, the sex organs begin to differentiate and by the end of the month, all parts of the body will be formed. At this point, the fetus weight around three ounces. The fetus continues to grow in both weight and length, although the majority of the physical growth occurs in the later stages of pregnancy.

The end of the third month also marks the end of the first trimester of pregnancy. During the second trimester or months four through six, the heartbeat grows stronger and other body systems become further developed. Fingernails, hair, eyelashes, and toenails form. Perhaps most noticeably, the fetus increases quite dramatically in size, increasing about six times in size.

So what's going on inside the brain during this important period of prenatal development? The brain and central nervous system also become more responsive during the second trimester. Around 28 weeks, the brain starts to mature faster with an activity that greatly resembles that of a sleeping newborn.

During the period from seven months until birth, the fetus continues to develop, put on weight, and prepare for life outside the womb. The lungs begin to expand and contract, preparing the muscles for breathing.

The prenatal period of development is a time of physical growth, but what's going on inside the brain is critical for future psychological development. The brain development that takes place during the prenatal period helps set the course for what will take place outside the womb.

While prenatal development usually follows this normal pattern, there are times when problems or deviations occur. Disease, malnutrition, and other prenatal influences can have a powerful impact on how the brain develops during this critical period.

But brain development does not end at birth. There is a considerable amount of brain development that takes place postnatally including growing in size and volume while changing in structure. The brain grows by about four times the size between birth and preschool. As children learn and have new experiences, some networks in the brain are strengthened while other connections are pruned.

Infancy

Infancy ranges in age from the moment of birth to about 2 years of age when the young child begins to use words to make sentences. In fact, the word "infant" means literally "one who is unable to speak." Infancy is unique in that it is the earliest stage of life outside of the womb and is viewed as the most important formative period of development. During this early stage of life, infants are remarkably dependent on their caregivers for all their needs. Prior to the emergence of single words, which occurs as the first year of life comes to an end, infants convey their needs to their caregivers nonverbally through facial and body expressions and verbally such as crying and cooing.

Very young infants spend a great deal of their time sleeping and when awake are occupied with bodily sensations and sensory experiences. As they get older, infants become more interested in exploring the objects in their environment and establishing relationships with the significant people in their world.

The single most significant aspect of human development is the impressive brain growth and plasticity that takes place during the first 2 years of life. The neural pathways of the human brain undergo major changes in response to environmental stimulation during infancy. Importantly, these changes in brain maturation along with environmental events contribute to the development of the ability to use and understand single words, which signals the emergence of language in the second year of an infant's life. As infants develop the ability to use language to communicate, it also enables them to think and conceptualize in the ways that we commonly identify as characteristic of only human beings. Play becomes central to an infant's exploration of his or her world. Infancy is also a period of marked changes in body size and motor skills. As the infant comes to the end of the second year of life, independent locomotion becomes firmly established and further characterizes the demarcation of infancy from later childhood stages. In spite of the uniqueness and importance of the infancy stage in human development, only recently are infants being considered worthy of systematic, scientific pursuit.

Over the last few decades, the scientific study of the infant world has had a tremendous growth spurt likely due to innovative investigative techniques applied to study a broad range of infant abilities in early perceptual, sensory, cognitive, language, motor, sensorimotor, social, emotional, and self-regulatory abilities than had been imagined 50 years earlier. However, regardless of the fact that new information on infant abilities has been amassing exponentially for the past 50 years, the contributions of the early theorists remain among the most influential in the field of infancy. By deeming children, including infants, worthy of systematic study, John Locke and Jean Jacques Rousseau laid the groundwork for modern developmental psychology even though they expressed different outlooks on what goes on in the mind of the infant.

Locke stressed the role of the environment as the main determinant of infant behavior, a precursor of modern behaviorism. This empiricist view has frequently been interpreted as support for "controlling" children, which many, including Rousseau, disagreed with. Rousseau represented the romanticist view, recommended "understanding" infants rather than seeking control of them. Infants, as depicted by Rousseau, are born with a natural ability to learn, although, in his view, they are born as "idiot automaton," knowing nothing.

As the 19th century began, the ideas of Charles Darwin fueled the romanticist viewpoint. In particular, Darwin's assertion that human development was duplicating human evolution although at an accelerated pace furthered the viewing of infants as objects to be studied. Interestingly, Darwin was also considered a pioneer infancy researcher in that he kept a detailed diary of his sons' first 2 years of development, one of the first known "baby biographies." The early romanticism versus empiricism controversy was replaced in the 19th century by one of the most widely debated topics in the field of developmental psychology: Which contributes more to development, environment or nature?

An early proponent of the nature theory, Arnold Gesell claimed the primacy of genetics in determining development. To capture what he considered the genetically determined unfolding of development, Gesell created scales to assess behavioral change in infants and young children. Contrary to Gesell, John B. Watson believed that children could be taught just about anything, given the right kind of nurturing environment. To highlight the impact of environmental contribution, Watson emphasized parental responsibility for infant outcome; if the outcome was negative, it was the parents' fault. Both Gesell and Watson made a lasting imprint on how infants are viewed. In fact, heated discussion of the nature-nurture viewpoints continued throughout the 1800s, 1900s, and still is being debated today. While many researchers have sought to provide evidence that only one of these viewpoints is correct, the most up-to-date interpretation from years of systematic study by many developmental psychologists is that environment and genetics together contribute to infant development.

Sigmund Freud believed that the value of understanding infant development lay in what it might reveal about the adult mind. While psychoanalytic theory stresses the importance of biologically determined aspects of psychological functioning, the importance of the environment, particularly as it encouraged the child's nature to unfold, was acknowledged as well. Freud's theories countered the extremist views of nature or nurture. Freud never used direct infant observation to understand the mind of the infant.

Rather, he used reconstructive techniques. Like Freud, Jean Piaget was ultimately interested in the working of the human mind throughout the life span, but in contrast to Freud, Piaget directly observed and experimented on infants to understand the progression of cognitive ability. Piaget's detailed descriptions of his own children led to his conceptualization of infant skills as inherited capabilities emerging as substages in an invariant order with each subsequent stage representing a stable reorganization of the infant in relation to his or her environment.

Throughout the last century, the focus of infant development has been to document the emergence and extent of a wide range of infant abilities. Theorists of the earlier centuries, such as Rousseau, claimed that infants were capable of very little. However, current scientific findings support the idea that infants have a myriad of capabilities evident from birth and even before. Contemporary infancy researchers have created innovative experimental paradigms that tap into the behavioral repertoire of infants in order to discover what goes on in the mind of infants. Dramatic findings from the past 50 years of systematic, scientific inquiry not only determined that infants are capable of learning more and learning earlier than previously believed, but also were dispensed readily to consumers because of the rise of mass media and electronic communication. Once in the public domain, research findings quickly became topics of major interest for parents, shaping the way babies were being raised. Producing intellectually precocious infants became somewhat of an obsession for many parents, resulting in less emphasis on rearing mentally healthy infants. The emphasis of infancy research has shifted somewhat in the past few years, however, to include the identification of factors associated with producing optimal psychological outcomes for infants and their families In addition to this recent interest in infant social, emotional, and behavioral development, contemporary infancy researchers continue to investigate a broad range of infant abilities.

The Scientific Study of Infant Development

Using the scientific approach, researchers have investigated various areas of infant development. To describe infancy, psychologists traditionally divide development into separate domains of perception and sensation, motor skills, cognition and language, social behavior, and emotional and behavioral development. However, despite the depiction of infant development as discrete areas, research on infant development would suggest that there is much interdependence of all of the domains.

Perception and sensation involves the development and use of the infant's senses, specifically vision, touch, hearing, smell, vestibular-proprioceptive movement, and taste. Although not fully developed at birth, perception and sensation are critical experiences for the infant; in fact, until infants can engage in active exploration of the environment, which occurs toward the latter part of the first year of life, they spend most of their time looking at, listening to, touching, smelling, and tasting their environment. The development of motor skills enables infants to become independent explorers of their environment. Investigating the development of perception and sensation in infants includes not only the study of the emergence of gross motor skills such as crawling but also fine motor skills such as hand-eye coordination. Motor development progresses from simple acts, such as turning over, to more complex motor skills, such as walking, to fine motor coordination of objects, such as little pieces of food, crayons, or toys.

Cognitive development refers to the study of mental processing skills used by infants to understand their world, with the development of representational and symbolic thinking critical markers for later optimal development. Although findings from scientific investigations prove that even newborns are not in a state of "blooming, buzzing confusion," as characterized by William James in the 1800s, it is more toward the end of the second year that infants behave in a way that indicates they are actually reasoning and planning actions mentally. Prior to that, infants do show the ability to form conceptual categories but do not have the cognitive skills to mentally represent a plan of action in thoughts or words in order to choose appropriate plans of action and eliminate less worthy plans. Processing of information becomes more sophisticated with the emergence of symbolic thinking, and social relationships are enriched as infants develop shared meaning with others through language.

Infants process and express social cues long before they ever use language to form relationships. Descriptions of mother-infant relationships by Daniel Stern in the 1980s depicted the nonverbal and verbal "dances" between caretakers and infants, which Stern described in terms of eye gaze, touch, and positive verbalizations such as cooing. Tiffany Field studied how mothers and infants develop shared experiences by analyzing face-to-face interactions during which infants were seen matching their own experiences with that of their caretakers. The interchange between social and emotional development becomes clear when considering the studies by Mary Ainsworth that showed that infants who are secure in their relations with their caretakers show good self-regulation of emotions upon separations and reunions.

Investigators studying emotional development during infancy focused on the emergence of feeling states, how emotions are expressed, and how infants interpret the emotions of others. Michael Lewis and colleagues evaluated infants' facial expressions and found that the emergence of basic primary emotions, such as joy, interest, sadness, and anger, is apparent from birth but secondary emotions such as shame and guilt emerge in the second year of life. Studying behavioral skills of infants involves the measure of inherited temperament and later learned patterns of behavior. A number of researchers have paid particular attention to the emergence of self-regulatory skills and how infants use these skills to cope with everyday stresses, such as separation and frustration, sleeping through the night, adjusting to new food tastes, and inhibiting one's impulses when told "no." Jerome Kagan and colleagues engaged in extensive longitudinal studies and determined that infant's feelings, affects, and emotions are moderated by individual, inherited temperament traits, such as behavioral inhibition, and that these temperament traits persist in one form or another into later childhood, adolescence, and adulthood.

Recent Scientific Advancements

The dramatic increase in our understanding of infant development over the past 50 years can likely be attributed to the growth of scientific approaches utilized to study infants as indicated earlier. It is generally agreed that the best way to investigate the world of infants is to observe them directly in a controlled environment using systematic experimentation. Use of a scientific approach yields better validity and reliability and can control for the effects of experimenter bias and subjectivity. Much of the research prior to the second half of the 20th century used less scientific means to study individual infants. For example, Piaget, among others, documented qualitative case studies from baby biographies. While many researchers agreed that Piaget ushered in a direct, rather than retrospective, approach to studying infant development, his investigative style was not scientifically rigorous, which may account for some of the discrepancies found by later researchers regarding the emergence of early cognitive skills. It is well acknowledged, however, that infants are not as easy to study as older children or adults.

The mode of communication relied on most frequently by researchers in the field of psychology to collect information is language expression, typically verbal and sometimes written. To systematically study infants, researchers had to determine how to develop methods that compensated for the infants' lack of mature expressive ability. Infants cannot describe their feelings, fill out self-report measures, complete standardized written tests, or respond to interview questions. Because it is so difficult to utilize typical methodology with infants, infancy researchers have deduced what is going on in an infant's mind by developing creative procedures for systematically measuring responses using behaviors within an infant's repertoire, such as crying, sucking, tracking objects visually, kicking, or orienting the head.

Habituation or Dishabituation

The habituation paradigm measures infant response to repeated exposure of the same visual or auditory stimulus. This paradigm is based on the premise that infants, like older humans and animals, will show reductions in attention as they encounter the same stimulus repeatedly, which is determined by assessing length of visual gaze to the familiar stimulus. Eventually infants will fail to attend when they have "habituated" to the stimulus as if they were bored. The gradual decline in looking time over repeated presentations or trials due to increasing familiarity with the same stimulus is known as habituation. Researchers also assess how quickly infants recover or "dishabituate" when changes are made to the original stimulus and infer from changes in looking behavior whether infants can detect differences. Typically, a criterion for initial looking time duration is determined and habituation occurs when subsequent presentations consistently yield durations shorter than the habituation criterion. Following habituation, the stimulus is changed. If the infant's looking time increases from the habituation criterion, signaling dishabituation, or recovery, it is inferred that the infant can tell the difference between the two stimuli. If the infant cannot detect a difference, looking time will be shorter than the habituation criterion.

Using this paradigm, Bennett Bertenthal and colleagues found that 5-month-old infants when presented with point lights of a person can discriminate when that person is moving from a random, disorderly pattern of the same person's point lights. Bertenthal interpreted this as suggesting that young infants have stored knowledge of the human form and its movements. Tiffany Field and colleagues used the habituation/dishabituation technique and found that even newborns could differentiate between happy, sad, and surprised facial expressions. This paradigm has also been used to investigate many other aspects of infant development including recognition of the mother's face, object categorization, and the detection of emotions and speech sounds.

Preferential Looking and Violation of Expectancies

Another creative approach to understanding infant behavior relies on head turning to determine preferences and is called the paired-preference approach. For example, in a number of preferential looking studies, infants are required to show preference between two visual stimuli presented side by side or two sounds presented to one or the other ear. Investigators try to determine which of the two stimuli is most preferred by the infant by judging where the infant is looking. In the 1960s when infancy researchers first began to use innovative experimental techniques, Robert Fantz and his colleagues used the preferential looking paradigm to document that infants could distinguish visual patterns and, in fact, demonstrated marked visual preferences by infants when presented with two different patterns side by side. To do this infants were introduced to competing patterns while in an infant seat or on their mother's lap and in a darkened room. Patterns were mounted as a display of flashing lights on a screen directly in front of the infant.

As the preferential looking methodology became more sophisticated, researchers such as Marshall Haith detected the precise position of the infant's gaze by using an electronic sensor to measure the angle of reflection of an invisible infrared light reflected off the infant's cornea. By using the preferential looking method, researchers have found that young infants prefer the sound of their mother's voice and the odor of their mother's breast milk compared to that of another woman. Recently researchers have used variations on preferential looking to cleverly detect cognitive abilities in infants not documented or even believed to exist earlier because of limits in the methodology of prior time periods. For example, in the 1990s Karen Wynn used preferential looking as part of a violation of expectancy paradigm to show infants could detect the outcome of the addition or subtraction of one discrete object from a small collection of two or three objects. Wynn interpreted this as evidence of precocious number concept and concluded that 5-monthholds discriminated between quantitative outcomes when their expectancy of addition or subtraction solutions was violated.

Classical and Operant Conditioning

The interest in behaviorism during the 20th century led a number of infancy researchers to try conditioning young infants to determine aspects of conditioned learning. Hans Papousek, for example, demonstrated classical conditioning in newborns by pairing a neutral stimulus (a sound) with an unconditioned response (head turning). The sound eventually became the conditioned stimulus triggering the head turning, which became the conditioned response. Specifically, Papousek paired a sound with the turning of an infant's head by touching the corner of the infant's mouth with a bottle. After repeated exposure, as soon as the sound was heard the newborns turned their heads in anticipation of contact with the bottle. Thus, the neutral stimulus, the sound, became a conditioned stimulus and the head turn became the conditioned response.

While the classical conditioning of an infant demonstrated that infants have the potential to learn, infancy researchers sought to go further and investigate whether infants can be instrumental in changing their own behavior to secure reinforcement, a technique referred to as operant or instrumental conditioning. Operant conditioning has been used by many infant researchers to assess whether infants can learn that their own behavior controls environmental stimuli, thus actively engaging in the learning process. In the 1970s, James B. Watson, one of the first infancy researchers to utilize this approach, conditioned infants to turn their heads to produce movement in an overhead crib mobile. In the 1980s Anthony DeCasper and William Fifer used newborn infants' nonnutritive sucking responses to activate a tape recording of either the mother's or an unfamiliar female's voice reading from a book. DeCasper and Fifer found that the newborns learned that different pause lengths between bursts of sucking would differentiate which recording would be turned on and as a function of what was learned infants consistently sucked in such a way that would turn on the mother's voice.

A series of studies by Carolyn Rovee-Collier and colleagues investigated infant learning and memory utilizing a paradigm termed mobile conjugate reinforcement, a variant of operant conditioning. Infants learned to produce movement in a crib mobile when placed supine in their cribs with a ribbon extending from one ankle to the bar of a mobile stand. Movement in a mobile attached to the mobile stand was contingent on the kicking of the infant's ankle. Infants readily learned to increase their ankle movements over an initial baseline and if presented with the same mobile at later increments of time demonstrated good short and long-term retention. Rovee-Collier and colleagues used mobile conjugate reinforcement to demonstrate memory for color, number of components, and even contextual determinants of memory, such as odor and music. Investigation of infant response to changes in the mobile suggested that infants differ in how they react to violations of the expected type of stimulation with some infants demonstrating extreme negative reactivity and others learning to compensate for the change.

Physiological Responses

Infancy researchers have also used physiological indices to expand on or substantiate behavioral measures of infant ability and from this infer what is going on inside the infant's mind. Two common ways that have been used to assess levels of physiological arousal under a variety of circumstances are by using instruments that measure heart rate and galvanic skin response. Recent technological advances have also made possible physiological measurements of electrical brain activities recorded by surface electrodes or brain scans. Using physiological measures has been particularly useful in providing researchers with a way to investigate infant abilities prior to the infant's capability of expressing the ability behaviorally. For example, depth perception was assessed in infancy using a visual cliff paradigm that required crawling. Based on this research by James and Eleanor Gibson and colleagues, it was concluded that at 6 months of age infants are capable of perceiving the drop-off between themselves and their mother. However, does depth perception emerge at 6 months of age or was research on the emergence of depth perception limited because the visual cliff paradigm could not be used with young infants who were not yet crawling? To study depth perception in younger infants, researchers cleverly attached heart monitors to the infants and looked at changes when young infants were merely placed next to the visual cliff. Moderate arousal signified by changes in heart rate was found in infants as young as 2 months, suggesting depth perception occurs earlier than previously determined.

A number of infancy researchers have studied emotional development using physiological measures to corroborate findings originally yielded by behavioral measures. Jerome Kagan and colleagues initially used behavioral responses to investigate how infants respond to unexpected or novel situations. They found that infants who respond with crying and high motor activity, a response dyad he termed "inhibited temperament," tend to develop into children who avoid people, objects, and situations that are novel or unfamiliar, whereas uninhibited infants tend to develop into children who spontaneously approach novel persons, objects, and situations. As he continued investigating inhibited temperament longitudinally, Kagan developed an interest in determining if physiological differences could further distinguish between inhibited and uninhibited temperament types. His next step was to utilize the latest developed technology and he measured functional MRI signal response within the amygdala, finding, as he suspected, variations in amygdalar responses to novelty. Adults who as infants were categorized as inhibited showed greater functional MRI signal response within the amygdala to novel versus familiar faces compared with those adults categorized as uninhibited during infancy. Kagan interpreted these findings as evidence of early appearing manifestations of brain functions relating to temperament that are preserved into early adulthood.

Physiological findings also broadened our understanding of how self-control of emotion develops during infancy. Stephen Porges developed a procedure called vagal tone to measure heart rate variability that occurs at the frequency of breathing. Suppression of vagal tone has been found to be associated with the activation of coping strategies in children. Susan Calkins used this measure to investigate relations between mother-infant interactions during which the mother's face remained still and infants' physiological responses. Infants showed suppression of vagal tone during the still-face interaction indicating the need for physiological regulation of distress. Infants who did not suppress vagal tone (did not activate coping strategies) during the still-face interaction showed less positive affect and higher reactivity and lower mother infant synchrony in normal play.

Infancy in Perspective

Learning about infant development is becoming so sophisticated that the questions that can be answered about infant ability seem limitless. Infants are clearly not idiots automaton as proposed by Rousseau centuries earlier, and new scientific inquiry confirms that Piaget, among others, underestimated the emergence of infant skills abilities. Researchers have even found novel ways to document perceptual and sensory abilities in the developing fetus. It has become clear that many recent research findings have had a dramatic impact on how parents regard their infants. Our recent history has shown that many parents influenced by findings of early skill development became determined to produce "smarter" babies as early in life as possible. To produce "superbabies," many parents enrolled their infants in programs of structured education before the age of 3 years. This also led to the phenomenon of the "supermom," the woman who raises super babies while holding down a job and performing as a "perfect" wife. Perhaps as a reaction to the overemphasis on achievement for both infant and mother, the early 21st century has seen a rise in concern for the psychological outcomes of infants and parents. The current research trend focuses on topics such as emotional intelligence and the goodness of relationships between parents and children. From an applied standpoint there is also growing emphasis on early detection of developmental problems and interventions that may alleviate or even prevent delays. Knowing when certain skills emerge during infancy can help clinicians determine mature or immature developmental status of infants and identify those infants at risk for future difficulty. In spite of centuries of study about infant development, it seems like our knowledge about this first stage of life outside the womb is still in its infancy, but it is clear that continued scientific research is valuable for our society.

Infant Perception

Infant perception is a process by which a human infant (age 0 to 12 months) gains awareness of and responds to external stimuli. At birth, infants possess functional sensory systems; vision is somewhat organized, and audition (hearing), olfaction (smell), and touch are fairly mature. However, infants lack perceptual knowledge, which must be gained through experience with the world around them. As infants' senses mature, they begin to coordinate information obtained through multiple sensory modalities. The process of coordination, known as intermodal perception, begins early and improves across infancy.

Basic Visual Function

Most basic visual functions are operational yet relatively immature at birth. Visual acuity, the ability to distinguish fine detail, is estimated at about 20/400 for most newborns. In healthy normally developing infants, acuity improves rapidly within the first few months. Contrast sensitivity, the ability to detect luminance differences between two adjacent areas (such as stripes on a grating), is also reduced in newborns relative to adults but develops as infants gain visual experience. Colour vision also develops, nearing the perceptual ability of adults by four to six months.

The perception of motion is an important part of an individual's visual interpretation of his or her environment. Objects and people in the environment move in many different ways (laterally, vertically, toward and away from the observer, and rotating) and at different velocities. Infants' responses to slow and fast motion velocities differ depending on age and the type of motion observed. Thus, separate perception mechanisms may exist for different types of motion. Moreover, infants' own motion also contributes to motion perception. Despite the complex nature of motion, nearly all types of motion perception develop by about six months in healthy infants.

Depth perception also gradually develops during the first several months. Infants first become sensitive at about two months to kinematic, or motion-carried information for distance, as when one surface moves in front of another. At about four months, infants are able to perceive depth via the difference in the optical projections at the two retinas to determine depth, known as stereopsis. Stereoscopic depth cues provide information about distances of objects in near space as a function of their relative horizontal positions in the visual field. At about seven months, infants are able to perceive depth in a flat, two-dimensional picture.

Visual Attention

Infants are born with a functional oculomotor (eye-movement) system. The muscles that move the eyes and the brain-stem mechanisms that control the eye muscles directly appear to be fully mature at birth, and infants make good use of these systems to scan the visual environment. Two developmental events seem to be particularly important to the control of visual attention: the emergence of smooth pursuit, at about two months, and increasing top-down control over saccadic, or scanning, eye movements, which can take much longer. Smooth pursuit helps an individual track moving targets in the environment and stabilize gaze. Saccades are used when inspecting visual stimuli. Both kinds of eye movements are believed to develop along with specialized brain regions, such as those involved in processing information about motion and objects.

Object Perception

Object perception is complex, involving multiple information-processing tasks, such as perceiving boundaries, shapes, sizes, and substances of objects. Understanding object boundaries first requires recognizing where one object ends and another object or surface begins. Detecting edges is critical for this process, and the intersection of edges provides information for the relative distance of object and surfaces. For example, where one edge is seen to lead into and end abruptly at another, the uninterrupted edge is usually nearer to the observer. Infants typically become capable of recognizing boundaries between three and five months.

Recognizing object boundaries alone does not necessarily reveal the complete size or shape of an object. In some cases, objects are partly hidden by other surfaces nearer to the observer. The perception of partly occluded objects as complete is first accomplished at about two months. Objects also have constant size and shape, even when viewed at varying distances and angles. Newborns, despite their limited visual experience, appear to have some sense of both size and shape constancy.

Face Perception

Newborns show a consistent preference for looking at faces relative to other stimuli throughout infancy. Newborns' ability to recognize facelike patterns suggests that they may have an inherent ability to perceive faces before having actually viewed a face. Alternatively, it may indicate that faces match infants' preferences for particular types of stimuli, such as those with specific spatial characteristics.

Infants are able to recognize familiar faces despite variations in expression and perspective. They also can discriminate gender in faces. Most infants show preferences for females; however, infants who are handled primarily by males express preference for male faces. Infants' sensitivity to facial expressions emerges early; for example, different intensities of smiling can be perceived by three months. By seven months, infants can discriminate an extensive range of the facial expressions, including happiness, anger, sadness, fear, and surprise, although it is unlikely that they understand the content of this range of emotions at this age. Researchers have identified several areas in the brain that are involved in face perception, including the middle fusiform gyrus in the right hemisphere and the amygdala. Experience with faces is thought to facilitate the development of brain areas that process facial information.

Auditory Perception

In the second trimester of pregnancy, the inner ear becomes fully developed, allowing the fetus to have limited auditory experiences in the womb. As a result, fetuses show distinct responses to sounds of various intensities and frequencies. Neonates' auditory perception appears to be influenced by prenatal experiences with sounds. For example, newborns prefer listening to their own mother's voice over the voice of another woman.

Despite the physical maturity of the cochlea about two-thirds of the way through gestation, sound conduction through the external and middle ear to the inner ear is inefficient at birth, hindering the transmission of information to the auditory neural pathway. Perception of low frequencies is poor in young infants relative to high frequencies. In fact, low-frequency discrimination does not mature until about 10 years, but discrimination of high frequencies is superior in infants relative to that of adults.

The most common measure used when testing intensity processing for pure tones is the absolute threshold, the smallest intensity of sound detectable in a quiet environment. The absolute threshold improves throughout infancy and reaches adult levels by puberty, and the higher the frequency, the earlier adult levels are achieved. For example, the absolute threshold level at 4,000 and 10,000 hertz (Hz) reaches adult levels by age five, whereas the level for 1,000 Hz requires 10 years or more to reach maturity. Between one and three months, the absolute threshold improves by 15 decibels (dB); between three and six months, a 15-dB improvement occurs for the threshold at 4,000 Hz.

In contrast to pure tones, many sounds in the environment are complex, made up of multiple frequencies and various intensities. For example, perception of timbre, such as hearing differences in the way different musical instruments sound, involves comparison of different intensities across frequencies. As early as seven months, infants can discriminate between sounds of different timbres with the same pitch, but adult levels of competence at discriminating a series of complex timbres are not reached until well into childhood.

The ability to locate the source of sounds is required to accurately perceive sound in the environment. Spectral shape and intensity and binaural comparisons provide information on positions in elevation (the vertical plane) and azimuth (the horizontal plane), respectively. Infants tend to use spectral shape more than binaural comparisons when locating the source of a sound, possibly because they are more sensitive to differences in sound frequency than to differences in sound intensity.

Once different types of auditory information have been received, they need to be organized into perceptually meaningful elements. For example, for a conversation to be followed speech produced by members of the family must be grouped together and noises from children playing outside must be filtered out. The process of grouping is partly functional in infants, but it is more easily disrupted in children than in adults. Part of this process is ignoring irrelevant sounds while attending to the relevant sound source. Infants, unlike adults, often seem to act as if they are not sure about disregarding irrelevant sounds. For example, studies with seven- to nine-month-old infants suggest that they cannot detect a pure tone when presented simultaneously with a wide-frequency noise band.

Speech Perception

Infants appear to have difficulty segregating speech from other competing sounds. Thus, when interacting with infants, adult caregivers often compensate for this difficulty by making major acoustic adjustments in their speech, such as the use of infant-directed speech, which contains exaggerated pitch contours, a higher register, repetitions, and simpler sentences.

A central question in this area concerns whether infants respond to phonetic differences in a manner similar to that of adults. Studies examining cross-language and native-language speech perception suggest that infants are born with universal sensitivity to the phonemes that are present in all languages. Phonemes are components of a language that distinguish words by forming the contrasting element in pairs of words, such as the /r/ and /l/ in rake and lake. There is a developmental loss of "unused" initial sensitivities. For example, a study of English-speaking adults, Hindi-speaking adults, and six- to eight-month-old infants from English-speaking families demonstrated that infants distinguished two distinct phonemes with similar sounds in both English and Hindi—/ta/ and /da/ in English and the retroflex /D/ and dental /d/ in Hindi—whereas adults distinguished only between different phonemes in their native language. These phonemes are all produced by placing the tongue against the alveolar ridge, just behind the teeth, and releasing it in time with voice onset. They vary with respect to the precise part of the tongue and alveolar ridge involved and to voice-onset timing.

Infants often exhibit preferences for speech sounds over non-speech sounds; the former can help in attending to signals in the environment necessary for language acquisition. But infants do not always prefer speech. In addition, speech preference does not appear to be a result of prenatal auditory exposure to human speech, and infants are attentive to other forms of communication, including sign language.

Newborns also are sensitive to prosody, the patterns of rhythm and intonation in speech, and may use prosody to discriminate one language from another. Prosody appears to be the primary way for young infants to perceive speech. This is especially useful in bilingual environments, because it helps infants avoid potential confusion.

Intermodal Perception

Adults experience the world through the integration of sensory impressions. Infants, to some extent, are capable of coordinating information perceived through different senses. Newborns can detect "arbitrary" auditory-visual relations that are presented during a period of familiarization (a particular shape paired with a particular sound). Most intermodal relations in the world, however, are quite specific rather than arbitrary. An example is speech, which can be simultaneously heard and seen in a talking face. Adults' phoneme perception is strongly influenced by watching faces, the so-called McGurk effect. When adults hear a syllable while looking at a face producing a different syllable, they tend to perceive the sound associated with the lip movements rather than the actual phoneme that they heard. Five-month-old infants are also susceptible to this effect.

Infants also can use the duration of events to integrate information across modalities and may be capable of abstracting amodal rhythmic structure from auditory-visual pairings. At five months, infants can detect changes in regularly or irregularly occurring rhythmic auditory or visual sequences regardless of whether the modality of presentation is changed. By four to five months, infants may be able to recognize and discriminate objects by using information that is perceived through vision and touch.

Language

The first words spoken by an infant may seem to mark the beginning of the infant's language development; however, by the time the first word has been spoken at about the age of 12 months, language development has been underway for more than a year. After birth, all normally developing children master the skills necessary for listening and speaking within a few years. Regardless of the language or languages spoken in the home, research has shown that language development proceeds in a remarkably similar fashion.

Before Birth

In the 12 weeks before birth, sounds from the world outside of the womb can be heard. By the 24th week of pregnancy, the auditory system of the growing fetus is well developed. Expectant mothers may feel movement by the fetus in response to a loud noise. The startle response can be consistently observed by the 28th week of pregnancy.

The early memories of speech sounds that are formed in the womb represent infants' very first experiences with language. Research conducted with newborns has shown that newborns treat some sounds as familiar while treating other sounds as unfamiliar. Treating a sound as familiar suggests that the newborn gained familiarity with the sound before birth. For example, in research reported in 1980, DeCasper and Fifer showed that soon after birth, newborns prefer to hear the sound of the mother's voice versus the sound of a stranger's voice. Similar research reported in 1988 by Jacques Mehler and colleagues showed that newborns only 4 days old treated sounds from the mother's language as familiar, whereas they treated sounds from another language that was not spoken in the home of the expectant mother as unfamiliar. In 1986, DeCasper and Spence reported one of the most compelling studies of this type. They instructed expectant mothers to read a particular Dr. Seuss book aloud during pregnancy. After birth, newborns showed a preference for hearing the familiar story over a different story that had not been read during pregnancy. A second group of newborns who had not heard either story before birth did not show a listening preference.

Listening

At birth, all newborns demonstrate the remarkable ability to distinguish speech sounds occurring in all the world's languages. This phenomenon has been referred to as categorical perception. The inborn ability to make fine-grained perceptual distinctions is not unique to humans. Chinchillas, which are small fur-bearing rodents, also demonstrate these perceptual abilities. Of course, chinchillas never acquire human language. An important difference between the perceptual abilities of children and other species is that the perceptual abilities of children change during the first year of life as a result of their listening experiences. By the end of the first year of life, children gradually lose the ability to distinguish speech sounds not occurring in the language or languages spoken in the home.

Young infants' ability to recognize syllables in speech has been shown to be influenced by the frequency with which they are experienced. Research conducted by Peter Jusczyk and colleagues showed that infants as young as 9 months could distinguish single syllables that were frequently experienced from those that were infrequently experienced. In contrast, infants who were 6 months old were unable to distinguish the two types of syllables. Furthermore, research conducted by Eleanor Saffran and colleagues has shown that infants who were 6 months old could distinguish two-syllable sequences, such as bida and kupa, when presented in a continuous stream of syllables, such as ibidakupadotigolabubidaku. Some two-syllable sequences occurred frequently; others occurred infrequently. The results suggested that infants' ability to recognize two-syllable sequences was influenced by the frequency with which the specific syllables occurred in the speech stream played for infants during the study.

Research studies confirm what many new parents may have guessed—children may understand some language even before they have produced their first words. Research conducted by Roberta

Golinkoff and Kathy Hirsch-Pasek and colleagues showed that young children who had only one to two words in their productive vocabulary demonstrated the ability to understand certain aspects of meaning contained in spoken sentences. Children were seated in between two television monitors. The children sat comfortably on a caregiver's lap and viewed two videos simultaneously. Both videos depicted the well-known Sesame Street characters Cookie Monster and Big Bird. In one video, Big Bird was carrying out an action and Cookie Monster was being acted upon. For example, Big Bird was feeding Cookie Monster or tickling Cookie Monster. In the other video, the roles were reversed. Cookie Monster was carrying out the action and Big Bird was being acted upon. As children viewed the videos, a spoken sentence was presented to the children, such as "Where is Big Bird feeding Cookie Monster?" The results showed that children preferred to look at the video that matched the meaning of the spoken sentence. Months before children are producing full sentences, they appreciate the fact that the one who performs an action, or the subject, is mentioned first in an English sentence, and the one who is affected by the action, or the object, is mentioned second.

Speaking

Infants' first spoken utterances after birth are most certainly crying. Crying can be viewed as the first important form of communication. In the first 3 months following birth, infants develop distinct cries to indicate hunger, discomfort, or anger. By the third month, children have begun laughing and cooing. When infants coo, they produce elongated vowel sounds, such as oooh and aaaah. In the months that follow, infants' productions become more and more complex. By the end of the first year of life, infants are generally producing their first words. Table summarizes the different types of vocalizations produced during the first year of life and the ages at which each type of vocalization is generally observed.

By the sixth month, infants begin to practice the sounds of language. This stage of language development has been referred to as the babbling stage. Children begin babbling by repeating a single syllable, such as babababa or dududu. This type of babbling is called canonical babbling. Later on, children's babbling becomes more complex, as they produce sequences that contain different syllables, such as bagada and dabuga. This type of babbling is called variegated babbling. Of the speech sounds that are produced during these babbling stages, the 12 most common speech sounds found in the world's languages make up 95% of children's babbled productions. Infants will babble speech sounds that do not occur in the language or languages that are spoken in the home. As the infant nears 1 year of age, the infant produces fewer and fewer speech sounds not represented in the language or languages of the home. It turns out that as children lose the ability to distinguish speech sounds that are not regularly experienced during listening, they are less and less likely to produce those speech sounds.

Table: Language Productions in the First Year.

Age	Type Of Utterances
New born	• Crying
1-3 Months	• Cooling ("oooh," "aaah") • Laughing • Distinct crying to indicate hunger, anger, or discomfort • Vocalizes in response to speech

4-6 Months	• Single syllables emerge • ("ba," "ga")
6-8 Months	• Canonical babbling • ("bababa," "dadada") • Attempts to imitate sound
8-12 Months	• Variegated babbling • ("bagadabu," "dabuga") • Babbling is produced with sentence like intonation
12 Months	• First words, mama, dada, baba

Children's first words may be mama or dada or the name of a favorite toy or pet. However, among a child's first words may be invented words. Such words are used consistently by the child to refer to a specific object or action, but are not used by adults. These word inventions are called idiomorphs. For example, the child may consistently refer to a favorite food with an invented word, such as gump. In the book Mirror of Language: The Debate on Bilingualism, Kenji Hakuta describes a child who used the word Whew! as a greeting, when others might say hello. A possible explanation for the child's choice of greeting was the fact that the child's mother often said Whew! When first entering the child's room in the morning, in response to an odor indicating that the child's diaper needed changing. Children's uses of idiomorphs are usually short-lived because they exchange their invented words for the words preferred by adults.

Table: Children's Phonological Errors.

Type of Error	Examples
Reduction	"ba" for "bottle"
Reduction with Reduplication	"baba" for "bottle"
Substitution	"tandy" for "candy"
Assimilation	"nance" for "dance"
Coalescencee	"paf" for "pacifier"

Parents and caregivers may find it relatively easy to decipher the intended meaning of children's production of words; however, there may be notable differences between children's pronunciations and those preferred by adults. Table displays five common phonological errors that children make when producing words.

Reductions occur when children omit sounds from the target word. Reductions may occur with reduplication, as when children's productions involve both a loss of sounds from the target word and a repetition of a syllable from the word. Substitutions occur when the infant replaces a phoneme with a different phoneme. Assimilations occur when the infant changes a speech sound in a word so that it is similar to a speech sound appearing later in the word. Coalescence errors occur when a word is shortened, by the loss of intermediate sounds.

The quality of children's productions improves over time; however, some sounds are mastered more quickly than others. For English-speaking children, it may take years to master the articulation of all the speech sounds. English-speaking children between the ages of 4 and 8 years may make errors in the articulation of a number of consonants. The initial consonants in the words red and long are typically mastered by the age of 5. The initial consonants in the words church, shirt, zoo, joke, van, and thumb are typically mastered by the age of 6. The initial consonant in the word them is typically mastered by the age of 7. The most difficult consonant in English is the intermediate consonant in the words treasure and measure; children typically master it by the age of 8. Although most children eventually achieve adult-like pronunciation on their own, some normally developing children may be referred to speech classes, sometimes called speech therapy. In speech therapy sessions, children receive directed instruction and practice for specific speech sounds.

Building a Vocabulary

The typical adult speaker of American English may know more than 40,000 words. Considering the fact that the child produces the first word at the end of the first year, the task of building an adult-sized vocabulary is a daunting one. In order for children to achieve an adult-sized vocabulary by the age of 18, it is necessary to learn at least six words a day, on average. Parents and researchers have observed that the acquisition of vocabulary by young children does not occur at a steady rate. Between 18 and 24 months, children's vocabularies may double or triple over a short period of time. This phenomenon has been called the word spurt. Researchers have discussed the possible explanations for the word spurt. One possibility is that children experience a naming insight, at which point they realize that everything has a name. Children then may set out to learn as many new words as possible. A second possibility is that there are internal changes occurring in children's understanding of words. These internal changes may facilitate the learning of new words. For example, children may come to understand that objects in the world can be grouped into different categories, such as animals, vegetables, fruits, tools, and many others. Children may set out to learn additional members of a category after the category label has been learned.

The earliest strategy used by children to learn words has been called referential learning. Children learn words that refer to concrete aspects of the environment. The vocabulary of the 18to 24-month-old contains far more nouns than other types of words, such as verbs and adjectives. One of the most effective strategies that children can use to learn new words involves asking an adult for help. Children may point to an object and ask, "What's that?" This has been called the original word game. The adult provides the answer. The child may then attempt to say the word, and the adult provides a correction, if needed.

Children employ other less obvious strategies when learning new words. When provided with a new word in response to the question—What's that?, children as well as adults show a strong tendency to assume that the new word refers to the entire object, rather than to a part of the object or some other aspect of the object, such as color or texture. This strategy has been called the whole object bias. The philosopher Quine discussed this bias in his well-known Gavagai Problem. The problem was formulated as a hypothetical case. Imagine you are in a country where you do not speak the language and no one in this country speaks your language. You are walking along with a person native to this country. A rabbit darts across the path, and your companion points toward the rabbit and utters, "Gavagai." What do you assume Gavagai means? Usually, gavagai is taken to mean rabbit, rather than other comparably plausible meanings, such as hopping, fur, ears, or white.

Children approach word learning with two additional biases. These are the taxonomic bias and mutual exclusivity assumption. The taxonomic bias refers to the fact that children generally assume that a new word refers to a type of object, rather than a specific object. For example, the child will assume that the word dog refers to a group of animals, not just Toto. The mutual exclusivity assumption refers to the fact that once an object has been associated with a particular label, it will not be assigned a second label. This assumption leads to useful inferences about unknown objects. Consider the case in which a child is shown two objects. Assume that the child has already learned the label of one of the objects and knows it to be a wrench. If the child is then told Hand me the hammer, the child will infer that hammer refers to the object that is not the wrench because a wrench cannot be both a wrench and a hammer.

As any parent can attest, children's usages of newly learned words may not always conform to the usages preferred by adults. A child may use a word, such as cow, to refer to cows as well as other types of animals, such as any four-legged animal. Such errors have been called overextensions. Other examples of overextensions include using the word, such as hot, to refer to any object that is forbidden or using the word, such as hat, to refer to any object placed on the head. When children produce overextensions, they use a word to refer to a set of objects that is larger than the set referred to by adults. In contrast, underextensions occur when children use a word to refer to a set of objects that is smaller than the set referred to by adults. For example, a child may use the word shoes to refer to a single pair of shoes, such as Mommy's shoes, rather than any and all pairs of shoes. Other examples of underextensions include when children use the word lights only to refer to the headlights on a car, rather than all types of light, and when children use the word milk to refer only to milk in a glass, rather than milk in any container.

Constructing Sentences

Children's single-word utterances may be produced with sentence-level intent. The term holophrase refers to children's single-word utterances that have meaning more complex than that of a single word. For example, the utterance Daddy may mean a variety of things. Daddy may name the presence of the person daddy. Daddy may be a request for Daddy to perform some action. Daddy may be a reference to a location, if Daddy were holding a desired object. Daddy may also refer to some meaning comparable to the meaning of an adult sentence, such as I want Daddy to come here.

By 24 months, children are regularly producing two-word utterances, such as Daddy go or eat cookie. These two-word utterances can be viewed as miniature sentences. Roger Brown showed that there are 11 types of semantic relations typically occurring in children's two-word utterances. Approximately 75% of English-speaking children's two-word utterances can be classified in these 11 categories. Research conducted by Dan Slobin has shown that these semantic relations also appear in other languages, including Samoan, Finnish, and Russian.

Between 24 and 36 months, children's utterances become more and more similar to the sentences produced by adults. During this time, children are producing longer utterances, on average, such as utterances that contain a subject, a verb, and an object. Furthermore, children begin producing words that contain grammatical word endings or morphemes, such as the suffix -ed, which is used to create the past tense form of verbs, as in walked and talked, and the suffix -s, which is used to create the plural form of nouns, as in cups and dolls. Classic research conducted by Jean Berko-Gleason showed that children learn to form new words, such as past tense verb forms and plural nouns, by learning rules. BerkoGleason devised the Wug test to demonstrate children's knowledge of word formation rules. In the task, a child is presented with a picture of an unusual bird-like creature. The child is told, "This is wug." There is an accompanying picture depicting two of the odd creatures. The child is told, "Now, there are two of them. There are two." Children are asked which word comes next. Children as young as 3 can provide the plural form of wugs, a specific word form that they could not have heard before because the word singular word wug was a word created for use. Berko-Gleason also tested children's ability to use the English rule for using the past tense suffix -ed. Children saw a picture of a man holding a large unusual object in his hands and moving the object from side to side. Children were told, "This man is ricking. Yesterday, he" Again, children as young as 3 can fill in the past tense form, which they could not have heard before.

Table: Semantic Relations of Two-Word Utterances.

Semantic Relation	Example
Nomination	That book
Recurrence	More ball
Nonexistence	All gone ball
Agent and action	Mommy sing
Action and object	Throw ball
Agent and object	Mommy book
Action and locative	Go store
Entity and locative	Book table
Possessor and possession	Daddy chair
Entity and attribute	Big house
Demonstrative and entity	That box

The learning of word formation rules may lead children to produce forms of words that adults would not produce. In English, there are some plural nouns and some verbs that are not formed by adding the suffixes -s or –ed. For example, the plural of the noun foot is feet, rather than foots. The past tense form of the verb eat is ate, rather than eated. When children discover the rule for forming plural nouns from singular nouns or the rule for forming past tense verbs from verb stems, they may sometimes apply the rule inappropriately, as when they say foots instead of feet or eated instead of ate. These errors are called over-regularization errors. It is typical for children to produce an over-regularized form of a word that was used correctly before the rule was learned. For example, many young children produce the correct forms of the verbs go went, gone in the first 24 months. Later, when the rule for forming past tenses is learned, children may produce errors, such as *goed or *wented. After rule learning occurs, children must then determine which words follow the rule (or are regular forms) and which words do not follow the rule (or are irregular forms). Children's productions of over-regularization errors become more and more infrequent in the year following the learning of particular word formation rule.

Children's mastery of complex sentence forms suggests that children master sentence production in a series of stages. Children initially appreciate what a particular type of word means, but then must figure out how to use the word appropriately in a complete sentence. Research conducted by Edward Klima and Ursula Bellugi suggests that children's use of wh–questions, such as what did you eat?, is mastered in a series of stages. The first stage occurs in the first half of the third year of life. During this time, children produce questions with the wh– word located at the beginning of the question, but the subject and the verb are ordered as they are in an affirmative sentence, as in Where I should put it? In the second stage, children appropriately order the subject and the verb in affirmative questions, as in Where should I put it? However, children do not use the appropriate subject-verb order for negative questions, as in Why you can't sit down? In the third and final stage, children produce questions with appropriate subject-verb order for negative as well as affirmative questions. Children are typically between 48 and 54 months when they are producing well-formed wh– questions.

Edward Klima and Ursula Bellugi's research also suggests that children's production of negative sentences progresses in a series of stages, progressing from an initial stage at which the meaning of a negative word, such as no, is learned to a final stage at which children are positioning a negative word or morpheme appropriately within a sentence. Young children's first negative sentences have the form No eat cookie. The negative word no is placed at the beginning of a sentence. In the second stage, the negative word is produced in the middle of the sentence immediately before the verb, as in Doggie no bite. In the third and final stage, the child uses the negative word contracted with the verb in a form that adults use, as in Doggie doesn't bite.

Hearing-impaired Children

Many children are born each year with some form of hearing impairment. About 1 in 1,000 children is born with a severe hearing loss. In the first months of life, the vocalizations of deaf infants and hearing infants may not be easily distinguished. Deaf infants will cry, coo, and begin to babble. The amount of babbling and the quality of the babbling produced by deaf infants may be reduced when compared with the babbling of hearing infants. Deaf infants are unlikely to produce repeated consonant-vowel syllables characteristic of the canonical babbling stage.

Deaf infants who are exposed to sign language from birth develop sign language skills in a series of stages similar to those observed when hearing infants develop spoken language skills. Signed languages such as American Sign Language (ASL), British Sign Language (BSL), and Chinese Sign Language (CSL) are unique languages, each having their own rules of grammatical structure. Deaf infants exposed to a signed language will spontaneously produce gestures that can best be described as manual babbling. They will later produce one-sign utterances and later multi-sign combinations. Just as with hearing children, as deaf children mature, their multi-sign combinations become more and more complex in terms of the grammatical properties of the sign sequences. Signing children also make errors in sign production that are similar to the spoken errors made by speaking children. Signing children may produce idiomorph signs, sign overextensions, sign underextensions, and sign over-regularizations. Children's signed sentences also become more and more complex over time.

References

- Developmental-psychology: verywellmind.com, Retrieved 2 March, 2019
- Naturevsnurture: simplypsychology.org, Retrieved 12 June, 2019

- Continuity-and-discontinuity-in-development, developmental-psychology-theories, developmental-psychology: psychology.iresearchnet.com, Retrieved 11 January, 2019
- Theories-of-intelligence: mindvalley.com, Retrieved 20 August, 2019
- Infancy, prenatal-development-and-infancy, developmental-psychology: psychology.iresearchnet.com, Retrieved 21 February, 2019
- Language-development, developmental-psychology: psychology.iresearchnet.com, Retrieved 25 May, 2019

2

Educational Psychology

The domain of psychology which deals with the scientific study of human learning is termed as educational psychology. Some of the important theories within this field are Piaget's theory of moral development, Lewin's field theory of learning and Tolman's sign theory of learning. This chapter has been carefully written to provide an easy understanding of these theories within educational psychology.

Educational psychology is the scientific field concerned with applying psychological theories and concepts to the understanding and improvement of teaching and learning in formal educational settings. In simpler terms, it is concerned with the study of how students learn and how teachers can help them to learn effectively. Educational psychology draws on and combines various psychological theories and principles – such as those related to human development, motivation, learning, behavior management and assessment, among others – in order to improve the conditions of teaching and learning. Educational psychologists study the process of learning not only among the general population but also among sub-groups such as gifted children and those with various learning disabilities.

The goal of educational psychology is not to provide specific prescriptions for teachers and other individuals who have an influence on a learner's educational attainment, as if there were only a few set ways in which one can optimize the processes of teaching and learning. Rather, research in this field is designed to uncover general principles which can be applied in various ways across diverse educational settings and learners. Research in educational psychology is designed to answer questions such as:

Educational psychologists, like their counterparts in other fields of psychology, are employed in a variety of settings. They may work in colleges and universities where they either serve as lecturers or conduct research on topics relevant to education and learning. Others serve as consultants, helping to develop classroom programmes, university courses and instructional materials for people in educational or work settings. They may also assist in developing and reviewing educational policies and standards. As this takes up a significant amount of time, some choose to use the services of professional proofreaders to double-check the quality of their works. It is no simple task to balance all of these things out as an educational psychologist but making use of all the tools available to you is the first step towards success.

Other educational psychologists are employed by primary and secondary schools, in which case they may work directly with students (individually or in groups) to help them overcome problems related to their education. These may be problems which affect learning directly, as in the case of a learning disability, or indirectly, such as emotional, social and behavioural problems. In cases where learners appear to be struggling, educational psychologists usually begin my assessing their unique learning, emotional and behavioural needs through the use of observation, test materials and other assessment methods. They may then consult and collaborate with teachers, parents and other relevant individuals to develop and implement effective approaches and provisions to support learning. They also assess the progress of learners over time to determine the effectiveness of intervention.

Perspectives

Behavioral

Applied behavior analysis, a research-based science utilizing behavioral principles of operant conditioning, is effective in a range of educational settings. For example, teachers can alter student behavior by systematically rewarding students who follow classroom rules with praise, stars, or tokens exchangeable for sundry items. Despite the demonstrated efficacy of awards in changing behavior, their use in education has been criticized by proponents of self-determination theory, who claim that praise and other rewards undermine intrinsic motivation. There is evidence that tangible rewards decrease intrinsic motivation in specific situations, such as when the student already has a high level of intrinsic motivation to perform the goal behavior. But the results showing detrimental effects are counterbalanced by evidence that, in other situations, such as when rewards are given for attaining a gradually increasing standard of performance, rewards enhance intrinsic motivation. Many effective therapies have been based on the principles of applied behavior analysis, including pivotal response therapy which is used to treat autism spectrum disorders.

Cognitive

Among current educational psychologists, the cognitive perspective is more widely held than the behavioral perspective, perhaps because it admits causally related mental constructs such as traits, beliefs, memories, motivations and emotions. Cognitive theories claim that memory structures determine how information is perceived, processed, stored, retrieved and forgotten. Among the memory structures theorized by cognitive psychologists are separate but linked visual and verbal systems described by Allan Paivio's dual coding theory. Educational psychologists have used dual coding theory and cognitive load theory to explain how people learn from multimedia presentations.

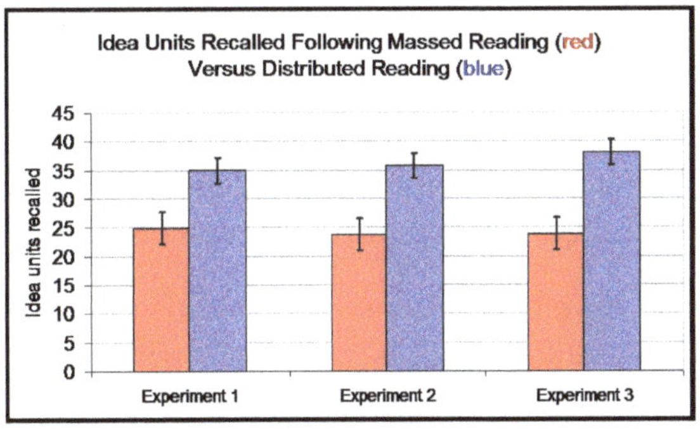

Three experiments reported by Krug, Davis and Glover demonstrated the advantage of delaying a 2nd reading of a text passage by one week (distributed) compared with no delay between readings (massed).

The spaced learning effect, a cognitive phenomenon strongly supported by psychological research, has broad applicability within education. For example, students have been found to perform better on a test of knowledge about a text passage when a second reading of the passage is delayed rather than immediate. Educational psychology research has confirmed the applicability to education of other findings from cognitive psychology, such as the benefits of using mnemonics for immediate and delayed retention of information.

Problem solving, according to prominent cognitive psychologists, is fundamental to learning. It resides as an important research topic in educational psychology. A student is thought to interpret a problem by assigning it to a schema retrieved from long-term memory. A problem students run into while reading is called "activation." This is when the student's representations of the text are present during working memory. This causes the student to read through the material without absorbing the information and being able to retain it. When working memory is absent from the reader's representations of the working memory they experience something called "deactivation." When deactivation occurs, the student has an understanding of the material and is able to retain information. If deactivation occurs during the first reading, the reader does not need to undergo deactivation in the second reading. The reader will only need to reread to get a "gist" of the text to spark their memory. When the problem is assigned to the wrong schema, the student's attention is subsequently directed away from features of the problem that are inconsistent with the assigned schema. The critical step of finding a mapping between the problem and a pre-existing schema is often cited as supporting the centrality of analogical thinking to problem solving.

Cognitive View of Intelligence

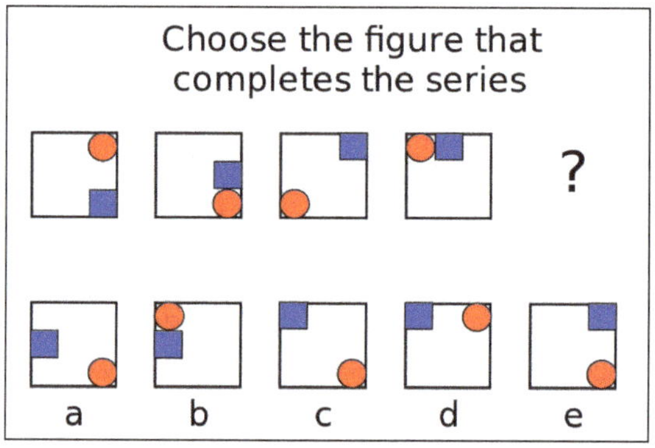

An example of an item from a cognitive abilities test.

Each person has an individual profile of characteristics, abilities and challenges that result from predisposition, learning and development. These manifests as individual differences in intelligence, creativity, cognitive style, motivation and the capacity to process information, communicate, and relate to others. The most prevalent disabilities found among school age children are attention deficit hyperactivity disorder (ADHD), learning disability, dyslexia, and speech disorder. Less common disabilities include intellectual disability, hearing impairment, cerebral palsy, epilepsy, and blindness.

Although theories of intelligence have been discussed by philosophers since Plato, intelligence testing is an invention of educational psychology, and is coincident with the development of that discipline. Continuing debates about the nature of intelligence revolve on whether intelligence can be characterized by a single factor known as general intelligence, multiple factors (e.g., Gardner's theory of multiple intelligences), or whether it can be measured at all. In practice, standardized instruments such as the Stanford-Binet IQ test and the WISC are widely used in economically developed countries to identify children in need of individualized educational treatment. Children classified as gifted are often provided with accelerated or enriched programs. Children with identified deficits may be provided with enhanced education in specific skills such as phonological awareness. In addition to basic abilities, the individual's personality traits are also important, with people higher in conscientiousness and hope attaining superior academic achievements, even after controlling for intelligence and past performance.

Developmental

Developmental psychology, and especially the psychology of cognitive development, opens a special perspective for educational psychology. This is so because education and the psychology of cognitive development converge on a number of crucial assumptions. First, the psychology of cognitive development defines human cognitive competence at successive phases of development. Education aims to help students acquire knowledge and develop skills which are compatible with their understanding and problem-solving capabilities at different ages. Thus, knowing the students' level on a developmental sequence provides information on the kind and level of knowledge they can assimilate, which, in turn, can be used as a frame for organizing the subject matter to be taught at different school grades. This is the reason why Piaget's theory of cognitive development was so influential for education, especially mathematics and science education. In the same direction, the neo-Piagetian theories of cognitive development suggest that in addition to the concerns above, sequencing of concepts and skills in teaching must take account of the processing and working memory capacities that characterize successive age levels.

Second, the psychology of cognitive development involves understanding how cognitive change takes place and recognizing the factors and processes which enable cognitive competence to develop. Education also capitalizes on cognitive change, because the construction of knowledge presupposes effective teaching methods that would move the student from a lower to a higher level of understanding. Mechanisms such as reflection on actual or mental actions vis-à-vis alternative solutions to problems, tagging new concepts or solutions to symbols that help one recall and mentally manipulate them are just a few examples of how mechanisms of cognitive development may be used to facilitate learning.

Finally, the psychology of cognitive development is concerned with individual differences in the organization of cognitive processes and abilities, in their rate of change, and in their mechanisms of change. The principles underlying intra- and inter-individual differences could be educationally useful, because knowing how students differ in regard to the various dimensions of cognitive development, such as processing and representational capacity, self-understanding and self-regulation, and the various domains of understanding, such as mathematical, scientific, or verbal abilities, would enable the teacher to cater for the needs of the different students so that no one is left behind.

Constructivist

Constructivism is a category of learning theory in which emphasis is placed on the agency and prior "knowing" and experience of the learner, and often on the social and cultural determinants of the learning process. Educational psychologists distinguish individual (or psychological) constructivism, identified with Piaget's theory of cognitive development, from social constructivism. A dominant influence on the latter type is Lev Vygotsky's work on sociocultural learning, describing how interactions with adults, more capable peers, and cognitive tools are internalized to form mental constructs. Elaborating on Vygotsky's theory, Jerome Bruner and other educational psychologists developed the important concept of instructional scaffolding, in which the social or information environment offers supports for learning that are gradually withdrawn as they become internalized.

Jean Piaget's Cognitive Development

Jean Piaget was interested in how an organism adapts to its environment. Piaget hypothesized that infants are born with a schema operating at birth that he called "reflexes". Piaget identified four stages in cognitive development. The four stages are sensorimotor stage, pre-operational stage, concrete operational stage and formal operational stage.

Major Psychological Schools of Thought

"Psychology has a long past but only a short history." With these few words, Hermann Ebbinghaus, one of the great thinkers in psychology, aptly captured the essence of this field's development. Since time immemorial, men and women have pondered over questions that are psychological in nature. From the early Egyptians to the ancient Greek philosophers, there has been no letup in efforts to understand human thought and behavior. Yet, in spite of its long past, the formal history of psychology dates back only 133 years to 1879 – the year when Wilhelm Wundt opened the doors of the first psychology laboratory in Leipzig, Germany. As a result of this significant move, Wundt is widely regarded as the founder of psychology. Yet, this was just the beginning of Wundt's contributions to the field. He went on to become the first of several spirited speakers to engage in an ongoing debate over what should be the focus of psychology. The history of psychology is indeed short, but it has never been short of drama. With that said, let the drama unfold.

Structuralism

Wundt's ideas formed the basis of the first school of thought (or perspective) in psychology, known as structuralism. In reality, though, it was one of Wundt's students, Edward B. Tichener, who formally established this psychological school of thought. Structuralism, as the name suggests, was centered on investigating the structure of the mind. Wundt believed that psychology should focus on breaking down consciousness into its basic elements, in much the same way a child would pull apart a toy to reveal its component parts. The idea of determining the specific structure of something so abstract and dynamic as the mind may seem absurd to many today. Yet, structuralists were confident that not only could they accomplish this goal, but that they could do so scientifically.

Wundt advanced the technique of introspection as the "scientific" tool that would enable researchers to unveil the structure of the mind. Introspection involves looking inwards; reflecting on, analyzing and trying to make sense of our own internal experiences as they occur. In employing this technique, trained subjects were presented with various forms of stimuli and asked to describe as clearly and "objectively" as possible what they experienced. Reports would then be examined to determine the basic elements of consciousness. For example, if you were presented with a slice of cake, it would not be enough to simply identify the type of food before you. You would also need to explain the basic elements of the cake that you able to sense. For example, you might describe the taste, smell, texture, colour, and shape of the cake in as much detail as possible.

Structuralism played a significant role in shaping the field of psychology during its formative years. Wundt and his followers helped to establish psychology as an independent experimental science and their emphasis on scientific methods of inquiry remains a key aspect of the discipline today. Nevertheless, structuralists could not escape criticism. Despite their noble attempt at scientific investigation, introspection was less than ideal because no two persons perceive the same thing in exactly the same way. Subjects' reports therefore tended to be subjective and conflicting. Some of the fiercest criticisms of structuralism came from the person of William James, one of the leading proponents of the functionalist perspective.

Functionalism

From the point of view of American scholar William James, structuralists were sorely misguided. The mind is fluid, not stable; consciousness is ongoing, not static. Attempts to study the structure of the mind would therefore be futile at worst and frustrating at best. A more fruitful endeavor, they argued, would be to study the function, as opposed to the structure, of the mind. Function in this sense can mean one of two things – first, how the mind operates – that is, how the elements of the mind work together – and second, how mental processes promote adaptation. Clearly influenced by the teachings of Charles Darwin and the principle of natural selection (survival of the fittest), James believed that mental processes serve vital functions that enable us to adapt and survive in a changing world. Thus, while the structuralists asked "what happens" when we engage in mental activity, the functionalists were more concerned with "how it happens" and "why."

Functionalism contributed greatly to the development of psychology. It extended both the subject matter of psychology as well as the range of methods use to acquire data. For example, thc functionalists' emphasis on adaptation led them to promote the study of learning since this is believed to improve our adaptability and chances of survival. Their concern with "why" certain mental processes occur also meant that they did extensive work on motivation. Functionalists are also credited with bringing the study of animals, children and abnormal behaviour into psychology, as well as an emphasis on individual differences. In addition, while the structuralists established psychology as a pure science, the functionalists broadened this narrow focus by also concentrating on the practical application of psychology to real-world problems. As it relates to research methods, functionalists added to the existing repertoire by utilizing mental tests, questionnaires and physiological measures, in addition to introspection.

Nevertheless, functionalists had their share of flaws. Like structuralists, they relied heavily on the technique of introspection with all the shortcomings previously mentioned and were criticized for only providing a vague definition of the term "function." Despite repeated verbal attacks aimed at each other, neither structuralism nor functionalism remained at the forefront of psychology for very long. Both made significant contributions to psychology but neglected one important influence on human thought and behaviour – the unconscious. Here is where Sigmund Freud made his great début.

Psychoanalysis

Mention the word psychology, and few persons would fail to recall Sigmund Freud. Like the structuralists and functionalists before him, Freud believed in studying covert behavior, but unlike his predecessors, Freud was not content with examining only conscious thought; he dived head-first into the unconscious. Freud compared the human psyche to an iceberg – only a small portion is visible to others with most of it lying below the surface. Freud also believed that many of the factors that influence our thoughts and actions lie outside of conscious awareness and operate entirely in our unconscious. Psychology therefore needed to study these unconscious drives, motives and impulses to arrive at a more complete understanding of the individual.

Not all modern psychologists subscribe to Freud's psychoanalytic theory but none can deny the significant impact that this man has had on psychology. He opened up whole new frontiers in psychology and proposed one of the most comprehensive theories of personality ever written, complete with explanations of how the unconscious mind works and how personality develops in the early years of life. Many later theorists were influenced directly and indirectly by Freud as they either built on, modified or reacted to his sometimes controversial views. Freud's work led to the development of the first form of psychotherapy – one which has been modified and used by countless therapists throughout the history of psychology. Even all this, to use Freud's analogy, is just the very "tip of the iceberg" as far as his contributions are concerned.

No other psychological school of thought has received as much attention, admiration and criticism as Freud's psychoanalytic theory. One of the biggest criticisms is that his theory falls short of being scientific as many of his concepts are not testable. Freud also failed to recognize how experiences after childhood contribute to personality development and focused mainly on psychological disorders rather than more positive, adaptive behaviours.

Behaviourism

Despite their differences, structuralism, functionalism and psychoanalysis all shared an emphasis on mental processes – events that are unseen to the naked eye. John B. Watson, a staunch supporter of behaviourism, strongly objected to this approach and prompted a revolution in psychology. Watson was an advocate of scientific scrutiny but for him, covert behavior, including mental processes, could not be studied scientifically. The emphasis, from his perspective, should only be on overt or observable behavior. Behaviourists believed that human behavior can be understood by examining the relationship between stimuli (events in the environment) and responses (observable behavior). They saw no need to employ subjective techniques such as introspection to infer mental processes over which even trained subjects and researchers could not agree. What was once the study of the mind thus became the study of observable behaviour.

B.F. Skinner, another famous behaviourist, supported Watson's view by advancing the idea that human behavior can be explained by reinforcement and punishment – observable, environmental factors – with no need to consider inner mental processes. Later behaviourists adopted a more balanced view of matters, embracing the study of both overt and covert behavior. These became known as cognitive behaviourists.

Watson's call for greater objectivity, radical as it was greatly propelled psychology along the path to becoming a science rather than a mere body of philosophical thought. Many of the learning theories used by psychologists today were also born out of the behaviourist school of thought and are frequently applied in behavior modification and the treatment of some psychological disorders (e.g. phobias). Nevertheless, the strict behaviourist view of Watson was in no way superior to the narrow emphasis of structuralists and functionalists on mental life alone. Indeed, "many aspects of human experience (e.g. thinking, intrinsic motivation, creativity) lie outside a strict behavioural definition of psychology". These too must be studied in order to gain a more complete understanding of the individual. This was one of the key arguments of another emerging school of thought known as gestalt psychology.

Gestalt Psychology

The word "gestalt" means "form, pattern or whole." Gestalt psychologists believed that psychology should study human experience as a "whole," not in terms of separate elements as the structuralists would contend. Their slogan, "the whole is greater than the sum of its parts" conveyed the idea that meaning is often lost when psychological events are broken down; only when these pieces are analyzed together and the whole pattern is visible do we find true meaning in our experiences. To use an example, imagine breaking apart the words you are now reading into individual letters and scattering them as you wish across the page. Would you be able to discern anything meaningful from them? Quite likely, you wouldn't. Only when the letters are properly combined to form words and then structured into sentences do you grasp any true meaning. The "whole" then becomes something different, something greater than the accumulation of its "parts."

Gestalt psychologists, such as Max Wertheimer, did extensive work on various aspects of cognition, including perception, problem-solving and thinking. Additionally, their insistence on studying individuals and experiences as wholes is still preserved in psychology today. Their work also led to the emergence of a form of psychotherapy widely practiced by modern psychologists.

Humanistic Psychology

With the rise of each school of thought mentioned previously, the face of psychology was gradually taking shape. Yet, not all were satisfied with the way things were progressing. Foremost among these were the humanistic psychologists, such as Carl Rogers, who were uncomfortable with the highly deterministic view of two of the major forces in psychology – psychoanalysis and behaviourism. Determinism is the idea that our actions are controlled by forces beyond our control. For the psychoanalysts, these forces are unconscious; for the behaviourists, they exist in our environment. Humanistic psychologists, however, viewed humans as free agents capable of controlling their own lives (as opposed to being controlled), making their own choices, setting goals and working to achieve them. Humanism asserted a positive view of human nature, stressing that humans are inherently good. A unique form of therapy also emerged out of this school of thought, with emphasis on helping people to achieve their full potential. This differed greatly from psychoanalysis which only focused on reducing maladaptive behavior.

Scopes of Educational Psychology

Scope of the subject implies its field of study. Speaking in specific terms, it means the areas of study that are included in a particular subject. The scope of Educational Psychology is securing greater and greater importance in the field of education. Educational psychology is the combination of two i.e. Educational and Psychology. So educational psychology is the study of behavior of the teacher, taught and person is connected to educational environment. Educational psychology is, therefore, that branch of educational content, which deals with human behavior and its modification.

The following are included in the scope of Educational Psychology:

Human Behavior

It studies human behavior in educational situations. Psychology is the study of behavior and education deals with the modification of behavior and hence, educational psychology pervades in whole field of education.

Growth and Development

It studies growth and development of the child. How a child passes through various stages of growth and what are the characteristics of each stage are included in the study of Educational Psychology.

Learning Process

It studies the law of learning: learning is a major phenomenon in education. It studies how learning can take place most effectively and economically.

Heredity and Environment

To what extent heredity and environment contribute towards the growth of the individual and how this knowledge can be used for bringing about the optimum development of the child, form a salient feature of the scope of Educational Psychology.

Personality

Educational Psychology deals with the nature and development of the personality of an individual. In fact, education has been defined as an all-round development of the personality of an individual; personality development also implies a well-adjusted personality.

Individual Difference

Every individual differs from another and it is one of the fundamental facts of human nature, which has been brought to light by Educational Psychology. This one fact has revolutionized the concept and process of education.

Intelligence and its Measurement

The scope of Educational Psychology includes the study of the nature of intelligence as well as its measurement. This is of great importance for a teacher or an educator.

Guidance and Counseling

This is one of the most important fields or areas of study included in the field of Educational Psychology. Education is nothing but providing guidance to the growing child. Thus, guidance forms an important aspect of Educational Psychology.

The following five areas were named by American Psychological Associations:

- Human growth and development, including the effect of heredity and environment on various aspects of individual,
- Learning: The nature of learning process, factors influencing the learning process etc.,
- Personality and adjustment: It include many sub-topics, such as, mental health of the students and teachers character,
- Measurement and evaluation, statistics,
- Techniques and methods of Educational Psychology.

Thus, Educational Psychology describes and explains the learning experience of an individual from birth to old age. Its subject matter is concerned with the conditions that affect learning.

Importance of Educational Psychology

The importance of educational psychology and teachers has the following points:

- Educational Psychology helps teacher to know that how learning takes place.
- It enables a teacher that how learning process should be initiated, how to motivate, how to memorize or learn.

- It helps teachers to guide the students in right direction in order to canalized student's abilities in right direction.
- It informs a teacher, about the nature of the learners and his potentialities.
- It helps a teacher to develop a student personality because the whole educational process is for student's personality development.
- It helps a teacher to adjust his methodologies of learning to the nature / demand of the learner.
- It enables a teacher to know the problems of individual differences and treat every student on his / her merit.
- It helps a teacher that how to solve the learning problems of a student.
- It helps a teacher that how to evaluate a students that whether the purpose of teaching & learning has been achieved.

Importance of Educational Psychology in Education

Following are the points which show the importance of education psychology in education. It also shows how educational psychology and education have importance for another another.

- Learner: Educational Psychology studies various factors which have impacts upon students, which may include home environment, social groupings, peer groups, his / her emotional sentiments, and mental hygiene etc. Various methods are used in order to get the desired data about the learner in order to know about him / her mentality and behavior and its manifestations.
- The Learning Process: Here educational psychology investigates that how information and knowledge be transferred and what kinds of methodologies should be used for that purpose.
- Learning Situation: Educational Psychology studies the factors which are situational in nature that how environment like of classroom be managed and how discipline be maintained. Besides it, it studies various Audio Video Aids & its role in facilitating the teaching learning process.
- Curriculum Development: Educational psychology helps curriculum developers that what kind of curriculum should be made and what kinds of content be given to teachers to transfer to the next generation.
- Evaluation Techniques: Educational psychology helps educators that what kinds of evaluation techniques should be used to test the learner that to what extend information and concept have been transferred.

Methods of Educational Psychology

The following points highlight the top six methods of educational psychology. The methods are: 1. Introspection 2. The Observational Method 3. The Experimental Method 4. The Clinical Method 5. The Genetic or Developmental Method 6. The Testing Methods.

Psychology, we have observed before is a systematic and scientific study of human behaviour. It has its special tools and procedures. These tools and procedures help us in gathering and organising its subject-matter or the essential facts about it. These procedures are called its methods.

These methods have to be scientific, consistent and systematic if the knowledge that we get through them is to be used for scientific purposes. Educational psychology uses all these main methods of psychology. Besides these methods, there are certain other methods that are used by educational psychologists in the collection and organisation of necessary data.

The following are some of its method:

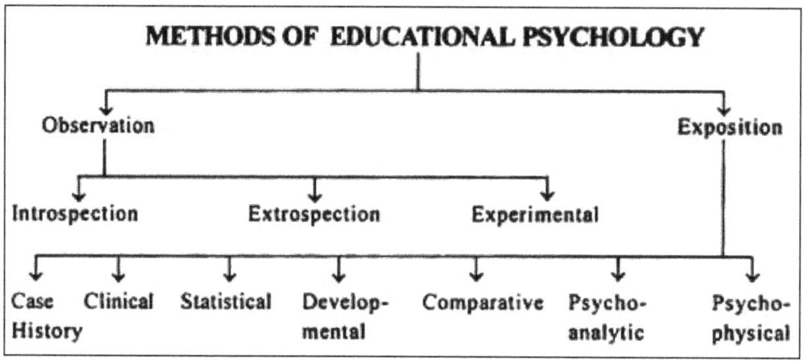

Method 1: Introspection

Introspection is one of the older methods and is peculiar to psychology. It means looking within, looking into the working of our own minds and reporting what we find there. In order words, it is a method of "self-observation "— observation by an individual of his own mental states directly by directing attention towards a particular experience with a particular purpose.

This kind of self-observation, therefore, is not a vague, unsystematic or haphazard observation. For example, a student has been asked to answer a question. He has to recall certain facts learned by him to organise them in a particular manner and then to report what way he tried to recall, what he thought and felt when trying to recall. Thus, it is a method in which the individual observes analyses and reports his own feelings, thoughts or all that passes in his mind during the course of a mental act or experience.

Advantages

The method has many advantages. It enables us to understand one's mental set at a certain time and thus throws light on behaviour, which is reflective of mental experience. Mere objective and direct observation of a person is not enough. We need to know what is going on in the mind of that person. An artist is painting a picture. We observe him carefully and find that, he is sitting absorbed in a certain posture, that he makes certain gestures or that he is mixing such and such colours.

But how he is doing it, what feelings and thoughts are passing his mind we can learn only when he introspects his own mind and reports. Then alone, we are in a position to understand fully his act or behaviour of painting. Again, the method does not entail any expenses. There is no need for any laboratory or apparatus. We obtain a direct knowledge of the mental experience of the individual.

Objections

Several objections have been raised against this method by later psychologists i.e., after Titchner. It is a purely private affair. The results of introspection are only subjective. Something is going on in another person's mind; it is not accessible to me or to you. Hence, it cannot be verified by other observers. What cannot be verified or repeated by others lack scientific validity. The essence of science is controlled observation under experimental conditions. Scientific results are always verifiable. Hence, introspection is regarded as an unscientific method.

Another difficulty of the method is that it may destroy the very experience or process it aims at studying. Our immediate memory can come to our rescue and we can recall the process to a large extent. Thus introspection actually becomes retrospection. Besides, this method cannot be found useful in studying children, animals, insane people and mental defective or those who are not good at linguistic expression. This is a limitation of the method.

Forms

One of the forms of introspection that is used in educational psychology is the anecdotal method. It consists of the recording of personal impressions about some aspect of pupil behaviour which seems significant to the observer. According to Brown and Martin, "anecdotes are descriptive accounts of episodes or occurrences in the daily life of the student." These accounts are written out of memory of the teacher or observer.

The method is open to criticism since the teacher or observer may have missed certain things or may not remember accurately. He may also be influenced by suggestion.

The questionnaire is another form of the introspective method, which is used in the appraisal of personal qualities, attitudes, opinions and beliefs of individuals. Galton used this method in his study of individual differences and Stanley Hall in his study of childhood and adolescence.

A questionnaire is a series of printed or written questions which the individual is supposed to answer. It is a useful device, which is frequently used by educational and vocational counsellors. But the usefulness of this method depends on how specific and clear the instructions are. In framing a questionnaire, one should be clear about the objectives in hand.

Questions should be so framed that the answers can easily be given or the right answer easily checked. The answers obtained are then compiled, classified and analysed or categorised and interpreted. The questionnaire is a type of introspective method because the answers of various questions evoke 'retrospective processes' as in pure introspection.

Method 2: The Observational Method

It is one of the most popular of methods used in psychology for collection of data. This method is also called the method of 'objective observation' as against introspection which is a method of self-observation. The individual's behaviour is observed by somebody other than that person himself. The behaviour observed may be expressed in the form of bodily changes, bodily action, gestures, facial expression and speech.

The psychologist may sit down and take notes of the behaviour of a subject under particular conditions. The method was used widely by child psychologists who would prepare running records of all that the child did during a certain period and in a certain situation. These observations enabled them to make certain generalisations about human behaviour in general.

Difficulties

Psychologists found that they could not keep pace with the speed of subjects' behaviour and thought as expressed by them. This problem was solved to a large extent by the introduction of type-recording, photographic films or by employing a number of stenographers to record the behaviour.

There was another problem besides the speed of behaviour. It was felt that the subject's behaviour can be affected by the presence of the psychologist in the room. The subject may become self-conscious and may not behave naturally, which he would have done had been alone in the room. This introduced the use of one-way screens and the system of observation-booths.

The subject would behave in the most natural manner without knowing that he was being observed or studied. Child development center and child guidance clinics are generally fitted with one-way glass screens or observations booths. Direct observation however, can be quite effective one the subject or subjects get used and adjusted to the presence of the psychologist.

Precautions

In order to have reliable and correct observations, there are certain precautions that should be borne in mind:

- Firstly, the observer must adopt an objective attitude. Our observations should be free from our own biases, prejudices and result from sustained attention.
- Secondly, it is necessary that before we form an estimate of an individual's behaviour, we should have made a number of observations of the same behaviour in similar conditions.
- Thirdly, if needed. We should pool our observations with those made by others.
- Fourthly, the problem that has to be observed is well-defined and observers are trained to distinguish between what is observed and what is interpreted.
- Fifthly, to ensure accuracy of observation and to reduce the effect of bias, the behaviour may be observed for a specific period of time, after it has been analysed into its various aspects.

This device is called "time sampling" i.e., the behaviour is sampled for a short and definite period of time and it is regarded as representative of the behaviour in general covered by the various analysable elements together. This device has been used by Iver James Robertson in his study. "A Two-year Old Goes to Hospital". He has observed the reactions of a hospitalised child to various situations and persons of suitable intervals, for a short period every time, with the help of a carefully drawn-up proforma to be filled in by the observer.

Method 3: The Experimental Method

The experimental method in psychology was made popular first by a German psychologist named

Wundt who opened the first psychological laboratory at Leipzing in 1879. The tremendous progress which psychology has made during the last 50 years is due to the use of this method.

Experimental investigations has thrown light on different ways of memorisation, the effect of different factors on learning, mental fatigue, image and imagination, span of attention, the effects of giving children practice or coaching on intelligence tests, transfer of training, the role of maturation in learning and the like.

According to Chapin "An experiment is an observation under controlled conditions." Festinger says, "The essence of an experiment may be described as observing the effect on a dependent variable of the manipulation of an independent variable."

Historical Background

The experimental method was first of all introduced by William Wundt in 1879 at Leipzig Laboratory. In 1880, Ebbinghaus conducted many experiments on memory. Rice and Common conducted many experiments on spelling achievements. Thorndike, Juad, Freeman, Kohler, Pavlov and Skinner etc. conducted many experiments in various fields.

The use of this method has raised psychology to the status of an experimental science like physics, chemistry and physiology, although the former cannot attain the degree of objectivity and verifiability that we can in the latter.

It will be desirable here to understand the essentials of the experimental method. "The essence of an experiment consists in controlling the condition under which a phenomenon occurs, then varying those conditions systematically and noting the results. In observation, we are content to take facts as we find them; but in an experiment we are not.

Thus, in this method all conditions or variable affecting the behaviour are held constant or unchanged or controlled: only one single specific condition is changed. This specific condition or variables is called "an independent variable"; other conditions or variables are called "dependent variables".

Supposing we want to study experimentally the day-to-day influence of room temperature on a group of students who are learning. We will have to use the same group at the same hour, with always a similar task to be done, with always the same conditions of seating, lighting, absence from distractions, interests or purposes, and direction giving; but with varying room temperature from sitting to sitting.

Thus, we will be able to state with confidence, after carrying out this experiment for a few days, that the most efficient mental work is accomplished, at least for those subjects, with room temperature, say at 70 °F.

Another important technique of experimentation in educational psychology is the use of control-group method. Suppose we want to study the effect of a period of intellectual activity after memorising a prose passage, on the amount of material remembered. We can have two groups of students or subjects. They will be equated in age, intelligence socio-economic or cultural status and also in their memorising ability.

The later will be ascertained through various tests and observations. Both these groups will be then given the task of memorising a prose passage. The passage having been memorised, group 'A' will be given some rest-pause for a certain period whereas group 'B' will be given some other intellectual task, say, of working out some mathematical problems during this interval.

At the end of the interval, the two groups will be compared in regard to the amount of material they can remember from the passage originally learned. Group 'A' is the control group and group 'B' is the experimental group. The comparison will either prove or disprove our hypothesis i.e., that the period of intellectual activity after the passage has been memorised improves or increases the amount of material remembered.

The same technique could be used to prove or disprove the hypothesis that the administration of glutamic acid, if given at a certain age and for a certain period, will increase the intelligence level of mentally deficient children. Subjects constituting the control group do not receive the drug whereas those of the experimental group do set it. Proving or disproving a hypothesis is technically described as 'testing' a hypothesis. A hypothesis is formed on the basis of available general knowledge insight and research inferences.

The following Characteristics of an experiment will further highlight the meaning of experimental method:

1. Observation under controlled conditions: An experiment consists of objective observation of actions performed under rigidly controlled or laboratory conditions. Control is the basic element in experimentation. In it the influence of extraneous factors that are not included in the hypothesis are prevented from operating and confusing the outcome which is to be appraised. Three types of control, namely (i) Physical control, (ii) Selective control, (iii) Statistical control are operated in an experiment.

2. Randomisation: As it very difficult to exercise complete control, efforts are made to assign cases in the experimental and control groups randomly.

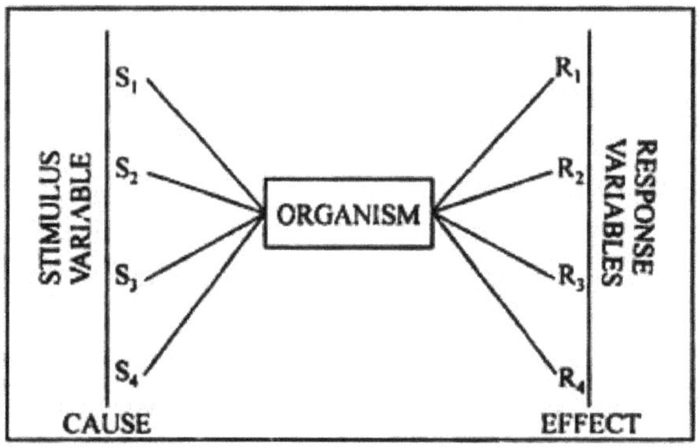

3. Replication: Replication implies conducting a number of sub- experiments within the framework of an overall experimental design.

The following are the essential features or requirements underlying the experiment:

1. Psychological laboratory: There should be psychological laboratory fully equipped with apparatus.

2. Experimenter: There is an experimenter or experimenters.
3. Subject: There is a subject or subjects on whom the experiment is performed. In physical sciences, experiments are performed on inorganic or dead subjects, whereas in psychology experiments are performed on living subjects.
4. Stimulus: By "stimulus", we mean any physical force in the environment which impinges (strikes) the organism to behave, or to react.
5. Response: Response is reaction to the stimulus. It can also be defined as change in behaviour which can be observed. So observable changes in behaviour is known as response.
6. Variables: The term "variable" means that which can be varied or changed or that which changes or varies itself. The stimulus is changed and the response changes. The former represents one type and the latter another type of variable. The first variable (stimulus variable) can be changed by the experimenter at will and is deliberately and systematically varied to find out how this is accompanied by changes in the second set of variables (response variables). The variation in the response variable is known to follow changes in the stimulus variable. However, there is no such definite relation in reverse direction.

In the worlds of James N. Shafer, the world 'variable' itself refers to any event or process that may assume different values. A person's height and weight would be examples of physical variables while intelligence and personality would be considered psychological variables.

There are mainly three types of variables:

Stimulus Variables

Independent variable is one which is systematically and independently varied or manipulated by the experimenter. For example, if we want to study the effect of noise on mental activity, then in this example noise is an independent variable since it is the variable from which we predict changes in mental activity.

Independent variables in psychology can be classified into following groups:

Environmental Variables

Perhaps the most common type of independent variable studied by psychologists is the variation of some aspect of the environment. In the above example, noise is an independent variable. Noise is an environmental condition.

Instructional Variables

A second type of variable often studied by psychologists is the kind of instruction given to the subjects. Depending on the instructions, a subject may have a set to respond in different ways. Instruction may influence his response. For example, student typists who work under instructions to emphasize accuracy may become better typists than students who are introduced to emphasize speed.

Task Variables

The experimenter may be interested in knowing the effect of manipulating aspect of the task itself. Difficulty of the task, length of the task, similarity of the task, meaningfulness of the task, pleasantness of the task may serve as independent variables.

Subject Variables

Subject variables involve characteristics of the individuals such as age, sex, intelligence, race and fatigue.

Organismic Variables

Organismic variables are those variables which are within the organism.

Some of the organismic variables are following:

- Habit strength, the strength of association between a certain S and certain R, based on previous learning.
- Drive such as hunger.
- Incentive like reward or punishment expected.
- Inhibition tending to diminish the momentary readiness for a response. Fatigue, satiation, distraction, fear and caution may cause inhibition.
- Individual differences due to age, sex, intelligence, interests, aptitudes, health and organic state.

Response Variables

The dependent variable is the variable that we predict will change with changes in the independent variable. In other words, dependent variable or response variable is that variable on which the effect is being studied. For example, we want to study the effect of punishment on learning. Here 'punishment' is stimulus variable and 'slow or quick speed of learning' is known as response variable.

Response variables can vary in the following ways:

- Accuracy: Measure of accuracy is almost inevitably a measure of errors.
- Speed or quickness:

  It can be measured in terms of:

  - Time limit: How much is done in the same time allowed?
  - Amount limit: How long does it take to do the assigned amount?

Probability or Frequency

When a particular response occurs sometimes but not on every trial. If there are two or more competing responses to the same stimulus or situation, the probability of each competitor can be determined in series of trials. The percentage or frequency of correct responses or errors is an index of discrimination.

Strength or Energy Response

The lesser the energy is consumed in attaining a certain result, the greater is the efficiency.

Response Latency

Response latency is the interval between a stimulus change and the occurrence of a response. It must be noted that in experiment, we hold all stimulus variables of influence constant except one and this one we can change and vary. The effects of these changes are observed, measured and recorded.

From the description of an experiment given above it will be clear that certain condition must be borne in mind for its success:

- We have to understand the organism and its nature fully. The human subjects on which the experiment is being performed may be an adult or a child or an adolescent.
- The maturation level reached by the organism must not be ignored.
- The state of the organism at the time of experiment must be considered. It is important to know if the organism is hungry, fatigued or bored.
- If the experiment involves danger to human subjects, it must be performed on the species close to human beings i.e., chimpanzees rather than rats.
- The condition or variable that affect the behaviour should be controlled and defined as perfectly as possible. These controls are called experimental controls. However, where experimental controls are not possible, various types of statistical controls may be used instead.

Characteristics of Experimental Method

- It enables us to study behaviour under controlled conditions.
- It is scientific in nature.
- The experimental method can be repeated without any difficulty.
- The results or conclusions arrived at by this method are reliable.
- Randomization.

Steps of Experimental Method

- Statement of the problem.

- Formulation of hypothesis.
- Designing the independent and dependent variable.
- Controlling the conditions of experiment.
- Selection of experimental design.

  Analysis of the result.
- Verification and confirmation of the hypotheses by the result of the experiment.

Merits of Experimental Method

- Reliable and Valid: Experimental method is most reliable, most valid, most systematic, most precise and most objective method of psychology.
- Exact Science: It is the experimental method which has made psychology a science and put it on scientific footing. As Woodworth states, "Experiment has made psychology an exact science." It gives us the exact results, as statistical techniques and calculations are used in it.
- Universal Application: This method has universal application. It can be applied in case of children as well as adults. Even animals can be studied with the help of this method. It becomes difficult to study all types of people with the help of other methods.
- Wide Applications: It has wide applications in all the branches of psychology especially in the intelligence measurement, personality measurement, attitude formation, individual differences and mental disorders.

  Experimental investigations have been thrown light on different methods and laws of learning and memory, effect of different factors of learning, memory, attention, interest, motivation, transfer of training, growth and development and finally development of personality.
- Quantitative Measurement: It has introduced quantitative measurement in psychology. Individual is studied internally by this method in a quantitative manner like the study of emotion, motivation, learning and perception etc.
- Special Activities: There are some special activities which can be studied only with the help of experimental method. For example, phenomena of conditioning can be studied only with the help of experimental method. Similarly reaction time of the subject cannot be tested with the help of any method except the experimental method.
- Pre-planned: It can be pre-planned and the experimenter can be fully prepared for the accurate observation.
- Variation and Repetition: The experimenter can control and create the conditions himself which influence the fact under investigation and can vary them systematically. He can repeat them as often as he wants. In observation, he has to wait for the natural phenomenon to occur. The experimenter can repeat the experiment for many times without any wait.

- Verification: It is given to verification. Results of the experiment can be verified.
- Utility in Education: Experimental method has been widely used in almost all the aspects of education i.e., in:
    - Determining the aim of education,
    - Curriculum,
    - Methods of teaching,
    - Framing the timetable,
    - Recruiting teachers,
    - Measuring the achievements of the pupils,
    - In guidance programme.

Demerits of Experimental Method

- Lengthy and Time Consuming: It is very lengthy, time consuming and energy consuming.
- Expensive: It is very expensive or costly as it requires well equipped laboratory or apparatus and experts to handle them. Prof. Woodworth says, "Experiment is a very costly affair."
- Difficulty in Controlling Variables: All the variables cannot be completely controlled. Experiments on heredity cannot be conducted on human beings under controlled conditions.
- Problem of Measuring Dependent Variable: Supposing that a suitable observable dependent variable is settled, still, there is the problem of measuring them. We do not have anything like a thermometer or an inch scale or weight box. We cannot say that such and such person has so much of anxiety. We can only say that such and such person is more worried today than yesterday or he is more worried than another individual. Our measures are purely ordinal and comparative. This also limits the scope of our generalisations.
- Artificiality: There is certain amount of artificiality of laboratory conditions and this artificiality does curb our results.
- A Gulf Between Laboratory and Life: In the laboratory, we control all other variables and arrive at a finding regarding the relation between a specific stimulus and a specific response. In actual life, several stimuli act at the same time and several responses appear. Hence there is a gulf between the laboratory experiments and life.
- A man who is hungry, thirsty, sick and has no money whose child has died and whose wife is in the hospital is a cold fact we get in life. But no laboratory has studied such a man and perhaps no laboratory will be able to do that though we may succeed in studying individually the effect of each one of the above facts.
- Every Phenomena cannot be Studied: Every phenomena cannot be studied in the laboratory e.g., to study the causes of abnormality and abnormal behaviour we cannot make

our subject mad. Similarly, we cannot retard the growth of a child to find out the causes of retardation.

- Restriction of Time and Place: In method of introspection and observation there is no restriction of time and place. But in experimental method, there is restriction of time and place. An experiment cannot be conducted at all times and all places. As Prof. Murphy states, "The restrictions of time, place and laboratory are a great obstacle in the study of human behaviour."

Method 4: The Clinical Method

The clinical method is also called case study method. It is used by clinical psychologists, psychiatrists, psychiatric social works and teachers in child guidance clinics or mental hygiene centers or in ordinary school situations. Generally, we use this method when we want to understand the causes and sources of people's fears, anxieties, worries, obsessions their personal, social, educational and vocational maladjustments.

A couple of students in your class are showing poor scholastic achievements or some behaviour problems. You want to understand the causes so that you may plan some treatment procedures. This method will be useful in such conditions. It may be noted that the clinical methods or "procedures are not designed to discover general behavioural trends, laws or relationships. Rather they are concerned with a unique individual who is trouble in and interest is focussed on the immediate, practical question of how to best help him. The starting point of a clinical investigation is an individual who needs or seeks help and the procedure ideally terminates with the better adjustment of the individual."

The clinical investigator may start with some hypothesis about the probable causes of the difficulty or troublesome behaviour. The tentative hypothesis is supported or disproved by the data collected through the use of case-history, interviews, visits to the home or school and psychological testing. From the data collected, certain deductions are made as to probable treatment. The employment of this method includes the use of case histories, interviews and psychological testing.

A case history traces the family and health, history, hereditary factors, classifies the developmental data, the educational progress, interpersonal and inter-parental or intra-parental relationships, and thus makes us understand the major forces and influences, which have developed and shaped the individual's personality.

The clinical method, in itself, cannot claim to the objectivity attained by the experimental method, but it may afford fruitful new hypothesis which can be tested by the better controlled experimental procedures.

Method 5: The Genetic or Developmental Method

This method, by laying emphasis on the developmental aspects of behaviour, seeks to find out the causes of that behaviour in its crude beginnings. It assumes that a full appreciation of such behaviour patterns of an adult requires the study of simple behaviour patterns in his childhood. These simple behaviour patterns grow more complex gradually as the individual grows in age.

An understanding of an adult can be facilitated if we begin with the learning behaviour in his childhood, go on to the study of such behaviour in his preadolescence and adolescence. This background should help us to arrive at some conclusions about the learning behaviour in adulthood.

The same can be said about the development of imagination, thinking and reasoning. This method seeks to answer such questions as: How do we become what we are? What do we inherit? How is inheritance modified in childhood, adolescence and adulthood? What changes take place in thought and behaviour at different stages of life? How does the perception develop?

Method 6: The Testing Methods

The testing methods comprise psychological tests, educational measurements, rating scales, checklists and questionnaires. Some writers characterise rating scales, checklists and questionnaires as field investigation methods as different from the testing methods. We know that the use of questionnaires as a form of the introspective method. Rating scales and checklists are often used as important devices of observing and evaluating personality or behaviour traits.

In rating scales we rate or judge an individual on the possession or absence of certain traits. The individual is given a place on the scale or a score which indicates the degree to which a person possesses a given behaviour trait.

For example, if we want to rate teacher- trainees on their sociability we might ask three or four supervisors to point out the place of each teacher trainee on the scale which may be as follows:

Avoids others	**Tolerates others**	**Likes others**	**Likes others well**	**Seeks others**

This scale has five degrees of the trait to be rated: This is a five point scale. Some scales have three or seven degrees. The descriptive words or phase used in the scale may be also given marks or scores, from zero to five.

The psychological tests are carefully devised and standardised tests for measuring aptitudes, interests, achievement, intelligence and personality traits. Intelligence tests measure the intellectual capacity of an individual and achievements tests throw light on the achievement of students in various subjects they are studying. Aptitude tests will enable us to evaluate the nature and degree of aptitude of a person for a certain subjects or profession.

In many teacher training colleges such test have been developed for selecting candidates for teacher training courses. Personality tests which are of various types shed light on general personality patterns, cluster of traits, moods temperament, emotionality, interpersonal relationships, needs and pressure and other qualities.

Language Development

We have been exploring the enigma of language — its power in helping us understand one another, and the mischief caused by misinterpretations.

Consider again this excerpt of a letter Wilbur Wright sent to Octave Chanute, the friend and mentor of the Wright brothers with whom they had a falling out — and Wilbur's eloquence in wanting to use language to discuss the feelings and avoid a rupture.

"My brother and I do not form many intimate friendships, and do not lightly give them up. I believed that unless we could understand exactly how you felt, and you could understand how we felt, our friendship would tend to grow weaker instead of stronger. Through ignorance or thoughtlessness, each would be touching the other's sore spots and causing unnecessary pain. We prize too highly the friendship which meant so much in the years of our early struggles to willingly see it worn away by uncorrected misunderstandings, which might be corrected by a frank discussion".

Language Beyond the Toddler Years

We ended last month discussing the concept of translation: the notion of putting words to feelings and feelings into words. This process of translating has benefits throughout life. It is of tremendous importance to put words to feelings and actions. Many people suggest adolescents are hard to understand. They are not. If one goes back to the basics, it all makes sense. What are the actions, the words? How can we translate from the actions and words back to the feelings? Are they distressed and angry? Are they curious and excited? Once we translate back to the feelings, and then accurately label these feelings, everything falls nicely into place. It starts with translating — translating words back into feelings.

To summarize, language represents a huge developmental leap. It is a stunning trip, from the child's expressing feelings and motives through facial expressions and vocalizations to a point where he or she can use words as symbols that shape direct and help form his or her personality and emotions. There are few things more exciting to watch or more of a privilege in which to participate.

Language, Translation and Later Development

Up to now, we have talked about the psychology of feelings primarily in the context of infancy and early childhood. It is time to put feelings into the larger scope of individual development and ages beyond childhood.

To make a very long story somewhat shorter, the basic built-in affects or feelings remain intact as we get older. These nine rapid affect responses are still there, but now the subjective sensations are describable with words. We gain more control over our feelings and responses. These feelings blend together with each other and with experience to create our more complex emotional life.

Studies using high-speed film show this relationship between our built-in responses and our conscious control. When subjects are asked to keep smiling even in the face of a slight pinprick, the high-speed film picks up the subjects' brief facial expressions of distress and anger in response to the pinprick before resuming the smile. The naked eye does not see this change of expression. The subcortical part of the brain (which is responsible for the preverbal built-in feelings and responses) as well as the cortex (our conscious efforts to understand and manage our feelings and responses) are both operating as we grow older.

This is why we have emphasized the importance of language and use of words in dealing with feelings. When words are linked with feelings in a young child, we are in essence helping the cortex do its job in better managing our feelings.

The cortex has the capacity to use symbols — words — for various biological responses and feelings. The cortex enhances our capacities to deal with our biological responses. Thus we gain greater tension-regulation, via the cortex, as we put words to feelings. Impulsive action lessen; awareness, thinking, and verbalizing increase. These opportunities for greater cortical involvement begin around 18 months in the child. This is what allows for greater self-awareness, self-consciousness, tension-regulation (or affect-regulation), words instead of actions.

Words and Feelings

The onset of language, or cortical involvement, is a double-edged sword, as infant-researcher Daniel Stern has put it. With the benefits come the liabilities, namely that words mean different things to different people, can be used to deceive and distort, and can split us from our underlying biological substrate. Thus, while our emotional life gets more complex as affects combine with each other and experience, it is useful to go back to the basics, the nine built-in feeling responses.

What does this mean, to go back to the basics? It means focusing on the affects, the feelings. It means translating backwards, in a sense: here are the words and actions, what are the feelings that motivated and caused the words and actions?

As we saw earlier: the young child says "I hate you I no like you!" What are the feelings? Distress and anger or with adolescents: a 15-year-old waiting for the train becomes bored, not anxious or excited. He begins fooling around with the various luggage tags on a pile of suitcases on a cart. His parents finally get upset and tell him to stop. But what's happening here? The stimulus-seeking brain is doing just what it's supposed to do — and the teenager is bored! Interest and enjoyment are not being triggered. So the answer is easy — translate back to the need for interest and enjoyment. What reading, or game, or music might be of interest? One sees this all the time — smaller children at restaurants or in the grocery stores, for instance.

Beyond Early Childhood: Adolescence through Adulthood

The nine basic feelings help make sense of all developmental phases—infancy through early childhood through adolescence through adulthood through old age. Focus on the positive affect of interest and enjoyment — this is effective in understanding and altering behavior at any age. Attend to the causes of negative affect and try to fix whatever has triggered distress, anger, shame, and so on — this too is important at any age.

As the child ages, however, the translation becomes different because of words. In infancy, one looks to facial expressions and vocalizations for clues to what feelings are being expressed. In later childhood, adolescence, and adulthood, one looks to words and actions, and then translates from these to the feelings.

Therapeutic Implications and Interpersonal Skills

This notion of translating from words back to the feelings also holds up clinically with patients. The effectiveness of psychotherapy involves the patient-therapist relationship and understanding and interpreting the patient's internal world. The key constant in work with patients is trying to understand the underlying feelings — the feelings which lie, consciously or unconsciously, behind a patient's words and actions. It is in helping people understand what they are feeling, what they are interested in and what they are distressed by, that gets them on track.

Many patients do not know who they are, what they really like or dislike. To some extent, they have developed what Winnicott called a False Self, a need to comply, a lack of sense of what is authentic and genuine to them. How this happens, and what we do clinically to help, is somewhat complicated. But in some sense it boils down to this: we are so eager to teach our children, to impart information, to socialize them, that we forget to learn about them and help them learn about themselves. Further, we often impose various religious systems on them to help them control their feelings and impulses and actions — usually because we don't understand how feelings really work. We are well-intentioned—without knowing how feelings work, we impose external systems to help us deal with a child's feelings, words, and behaviors.

Elicit Rather than Impose

There is another option – that is, being open to how feelings do seem to work internally. And with that in mind, we have to turn much of the foregoing on its head—we need to learn from the child! Rather than continuing to impose our systems and likes and dislikes, we need to learn what the child likes, dislikes, is interested in or bored by.

This is what lies behind Stanley Greenspan's Floortime concept. The parent acts as a benign assistant to the play; he/she validates the child's interests and play. In this way, the parent learns about their child, and the child learns what he/she likes and dislikes—i.e. who they are! This is a reciprocal process—the child learns from us, and we learn from the child.

In the midst of our desire to socialize the child we often forget to learn from her. The concept underlying much of this is that the child is separate from us, a separate new individual, with her own likes and dislikes — and who she is, and how she is different from and similar to us, is crucial to her development. This learning from her is crucial in terms of her learning about herself. And her learning about herself is crucial in developing a career she enjoys and can commit to 110 percent, finding a partner whom she loves, and so on.

Feelings, Actions and Interpersonal Skills

We have discussed the importance of linking feelings and words. This process has benefits in enhancing tension-regulation and self-soothing, promoting verbalization, and increasing thoughtfulness, rather than impulsive action.

However, we also need to remember that verbalizing—using words—is also an action. We strive for as much self-awareness as possible — internal freedom to have whatever thoughts and feelings come to our mind. We want to be playful with our various feelings and fantasies inside of our selves. This awareness permits us greater control over our actions and behaviors. Suppressing and repressing our inner feelings can make it more difficult to control ourselves. We have a better chance of controlling our behaviors if we are aware of our feelings and what is motivating us.

Similarly, in terms of interpersonal skills, it is useful to appreciate that our words are actions. We can hurt or heal with words. So, while one promotes linking words with feelings, one also needs to be aware of the impact on others of the words and verbalizing. As Aristotle said, “Anyone can become angry—that is easy. But to be angry with the right person, to the right degree, at the right time, for the right purpose, and in the right way—that is not easy”.

Typical Stages of Language Development

Receptive Language

Receptive language development refers to how children develop listening skills and an understanding of the language they are hearing.

Birth

Language learning starts at birth. Even new babies are aware of the sounds in the environment. They listen to the speech of those close to them, and startle or cry if there is an unexpected noise. Loud noises wake them, and they become “still” in response to new sounds.

0-3 Months

Between 0-3 months babies learn to turn to you when you speak, and smile when they hear your voice. In fact, they seem to recognise your familiar voice, and will quieten at the sound of it if they are crying. Tiny babies under three months will also stop their activity and listen closely to the sound of an unfamiliar voice. They will often respond to comforting tones whether the voice is familiar or not.

4-6 Months

Between 4 to 6 months babies respond to the word “no”. They are also responsive to changes in your tone of voice, and to sounds other than speech. For example, they can be fascinated by toys and other objects that make sounds, enjoy music and rhythm, and look in an interested or apprehensive way for the source of all sorts of new sounds such as the toaster, birdsong and the whirr of machines.

7-12 Months

During the 7 to 12 month timeframe, the baby will listen when spoken to, turns and looks at your face when called by name, and discovers the fun of games like “peep-oh” and “pat-a-cake”. They will begin to recognise the names of familiar objects (“Daddy”, “car”, “eyes”, “phone”, “key”) and begin to respond to requests (“Give it to Granny”) and questions (“More juice?”).

1-2 Years

Now your child points to pictures in a book when you name them, and can point to a few body parts when asked (nose, eyes, tummy). He or she can also follow simple commands (“Push the bus!”, “Don’t touch; it’s hot!”) and understand simple questions (“Where’s the toy?” “Who likes chocolate?”, “What’s in your bag?”). Your toddler now likes listening to simple stories and enjoys it when you sing songs or say rhymes. This is a stage in which he or she will want the same story, rhyme or game repeated many times.

2-3 Years

By now your toddler will understand two stage commands ("Get your coat and put your shoes on") and understand contrasting concepts or meanings like hot / cold / stop / go / in / on and nice. He or she notices sounds like the telephone or doorbell ringing and may point or become excited, get you to answer, or attempt to answer themselves.

3-4 Years

Your three or four year old understands simple "Who?", "What?" and "Where?" questions, and can hear you when you call from another room. This is an age where hearing difficulties may become evident. If you are in doubt about your child's hearing, speak to your GP who will refer you to a clinical audiologist.

4-5 Years

Children in this age range enjoy stories and can answer simple questions about them. He or she hears and understands nearly everything that is said (within reason) at home or at pre-school or day care.

Expressive Language

Expressive language refers to how children learn to speak and use Language.

Birth

Newborn babies make sounds that let others know that they are experiencing pleasure or pain.

0-3 Months

Your baby smiles at you when you come into view. He or she repeats the same sound a lot and "coos and goos" when content. The baby uses a different cry for different situations to help you differentiate between what they need. For example, one cry says "I'm hungry" and another says "I have a pain".

4-6 Months

Gurgling sounds or "vocal play" occur while you are playing with your baby or when they are occupying themselves happily. Babbling really gets going in this age range, and your baby will sometimes sound as though he or she is talking. This speech-like babbling includes many sounds, often these are bilabial (two-lip) sounds e.g. 'p', 'b' and 'm'. They also use different pitches. Your baby can tell you, using sounds or gestures that they want something, or want you to do something. He or she can use very "urgent" noises and facial expressions to spur you into action.

7-12 Months

The sound of your baby's babbling changes. This is because it now includes more consonants, as well as long and short vowels. He or she uses speech and/or sounds other than crying to get your attention and hold on to it. Your baby's first words may be spoken (they may not be very clear yet). Examples of typical first words are: "MaMa", "Doggie", "Night Night", "Bye Bye", "No").

1-2 Years

Now your baby is accumulating more words as each month passes. He or she will even ask 2-word questions like "Where ball?" "What's that?" "More choc", and combine two words in other ways to make other sentence types ("Birdie go", "No doggie", "More push"). Words are becoming clearer as more initial consonants are used.

2-3 Years

Your two or three year old's vocabulary is increasing quickly. He or she seems to have a word for almost everything. Utterances are usually one, two or three words long and family members can usually understand them. Your toddler may ask for, or draw your attention to something by naming it ("Dog") or one of its attributes ("Red!") or by commenting ("Wow!").

3-4 Years

Sentences are becoming longer as your child can combine four or more words. He or she talks about things that have happened away from home, and is interested in talking about pre-school, friends, outings and interesting experiences. Speech is usually fluent and clear and people outside of the family can understand what your child is saying most of the time.

4-5 Years

Your child speaks clearly and fluently in an easy-to-listen-to voice. He or she can construct long and detailed sentences ("We went to the zoo but we had to come home early because Sally wasn't feeling well". He or she can tell a long, involved imaginative story sticking to the topic, and using "adult-like" grammar. Most sounds are pronounced correctly, though he or she may be lisping as a four year old, or, at five, still have difficulty with "r", "v" and "th".

Your child can communicate easily with familiar adults and with other children. Your child may tell fantastic, dramatic, inventive, "tall stories" and engage strangers in conversation when you are out together.

Piaget's Theory of Moral Development

Piaget was principally interested not in what children do (i.e., in whether they break rules or not) but in what they think. In other words he was interested in children's moral reasoning. Piaget was interested in three main aspects of children's understanding of moral issues. They were Children's understanding of rules. This leads to questions like:

- Where do rules come from?

- Can rules be changed?
- Who makes rules?

Children's understanding of moral responsibility. This leads to questions like:

- Who is to blame for "bad" things?
- Is it the outcome of behavior that makes an action "bad"?
- Is there a difference between accidental and deliberate wrongdoing?

Children's understanding of justice. This leads to questions like:

- Should the punishment fit the crime?
- Are the guilty always punished?

Piaget found that children's ideas regarding rules, moral judgements and punishment tended to change as they got older. In other words just as there were stages to children's cognitive development so there were also universal stages to their moral development.

Piaget suggested two main types of moral thinking:

- Heteronomous morality (moral realism).
- Autonomous morality (moral relativism).

Heteronomous Morality (5-9 yrs)

The stage of heteronomous morality is also known as moral realism – morality imposed from the outside. Children regard morality as obeying other people's rules and laws, which cannot be changed.

They accept that all rules are made by some authority figure (e.g. parents, teacher, God), and that breaking the rules will lead to immediate and severe punishment (immanent justice).

The function of any punishment is to make the guilty suffer in that the severity of the punishment should be related to severity of wrong-doing (expiatory punishment).

During this stage children consider rules as being absolute and unchanging, i.e. 'divine like'. They think that rules cannot be changed and have always been the same as they are now. Behavior is judged as "bad" in terms of the observable consequences, regardless on the intentions or reasons for that behavior. Therefore, a large amount of accidental damage is viewed as worse than a small amount of deliberate damage.

Research Findings

Piaget told the children stories that embodied a moral theme and then asked for their opinion. Here are two examples:

- There was once a little girl who was called Marie. She wanted to give her mother a nice surprise and cut out a piece of sewing for her. But she didn't know how to use the scissors properly and cut a big hole in her dress.

- A little girl called Margaret went and took her mother's scissors one day when her mother was out. She played with them for a bit. Then, as she didn't know how to use them properly, she made a little hole in her dress.

The child is then asked, "Who is naughtier?" Typically younger children (pre-operational and early concrete operational i.e. up to age 9-10) say that Marie is the naughtier child.

Although they recognise the distinction between a well-intentioned act that turns out badly and a careless, thoughtless or malicious act they tend to judge naughtiness in terms of the severity of the consequence rather than in terms of motives. This is what Piaget means by moral realism.

Piaget was also interested in what children understand by a lie. Here he found that the seriousness of a lie is measured by younger children in terms of the size of the departure from the truth.

So a child who said he saw a dog the size of an elephant would be judged to have told a worse lie than a child who said he saw a dog the size of a horse even though the first child is less likely to be believed.

With regard to punishment Piaget also found that young children also had a characteristic view. Firstly they saw the function of punishment as make the guilty suffer. Paint called this retributive justice (or expiatory punishment) because punishment is seen as an act of retribution or revenge.

If you like young children have a very Old Testament view of punishment ("an eye for an eye"). Punishment is seen as a deterrent to further wrongdoing and the stricter it is the more effective they imagine it will be.

They also believe in what Piaget called immanent justice (that punishment should automatically follow bad behavior). For example one story he told was of two children who robbed the local farmer's orchard (today we might take the example of children who robbed cars).

The farmer saw the children and tried to catch them. One was caught and the farmer gave him a thrashing. The other, who could run faster, got away. However on the way home this child had to cross the stream on a very slippery log. This child fell off the log and cut his leg badly.

Now when you ask younger children why the boy cut his leg they don't say, "because the log was slippery," they say, "because he stole from the farmer". In other words young children interpret misfortune as if it were some kind of punishment from God of from some kind of superior force.

For young children justice is seen as in the nature of things. The guilty in their view are always punished (in the long run) and the natural world is like a policeman.

Piaget (1932) described the morality described above as heteronomous morality. This means a morality that is formed out of being subject to another's rules. Of course for young children these are the rules that adults impose upon them. It is thus a morality that comes from unilateral respect. That is to say the respect children owe to their parents, teachers and others.

However as children get older the circumstances of their lives change and their whole attitude to moral questions undergoes a radical change. An example of this is is how children respond to a question about the wrongdoing of a member of their peer group.

Young children typically "tell" on others. They believe their primary obligation is to tell the truth to an adult when asked to do so. Older children typically believe that their first loyalty is to their friends and you don't "grass" on your mates. This would be one example of the two moralities of the child.

Autonomous Morality (9-10 yrs)

The stage of autonomous morality is also known as moral relativism – morality based on your own rules. Children recognize there is no absolute right or wrong and that morality depends on intentions not consequences.

Piaget believed that around the age of 9-10 children's understanding of moral issues underwent a fundamental reorganisation. By now they are beginning to overcome the egocentrism of middle childhood and have developed the ability to see moral rules from other people's point of view.

A child who can decentre to take other people's intentions and circumstances into account can move to making the more independent moral judgements of the second stage. As a result children's ideas on the nature of rules themselves, on moral responsibility and on punishment and justice all change and their thinking becomes more like that of adults.

Children now understand that rules do not come from some mystical "divine-like" source. People make rules and people can change them – they are not inscribed on tablets of stone. With regard to the "rules of the game" older children recognise that rules are needed to prevent quarrelling and to ensure fair play.

Indeed sometimes they even become quite fascinated with the whole issue and will for example discuss the rules of board games (like chess, Monopoly, cards) or sport (the off-side rule) with all the interest of a lawyer. They also recognise that rules can be changed if circumstances dictate (e.g. "You've got one player less so we will give you a three goal start") and if everybody agrees.

With regard to issues of blame and moral responsibility older children don't just take the consequences into account they also consider motives. Children begin to realize that if they behave in ways that appear to be wrong, but have good intentions, they are not necessarily going to be punished. Thus for them a well-intentioned act that turned out badly is less blameworthy than a malicious act that did no harm.

So children of 10 and over typically consider Margaret the naughtier child. Although Marie made a much bigger hole in her dress she was motivated by the desire to please her mother whereas Margaret may have caused less damage but did not act out of noble intentions.

It all goes to show, in Piaget's opinion, that children are now able to appreciate the significance of subjective facts and of internal responsibility.

Children's views on lying also change. The seriousness of a lie is judged in terms of betrayal of trust. They now recognise that all lies are not the same and, for example, you might tell a "white lie" in order to spare someone's feelings.

They also recognise that if someone says something that they know not to be the case this doesn't necessarily mean the other person is telling a lie. It could be that they made a mistake or that this is a difference of opinion. Overall lying is now considered wrong not because you get punished for it by adults (the younger children's view) but because it is a betrayal of trust and undermines friendship and co-operation. With regard to punishment the emphasis now moves from retribution to restitution. Its purpose is not primarily to make the guilty suffer but to put things right again.

In other words punishment should be aimed at helping the offender understand the harm (s)he has caused so that (s)he will not be motivated to repeat the offence and, wherever possible, punishment should fit the crime – say for example when a vandal is required to make good the damage (s)he has caused.

Older children also recognise that justice in real life is an imperfect system. Sometimes the guilty get away with their crimes and sometimes the innocent suffer unfairly. For younger children collective punishment is seen as acceptable.

For example they would not disagree with a whole class being punished for the misdeeds of a single child. For the older children it is always considered wrong to punish the innocent for the misdeeds of the guilty.

Overall Piaget describes the morality of the older child as an autonomous morality i.e. a morality that is subject to its own laws. The change is partly seen as a result of the child's general cognitive development partly due to declining egocentrism and partly to the growing importance of the peer group.

The reference group for children's moral beliefs is increasingly focused on other children and disputes between equals need to be negotiated and compromises made. In place of the unilateral respect the younger children owed to their parents an attitude of mutual respect governs relations between peers.

Critical Evaluation

Piaget's theory of children's moral development can be seen as an application of his ideas on cognitive development generally. As such his theory here has both the strengths and weaknesses of his overall theory:

1. Reliability: Piaget uses qualitative methods (observation and clinical interviews). His research is based on very small samples. His methods are not standardised and therefore not replicable.

   It is impossible to say from his research how generalizable the results are. His is exploratory research, which is useful for generating new ideas rather than for the rigorous testing of hypotheses.

2. Validity: Is Piaget testing what he thinks he is testing? This isn't clear. For example in his story of the broken cups Piaget claims to find a difference in children's views of what is

right or fair. However it may be that the answer the children give is based on their view of what would actually happen in such circumstances not what they think should happen.

3. Underestimating children's rate of development: Piaget argues that the shift from "moral realism" to "moral relativism" occurs around the age of 9 to 10 and that children younger than this do not take motives into account when judging how much someone is to blame. Other research suggests that children develop an understanding of the significance of subjective facts at a much earlier age. Nelson found that even 3-year olds could distinguish intentions from consequences if the story was made simple enough.
4. What do children's replies to a story actually mean?: This again isn't necessarily clear. Do they understand the story? Are they able to remember it correctly? Do they give the answer that they think will please the experimenter? Is their reply governed by the substantive aspects of the story (what actually happens) or by the moral principle embedded in it?
5. Does Piaget tell us what we want to know?: Piaget's research is about children's moral reasoning. Many psychologists argue that what is far more important is not what children think about moral issues but how they actually behave. And we should not forget that there is no one to one relationship between attitudes and behavior. La Pierre proved that in his research with the Chinese couple driving round America.

Language Development of a Child Factors

The following points highlight the eight main factors influencing language development of a child:

General Health and Physical Status

General physiological condition and Motor development influence language development. Severe and prolonged illness and poor health particularly during the first two years of life retards the development of speech undoubtedly. Due to illness the child is separated from others and hence cannot learn to speak.

He also lacks self-confidence because of constant illness and weak health which may retard his spontaneous desire for effective self-expression. Since the child feels unwell most of the time there is no enthusiasm to talk and communicate with others. Slightly deaf children and children who are hard of hearing may have slow speech development.

Delay in speech development may be due to deafness. If a child does not start his first word by the requisite time his ear and vocal cord should be examined by a specialist. A healthy body produces a healthy mind. A healthy child is always happy, active and full of life and progressive. He has a wholesome personality, curiosity and interest in the environment, motivation and desire to learn.

A sickly child shows regression and backwardness in all types of development. Hence all satisfactory step should be taken to improve the health condition of the baby so that retarded language development can be checked before it does further harm to the baby.

Intelligence and Cognitive Development

Language and intellectual development are so highly correlated that it is said 'The child's speech is the best single indicator of his I.Q.' This is absolutely true. A child who is early in speech is above normal in I.Q. on the contrary, a delay in some months due to illness or other factors does not mean that he is dull.

This delay may be due to other factors as well. The ability to know the meaning of words and to gain from language symbols suffers because of difference in I.Q. Mentally alert young children usually talk early. They also understand or comprehend early what is communicated to them through language.

They very quickly grasp and understand what is told to them and recognize objects and people in their immediate environment call them by name. They can express their needs and desires in correct and simple sentences.

Some children may be slow beginners, but subsequently develop mastery in language development. This delay may not be due to low intellectual development, but other factors. Keeping other factors constant, babbling at an early stage indicate higher intellectual growth.

Growth of vocabulary depends to a considerable extent on cognitive growth. In a dull child integration in language development is very poor, while an intelligent child shows great integration.

Studies and experience show that children with superior intelligence are better in vocabulary linguistic growth and sentence construction. They also show competency in the structure of sentence, length of sentences uttered and application of the words rightly. Studies of Cruickshank Johnson show that the lower the I.Q., the poorer is the speech.

Learning and Maturation

Child's language development depends a lot on learning and maturation. Infact, the interaction of these factors is crucial in determining the language development of the child. With the increase in age the vocal cord of the child matures and his learning also increases. By the interaction of these two factors language develops.

Whatever training might be given to a neonate or a three four months old baby until his vocal cord and speech muscles are not properly developed, he cannot speak a word. The fact that most of the children start speaking between 18th to 28th months suggest the strong influence of maturation in the language development.

The nervous system and the speech muscles are adequately developed by this time to start speaking. Another proof of the role of maturation in language development is that irrespective of culture, race, religion and geographical differences certain phases of speech development have a fixed sequence and they occur within a fixed range of age inspite of the individual differences.

Hence after proper maturation when the child is taught, motivated and reinforced to speak, he gains from it. Thus learning helps in language development only after a certain age, only after maturation of speech organs. Learning undoubtedly facilities language development.

If the child is not provided with proper facility, reinforcement and motivation to speak through various measures, if nobody communicates or interacts with him and he is left to live alone, his language development is affected due to want of proper training.

Hence both maturation and learning are essential for language development. Language development suffers severe setback if either one of these is deficient.

Environment

It has been established through research that favourable and stimulating environmental conditions improve the development of early speech and unfavourable environment retards it. It has been observed that orphans adopted in foster homes have better language development than orphans staying in institutions or orphanages having unstimulating environments.

The role of environment is therefore of extreme importance in the development of language. Even the effects of unstimulating environment on speech development are quite lasting and more or less permanent. The verbal ability is restricted and inhibited in poor and an illuminating environment where the child does not get any encouragement to speak.

Social class which is mostly linked to environment influences language development. Irwin, a Professor of Psychology in the University of Iowa, USA has found that by increasing the stimulation of the environment of a young child in lower class background will lead to heightened interest in language and would lead to improvement in speech.

The caretakers in the institutions usually speak less and hence never stimulate the children to speak or communicate. Due to poor environment also there is delay in the organisation of language and cognitive development. Greater opportunity to talk with adults increase the scope of language development.

Sex

During the first of life effect of gender is not observed in language development i.e., boys and girls show similar development in language. But from second year girls show better speech development than boys; girls show greater mastery of speech sounds and talk fluently than boys.

This difference becomes more pronounced with passing of age and with the difference in Socioeconomic status. Closeness of mother daughter relationship perhaps does help the girl child to have better speech development than the boy child. Boys commit more grammatical mistakes and their pronounciation is also less accurate than girls. This difference in the language development of boys and girls is enduring.

Relationship with Family Members

The relationship of the child with his family members has lasting and enduring effect on his speech development. Excessive love and over protection of parents on the one hand and faulty child rearing practices, careless handling of the child, lack of proper parenting, continued and constant tension between parents and children, particularly mother and children lead to tension, anxiety and emotional problems.

The child feels insecured. In family children come in closer personal contact than in institutions. Those children who are reared by foster mothers or baby seaters from a very early age they lack closeness with the mother and family tie. They are slow in learning and retarded in their language development throughout their life.

Too much pampering of the child by parents has negative effect on language development. Over protected and anxious mothers allow their children to speak less and restrict their language. Democratic and flexible attitude of mothers encourage the children to speak more.

Number of Family Members

This has got significant effect on language development. Some view that in a single child family the language of the child well-developed, polished and free of mistakes compared to a family with large number of children where because of competition there is more conflict and defects in language development are observed.

But another group of Psychologists argue that when there are large number of children in a family, the children get a chance to talk with each other. which facilities their language development.

Bilingualism

Bilingualism develops when a baby is compelled to learn two languages in the early childhood. When a child speaks in native language at home and another foreign language at school or even when he hears two languages at home (when the father and mother speak different languages) his language development is retarded for the simple reason that it creates confusion in the small baby and his thinking power is affected.

Hence language development is delayed and adverse effect is observed on the vocabulary, spoken language etc. of the child. Due to transfer of training principles, one word of one language is used in the second language leading to faulty sentence constriction.

It is therefore not desirable to teach two more than one language to the child before he enters school (5-6 years age). By learning two languages before school going age, it becomes difficult for the child for adjustment. Defects in sentence construction and comprehension is also observed.

When two languages compete with each other because of competition of responses there is negative effect. The child's emotional and social adjustment is also affected due to bilingualism. Realising the adverse effects of bilingualism Thompson has remarked "There can be no doubt that the child reared in a bilingual environment is handicapped in his language growth."

When father and mother speak in different languages at home, it further affects the child's language development than when parents speak one language only. Children of immigrant parents are usually subjected to bilingualism.

Kohlberg's Stages of Moral Development

Lawrence Kohlberg expanded on the earlier work of cognitive theorist Jean Piaget to explain the moral development of children. Kohlberg believed that moral development, like cognitive development, follows a series of stages. He used the idea of moral dilemmas—stories that present conflicting ideas about two moral values—to teach 10 to 16 year-old boys about morality and values. The best known moral dilemma created by Kohlberg is the "Heinz" dilemma, which discusses the idea of obeying the law versus saving a life. Kohlberg emphasized that it is the way an individual reasons about a dilemma that determines positive moral development.

After presenting people with various moral dilemmas, Kohlberg reviewed people's responses and placed them in different stages of moral reasoning. According to Kohlberg, an individual progresses from the capacity for pre-conventional morality (before age 9) to the capacity for conventional morality (early adolescence), and toward attaining post-conventional morality (once Piaget's idea of formal operational thought is attained) which only a few fully achieve. Each level of morality contains two stages, which provide the basis for moral development in various contexts.

Kohlberg identified three levels of moral reasoning: pre-conventional, conventional, and post-conventional. Each level is associated with increasingly complex stages of moral development.

Level 1: Preconventional

Throughout the preconventional level, a child's sense of morality is externally controlled. Children accept and believe the rules of authority figures, such as parents and teachers. A child with pre-conventional morality has not yet adopted or internalized society's conventions regarding what is right or wrong, but instead focuses largely on external consequences that certain actions may bring.

Stage 1: Obedience-and-Punishment Orientation

Stage 1 focuses on the child's desire to obey rules and avoid being punished. For example, an action is perceived as morally wrong because the perpetrator is punished; the worse the punishment for the act is, the more "bad" the act is perceived to be.

Stage 2: Instrumental Orientation

Stage 2 expresses the "what's in it for me?" position, in which right behavior is defined by whatever the individual believes to be in their best interest. Stage two reasoning shows a limited interest in the needs of others, only to the point where it might further the individual's own interests. As a result, concern for others is not based on loyalty or intrinsic respect, but rather a "you scratch my back and I'll scratch yours" mentality. An example would be when a child is asked by his parents to do a chore. The child asks "what's in it for me?" and the parents offer the child an incentive by giving him an allowance.

Level 2: Conventional

Throughout the conventional level, a child's sense of morality is tied to personal and societal relationships. Children continue to accept the rules of authority figures, but this is now due to their belief that this is necessary to ensure positive relationships and societal order. Adherence to rules and conventions is somewhat rigid during these stages, and a rule's appropriateness or fairness is seldom questioned.

Stage 3: Good Boy and Nice Girl Orientation

In stage 3, children want the approval of others and act in ways to avoid disapproval. Emphasis is placed on good behavior and people being "nice" to others.

Stage 4: Law-and-Order Orientation

In stage 4, the child blindly accepts rules and convention because of their importance in maintaining a functioning society. Rules are seen as being the same for everyone, and obeying rules by doing what one is "supposed" to do is seen as valuable and important. Moral reasoning in stage four is beyond the need for individual approval exhibited in stage three. If one person violates a law, perhaps everyone would—thus there is an obligation and a duty to uphold laws and rules. Most active members of society remain at stage four, where morality is still predominantly dictated by an outside force.

Level 3: Postconventional

Throughout the postconventional level, a person's sense of morality is defined in terms of more abstract principles and values. People now believe that some laws are unjust and should be changed or eliminated. This level is marked by a growing realization that individuals are separate entities from society and that individuals may disobey rules inconsistent with their own principles. Post-conventional moralists live by their own ethical principles—principles that typically include such basic human rights as life, liberty, and justice—and view rules as useful but changeable mechanisms, rather than absolute dictates that must be obeyed without question. Because post-conventional individuals elevate their own moral evaluation of a situation over social conventions, their behavior, especially at stage six, can sometimes be confused with that of those at the pre-conventional level. Some theorists have speculated that many people may never reach this level of abstract moral reasoning.

Stage 5: Social-Contract Orientation

In stage 5, the world is viewed as holding different opinions, rights, and values. Such perspectives should be mutually respected as unique to each person or community. Laws are regarded as social contracts rather than rigid edicts. Those that do not promote the general welfare should be changed when necessary to meet the greatest good for the greatest number of people. This is achieved through majority decision and inevitable compromise. Democratic government is theoretically based on stage five reasoning.

Stage 6: Universal-Ethical-Principal Orientation

In stage 6, moral reasoning is based on abstract reasoning using universal ethical principles. Generally, the chosen principles are abstract rather than concrete and focus on ideas such as equality, dignity, or respect. Laws are valid only insofar as they are grounded in justice, and a commitment to justice carries with it an obligation to disobey unjust laws. People choose the ethical principles they want to follow, and if they violate those principles, they feel guilty. In this way, the individual acts because it is morally right to do so (and not because he or she wants to avoid punishment), it is in their best interest, it is expected, it is legal, or it is previously agreed upon. Although Kohlberg insisted that stage six exists, he found it difficult to identify individuals who consistently operated at that level.

Critiques of Kohlberg's Theory

Kohlberg has been criticized for his assertion that women seem to be deficient in their moral reasoning abilities when compared to men. Carol Gilligan, a research assistant of Kohlberg, criticized her former mentor's theory because it was based so narrowly on research using white, upper-class men and boys. She argued that women are not deficient in their moral reasoning and instead proposed that males and females reason differently: girls and women focus more on staying connected and maintaining interpersonal relationships.

Kohlberg's theory has been criticized for emphasizing justice to the exclusion of other values, with the result that it may not adequately address the arguments of those who value other moral aspects of actions. Similarly, critics argue that Kohlberg's stages are culturally biased—that the highest stages in particular reflect a westernized ideal of justice based on individualistic thought. This is biased against those that live in non-Western societies that place less emphasis on individualism.

Another criticism of Kohlberg's theory is that people frequently demonstrate significant inconsistency in their moral judgements. This often occurs in moral dilemmas involving drinking and driving or business situations where participants have been shown to reason at a lower developmental stage, typically using more self-interest driven reasoning (i.e., stage two) than authority and social order obedience driven reasoning (i.e., stage four). Critics argue that Kohlberg's theory cannot account for such inconsistencies.

Learning and Maturation

A new born baby is the most helpless creature in the world. His head is too large for his body His legs and feet are too small. He cannot stand or even hold his head up. His hands are no good for any kind of skill. He has no teeth. His voice may be loud, but it is too monotonous for human speech. He has eyes and ears, but makes no real use of them. He sleeps most of the time. His brain seems to be inactive inspite of his big head.

But the baby is capable of development. He has the power of growth. His legs and hands grow to the length appropriate for a human being. His muscles grow to a size and strength sufficient for standing, walking and running. His teeth already present in rudimentary form grow and harden and break through his gums at the proper ages. His mouth and larynx grow into flexible speech organs. His brain will not only grow in size, but also in fineness of microscopic structure and so become capable for playing its part in various human activities. This growth of any organism from an immature to mature state is called maturation.

A question may be asked if it were possible to speed up a child's growth and have it complete in a single week, would that week-old grownup be a true adult a competent adult? In a week's time it would be impossible for him to know much about the world, or to master the language and the thousands of skilful acts which the adult is normally required to perform. For this we must add to the power of growth another important capacity which may be called the power of learning.

Learning is extremely important for acquiring new knowledge, skills and attitudes that are necessary for an effective life. Both growing and learning are equally significant. Woodworth and Marquis have rightly said, "While many animals reach maturity in a few weeks or months after being born, it takes the human being about 18th years, and during all these years he is learning. What he is as an adult depends on how well he has grown and on what he has learned".

Maturation and learning go hand in hand in the process of human development, growth of the structures of the body makes it possible to perform several activities and these activities make learning possible. Most of the abilities of the adult are, therefore, dependent on both maturation and learning. There are some abilities which do not depend on learning.

The first stage of development must consist wholly of maturation. An organ must have developed to a certain point before it can begin to function. For example, the heart could not start pumping blood into the arteries until it had developed for enough to be a workable pump.

Similarly, no air can possibly enter the child's lungs before birth and after birth they are well enough developed to play their part in breathing. Even the muscle first makes its appearance long before birth, as a little bud consisting of embryonic cells which have no contractile power. These cells multiply and combine muscle fibres which can contract. In the meantime, a nerve is growing out from the nerve centre to the muscle and developing adequately for enabling muscle to receive nerve impulse. Thus it continues to mature by gaining strength for proper functioning.

Once maturation has provided an organ that can work or function, it has to be strengthened by exercise. It is a fact that repeated exercise will build up strength of a muscle, but gain in strength may be due to better circulation, oxygen supply, and stimulation from the brain and so on.

The individual develops all the new knowledge and skill, acquires new understanding and attitudes through learning. In all mental activities whether, thinking, reasoning or imagining learning plays an important part. Woodworth and Marquis have mentioned, "All knowledge and skill all habits good or bad, all acquaintance with people and things, all attitudes built up in your dealing with people and things, have been learned".

Exercise or activity is necessary for learning. It may be a motor activity as in playing the football or sensory activity as in listening to a song; there must be activity in some kind or other. There is a saying "we learn by doing" which is true enough, but does not fully cover the ground. To make it complete we have to say "we learn by doing and getting results". When a young football player succeeds playing football by giving goals, result encourages him to do the same thing again.

Therefore, there is another saying, "Nothing succeeds like success. This implies reinforcement. Reinforcement is the individual's reaction to the results of his own activity. Results are important to him in all his dealings with the environment. He is encouraged to do that work where it is recognized rewarded. This leads to his better performance.

Thus there are mainly four factors of development; maturation, exercise, reinforcement and learning. These are all inter-related and it is difficult to assess their importance individually in the transformation of the infant's behavior into that of the adult. Up to the time of birth maturation plays the major role, then through exercise and reinforcement mostly birth learning occupies in important place in the development of behavior.

Of course after birth learning comes in a very big way, but we should not assume that maturation stops short. Maturation certainly has much to do with the development of teeth, bones and also of the cerebral cortex which is so immature at birth as perhaps to be nonfunctional. The child's increasing strength and skill are thus partly due to maturation and party due to learning.

The pecking behavior of young chicks can be taken as an illustration of the relation between maturation and learning. As soon as the chick comes out of the shell, it can peck at the kernels of grains scattered on the ground. But it succeeds to seize and swallow grains only in 20 per cent of the total times of pecking. Its scores however improve rapidly from day to day and experiments indicate that some of this improvement is due to continued maturation after hatching, while most of it is due to practice and learning.

Maturation thus prepares the way for learning. Each step in maturation enables the child to conduct new activities in which learning takes place. When the baby's teeth, for example, come through (maturation), he starts biting and chewing (learning).

It is controversial whether the child learns to walk or matures to walk. The adult can stimulate the child to walk and protect him from bad falls. But if the child learns to walk, he does so through his own efforts. Many animals walk as soon as they are born as maturation does the spade work for them earlier. But the human child's growth is slower and Saturation is delayed. That is the human child's legs and feet not mature enough for any efficient walking movement.

Besides, consideration of maturation of the child's brain is necessary before he can learn the complicated skills of walking.

On the whole the development of the individual from infancy to adulthood is a continuous process. His adult characteristics depend on his previous growth and experience.

Maturation is the growth of the cells and organs of the body and learning takes place through experience or interaction of the individual, with his environment. Behavioral development or transformation depends on maturation to provide mechanism that will function and on learning that is resulted out of such functions of the mechanism. For fine, both maturation and learning are responsible for all-round development of the individual.

Lewin's Field Theory of Learning

Kurt Lewin, unlike Pavlov, Skinner and Gestltian psychologists, conducted experiments on the study of behaviour of children. He utilised an elaborate experimental set-up with a view to control the child's total environment during the course of the investigation for getting detailed information.

Lewin emphasised the study of behaviour as a function of the total physical and social situation. Lewin holds that psychological laws need not be formulated solely on the basis of statistical averages. Rather the individual case is equally important.

Even if all general psychological laws were known, we would still need to understand the specific individual and 'total situation' in which he exists before we could make any prediction about his behaviour. Thus Lewin favours an idiographic psychology in which the focus is on the individual, as opposed to nomothetic psychology, where the emphasis is on Statistical average.

Lewin describes his viewpoint in the following formula:

$B = f(p,e)$

B represents behaviour

f is a function

p is the person

e is the total environment situation.

Lewin explains the individual behaviour on the basis of life-space. An individual's life-space depends on his psychological force. It includes the person; his drives, tensions, thoughts and his environment, which consists of perceived objects and events. Lewin represents his theory through a diagram in which an individual is in the centre. He moves through his life-space which consists of the totality of facts that determine his behaviour at a given time.

A life-space contains the individual himself, the goals he is seeking (positive valence) or avoiding (negative valence), the barriers that restrict the individual's movements and the path he must follow to reach his goal.

Desire creates tensions in the individual and tensions come to a balancing state and the person acts. After the goal has been achieved, the organism (individual) returns to a state of repose until a new desire activates him.

In Lewin's theory, threat, goal and barrier are the main factors. An individual who has to achieve some goal has to cross a barrier. The barrier may be psychological or physical. Because of the changes in the barrier in the life- space of an individual, continuous reconstruction takes place.

Lewin's theory is called field theory as to a psychologist field means the total psychological world in which a person lives at a certain time. It includes matters and events of past, present and future, concrete and abstract, actual and imaginary – all interpreted as simultaneous aspects of a situation. Lewin states that each person exists within a field of forces. The field of forces to which the individual is responding or reacting is called his life-space.

Lewin's theory regards learning as a relativistic process by which a learner develops new insight or changes old ones. According to the theory, learning is not a mechanistic process of connecting stimuli and responses within a biological organism. Field psychology explains development of insight as a change in cognitive structure of life-space.

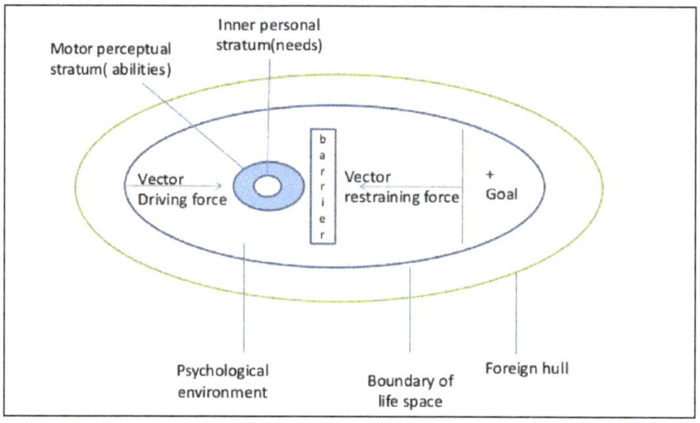

Figure: Lewin's Theory of Learning.

Lewin's theory regards learning as a relativistic process by which a learnt develops new insight or changes old ones. According to the theory, learning is not a mechanistic process of connecting stimuli and response within a biological organism. Field psychology explains development of insight as a change in cognitive structure of life-space.

Lewin's theory may be explained as under:

Suppose a person P is moving towards a goal of getting social recognition. But to achieve the goal, he has to apologies. New asking for apology is the barrier coming in his way. The barrier may be physical or psychological forces preventing him from reaching the goal. These forces organise themselves into a pattern which determines his future behaviour.

Lewin has classified learning into the following categories:

1. Learning is a change in cognitive structure.
2. Learning is a change in motivation, i.e., in valences and values.
3. Learning is acquisition of skills.
4. Learning is a change in group belonging.

Learning of all types involves change in perception.

Changes in cognitive structure are caused by the forces in the psychological field – needs, aspirations and valences.

Lewin thinks that level of aspiration depends upon the potentialities of an individual and on the influences of the group to which he belongs. Too higher or too level of aspiration discourages learning.

Main Concepts of Lewin's Field Theory

Lewin's system leans heavily on concepts derived from topology, a branch of higher mathematics that deals with transformation in space, from vector analysis, or the mathematics of directed lines and from the sciences of chemistry and physics concepts as Valence, equilibrium and field force. Lewin's most important publication is Principles of Topological Psychology.

The main concepts used in Lewin's field theory are as follows:

Topology

It is also called topological. Two basic concepts which topological space denotes are:

1. Connectedness, and
2. Part-whole relationships.

Topological concepts are used to represent the structure of life- space in such a way as to define the range of possible perceptions and actions. This is accomplished by showing the arrangements of the functional parts of life-space. The parts are shown as various regions and their boundaries. When an individual structures his life-space, he divides it into regions.

Vector

The term vector represents a force which is influencing movement towards a goal or away from it. If there is only one vector (force), there is movement in the direction of the vector. However, if there are two or more vectors acting simultaneously in different directions, the movement is in the direction of the resultant force.

Life-Space

It is also called the psychological field. The psychological field is the space in which the person moves psychologically. It contains the whole of one's psychological reality – one's self and what one thinks of or what one gains from one's physical and social environment.

The Person in Life-Space

The person is often represented as a point moving about in his life-space, affected by pulls and pushes upon him, circumventing barriers in his locomotion in his own life-space.

Valence

When a person is attracted by an object, that object is said to have a positive valence. When a person is repelled by an object that is said to have a negative valence. The person tends to move towards a region in life- space that has positive valence and he tends to move away from a region in life-space that has negative valence. Because life-space may contain regions with several valences active at a time, these give rise to conflict, especially when the opposing forces are approximately in balance.

Lewin specifies three chief kinds of conflict:

1. Two Positive Valence: Such as when a child has to choose between going to picnic and playing with his friends.
2. A Simultaneous Positive and Negative Valence: Such as when a child is offered for a reward for the school task he does not wish to perform.
3. Two Negative Valence: Such as when a child is threat-end with punishment if he does not do a task which he does not wish to perform.

Distance and Direction

When there is a close correspondence between life-space and physical space, physical distances and directions may be used for experimental purposes as approximations of distances and directions in life space.

Behaviour

Lewin regards behaviour as a function of present life space. He insists that behaviour depends upon the present and not upon the past or future.

Barrier

It is a dynamic part of an environment which resists motion through it. It stands in the way of a person's reaching his goal.

Goal

Goal is a region of valence-region of life-space to which a person is psychologically attracted.

Tension

It is very closely to and is descriptive of psychological needs. Release of tension may be achieved either through reaching a goal or through reconstructing a life-space.

Cognitive Structure

It is an environment including a person as known by the person. It is synonymous with insight or understanding.

Classroom Implications of Field Theory

Taking into consideration, the field theory as a whole, the classroom teaching-learning implications include the significance of seeing the total situation at the beginning of the lesson or an activity. The teacher should preview the activities involved and the problem to be encountered. Moreover, from the point of view of a field theorist, the teacher should keep in mind that the student, the teacher himself, other teachers, the school and the peer group- are all parts of the total situation.

The need for seeing the whole and details of the situation is very necessary. The teacher must assist the students to perceive the goal and the barrier. The goal must be presented in an easier and simplified way. Sometimes partial insight of a situation may provide partial relief from tension.

Following are the major educational implications of this theory:

Reward and Punishment

According to Lewin, the learner because of attraction to rewards may resort to shortest methods.

For example, to get distinction in the examination (record) the student may like to cheat (shortcut method). It is, therefore, necessary to put some barriers over the reward situation, to avoid access to such short methods.

In the case of punishment, however, there is a tendency to leave the field because of the unpleasantness of the task, unless some strong barriers are there to keep one in the field. Reward activities often become interesting and are liked so that motivation is no longer extrinsic while the activities controlled by the threat of punishment tend to become extremely hated.

Success and Failure

Psychological analysis of success from the point of view of the learner shows the following possibilities:

1. To reach a goal constitutes success.
2. To get within the region of the goal may be a success experience.
3. To make some progress in the direction of the goal also constitutes a success experience.
4. To select a socially approved goal is also a success experience.

Psychological success or failure depends upon ego involvement and the level of aspiration. Success in easy task is not a success experience, since it does not involve the ego of the person. Similarly, failure in a very difficult task is no failure experience.

Motivation

The repetition of an activity brings change both in the cognitive structure and in the need-tension systems. As a result of this goal, attractiveness changes. Lewin calls goal attractiveness valence and valence change.

The valence may change in any of the following ways:

1. Attractive goals may lose attention if the activity related to them is repeated to the points of satiation.
2. Choice of goals is influenced by previous experiences of success and failure.

Memory

The field theory states the following regarding memory:

1. Tasks which have no sense in completion are not remembered.
2. Unfinished tasks are remembered better than finished tasks because of psychological tension.
3. Tasks which lead to the satisfaction of many needs are remembered better than tasks which lead to the satisfaction of one need.

Tolman's Sign Theory of Learning

Basis of Learning according to Sign Theory Edward C. Tolman, like behaviourists rejected the idea of introspection as a method of studying human behaviour. On the contrary, he believed the objective method of collecting data. He remarked that we do not only respond to the stimulus but we act on beliefs, and express attitudes. Behaviour can be modified by experience and training.

Tolman's theory combines the advantages of stimulus-response theories and cognitive field theories. Tolman published his major work entitled. Purposive Behaviour in Animals and Men and recorded the results of his experiments. He revised his theory in 1949. According to the findings of these experiments, the learner does not reach the goal in fixed sequence of movements but changes his behaviour according to the variation in conditions. Tolman's theory of learning is known by several names such as "sign significance theory", "expectancy theory", "purposive behaviourism" or simple "sign theory".

The main features of this theory are as follows:

- It accepts behaviourism as basis:

  Main characterstics of behaviour are:

  - Behaviour is goal-directed i.e. it is purposive.
  - Behaviour makes use of environmental factors as means for getting at the goal.
  - Behaviour consists of the formation of cognitive maps.
  - The organism has a selective preference for the "principle of least effort", for arriving at the goal.
  - Molar behaviour is docile.
- According to Tolman, the behaviour depends upon:
  - The need system.
  - The belief value matrix.
  - The behaviour space.
- This theory takes into consideration that learning is based upon some signs or clues leading to the goal. The organism learns not the movement patterns, but the sign-significative relations.

Educational Implications

Typical Learning Problems

- Capacity: The learning of a task depends upon the capacity of the learner.
- Practice: Tolman believes that practice or exercise cannot help the learner in the initial

selection of a right response. Mere frequency without belongingness does not establish a connection.

- Motivation: Motivation does not help in learning something new. It simply encourages the performance as such.
- Understanding: Tolman believes in learning by creative inference, inventive ideation and so on. Insightful learning is emphasized.
- Transfer: Transfer of training depends upon applicability of the essential relationship perceived by the learner in one situation to some other situation.
- Forgetting: Repression and ratio-active inhibition cause forgetting Tolman attributes forgetting to the resistance of cathexis (relationship between a drive and object) also.
- Laws of Learning: Tolman stated the following laws of learning:
    - Law of Capacity: This relates to traits, characteristics and aptitudes of the learner which determine type of tasks and situations which can be mastered successfully.
    - Law of Stimulus: It deals with conditions inherent in the material itself such as belongingness of its parts and how successfully it leads to insightful solution.
    - Law of Manner: It is concerned with the manner of presentation of material such as frequency of presentation, distribution of practice and use of rewards.

References

- What-is-educational-psychology: whatispsychology.biz, Retrieved 5 April, 2019
- Deci, Edward L. (1991). "Motivation and Education: The Self-Determination Perspective". Educational Psychologist. 26 (3 & 4): 325–346. doi:10.1207/s15326985ep2603&4_6, Retrieved 15 July, 2019
- Major-psychological-schools-thought: whatispsychology.biz, Retrieved 26 January, 2019
- Importance-of-educational-psychology-for-teachers, social-sciences: studylecturenotes.com, Retrieved 6 May, 2019
- Methods-of-educational-psychology, educational-psychology-psychology: psychologydiscussion.net, Retrieved 27 March, 2019
- Language-development: psychologytoday.com, Retrieved 17 July, 2019
- Typical-stages-of-language-development: educational-psychologist.co.uk, Retrieved 19 January, 2019
- Piaget-moral: simplypsychology.org, Retrieved 9 February, 2019
- Language-development-of-a-child, social-psychology: psychologydiscussion.net, Retrieved 30 April, 2019
- Learning-and-maturation, psychology: preservearticles.com, Retrieved 14 August, 2019
- Tolmans-sign-theory-of-learning-education, learning-theory: psychologydiscussion.net, Retrieved 5 June, 2019

3

Motor Development

The development of a child's muscles, bones as well as the ability to move around is termed as motor development. The different motor skills which fall under this field are broadly divided into gross motor skills and fine motor skills. The chapter closely examines these key motor skills as well as their principles of development to provide an extensive understanding of the subject.

When babies are born, they are not able to move much on their own. Over time, a baby learns to move many parts of its body and control its muscles so it can hold its head up, sit up by itself, stand up, or pick up a toy. The process of motor development, however, does not happen overnight. Like many things, learning about the body and making it move takes time. Motor development is the process of learning how to use muscles in the body to move. The progression of acquiring motor skills goes from simple to complex.

Motor development happens in a predictable sequence of events for most children, but each child varies in age when each skill is mastered. For example, although most children begin to walk independently around twelve to fourteen months, some children are walking as early as nine months. Further, children differ in terms of the length of time it takes to develop certain motor skills, such as the baby who sits up, virtually skips crawling, and begins walking.

Transition from Reflex Movement to Voluntary Movement

At birth, babies have very little control over their bodies. They spend most of their time curled up in what is called a fetal position. This position is how the baby lay in the womb during the nine months of the mother's pregnancy. In addition to the fetal position, primitive reflexes dominate virtually all of a newborn baby's movements. Babies are born with these reflexive movements as a means for basic life preservation. The reflexes, which are controlled by lower levels of the brain, eventually give way to more sophisticated voluntary movements monitored by higher levels of the brain.

The first voluntary task of a newborn is learning to bring the arms and legs out straight in order to lie flat. This maneuver takes a lot of muscular energy, so the baby begins moving arms and legs around during the waking hours to develop coordination and strength. As babies move their bodies more in the first months of life, motor pathways begin to form in the brain. These pathways allow a baby to eventually perform motor movements without conscious thought.

Principles of Development

The process of motor development depends heavily on the maturation of the central nervous system and the muscular system. As these systems develops an infant's ability to move progresses. The sequence of motor development follows an apparently orderly pattern. Arnold Gesell, a noted researcher in the field of child development, indicated through his studies that development does not proceed in a straight line. Instead, it swings back and forth between periods of rapid and slower maturation. Gesell and his colleagues also discovered from their infant observations made in the 1930s and 1940s that infant growth does indeed follow distinct developmental directions: cephalocaudal, proximal-distal, and general to specific.

Cephalocaudal Principle

First, most children develop from head to toe, or cephalocaudal. Initially, the head is disproportionately larger than the other parts of the infant's body. The cephalocaudal theory states that muscular control develops from the head downward: first the neck, then the upper body and the arms, then the lower trunk and the legs. Motor development from birth to six months of age includes initial head and neck control, then hand movements and eye-hand coordination, followed by preliminary upper body control. The subsequent six months of life include important stages in learning to control the trunk, arms, and legs for skills such as sitting, crawling, standing, and walking.

Proximal-Distal Principle

Second, children develop their motor skills from the center of their bodies outward, near to far or proximal-distal. This principle asserts that the head and trunk develop before the arms and legs, and the arms and legs before the fingers and toes. Babies learn to master control of upper arms and upper legs, then forearms and legs, then their hands and feet, and finally fingers and toes. An example of this is an infant's need to control the arm against gravity before being able to reach for a toy.

General to Specific Principle

Lastly, the general to specific development pattern is the progression from the entire use of the body to the use of specific body parts. This pattern can be best seen through the learned process of grasping. Initially, infants can grossly hold a bottle with both hands at about four months of age. After practice and time, twelve-month-old infants can hold smaller toys or food in each hand using a pincher grasp. This finger and thumb grasp is more precise than the grasping skill of an infant at four months. Just as the child develops a more precise grasp with time and experience, many other motor skills are achieved simultaneously throughout motor development. Each important skill mastered by an infant is considered a motor milestone.

Motor Milestones

Motor milestones are defined as the major developmental tasks of a period that depend on movement by the muscles. Examples of motor milestones include the first time a baby sits alone, takes a step, hold a toy, rolls, crawls, or walks. The timing of the accomplishment of each motor milestone will vary with each child. "Motor milestones depend on genetic factors, how the mother and father progressed through their own development, maturation of the central nervous system, skeletal and bone growth, nutrition, environmental space, physical health, stimulation, freedom and mental health". Within the motor milestones exists two forms of motor development: gross motor development and fine motor development. These two areas of motor development allow an infant to progress from being helpless and completely dependent to being an independently mobile child.

Gross Motor Development

Gross motor development involves skills that require the coordination of the large muscle groups of the body, such as the arms, legs, and trunk. Examples of gross motor skills include sitting, walking, rolling, standing, and much more. The infant's gross motor activity is developed from movements that began while in the womb and from the maturation of reflex behavior. With experience, the infant slowly learns head control, then torso or trunk control, and then is rolling, sitting, and eventually walking. The first year of a baby's life is filled with major motor milestones that are mastered quickly when compared to the motor milestone achievements of the rest of the baby's development. In addition to the development of gross motor skills, a baby is simultaneously learning fine motor skills.

Fine Motor Development

Fine motor development is concerned with the coordination of the smaller muscles of the body, including the hands and face. Examples of fine motor skills include holding a pencil to write, buttoning a shirt, and turning pages of a book. Fine motor skills use the small muscles of both the hands and the eyes for performance. For the first few months, babies spend a majority of time using their eyes rather than their hands to explore their environment. The grasping reflex, which is present at birth, is seen when a finger is pressed into the baby's palm; the baby's fingers will automatically curl around the person's finger. This grasping reflex slowly integrates and allows the development of more mature grasping patterns. At four months, babies will begin to more frequently reach out for toys with their arms and hands. The reach looks more like a swipe because the baby is learning how to control the arm and hand. Over time, babies learn how to make smoother and coordinated movements with their arms and hands.

Assessment of Gross Motor and Fine Motor Development

Many assessment tools exist to measure a child's performance in regard to gross and fine motor skills. Each assessment requires good observational skills from the evaluator, who is typically a developmental pediatrician, nurse, educator, occupational therapist, or physical therapist. Some assessments call for each item to be administered in a formal standardized manner, so that each child is tested the same way every time. These tests are also called normative-based because they compare individual performance to that of other children. Other measures encourage professionals to ask parents questions about their child and are based on informal observations of the child at play. These more informal tests are referred to as criterion-based assessments because they compare individual performance to a criterion or standard. Regardless of the type of assessment, each measure has the common purpose of evaluating the child's current ability to perform motor-related tasks. Professionals use the results of these assessments to decide whether intervention is needed and also to guide goal setting and outcome measurement.

Delays in Gross Motor and Fine Motor Development

When children are not able to perform the motor skills at the appropriate milestones, their motor development may need to be evaluated by a professional. When motor skills do not progress along a normal trend, a child may be at risk for missing out on potential learning and social experiences. Children who demonstrate potential motor delays are at risk for continuing these delays throughout later development. For example, a child who demonstrates weak hand strength and has difficulty coordinating finger movement may have trouble with handwriting in school.

Early Intervention

After 1986, legislation was passed at the state level to set up services that assist families who suspect their child may have some developmental delays. These services are called early intervention systems. The main purpose of early intervention is to offer evaluation and treatment to children from birth to age three and to their families. The professionals involved with early intervention are members of a team who test a child's skills to see where the child's current skills are in relation to the chronological age. Children who are not doing many motor activities typical of their age may be considered at risk or delayed. These children may not have the strength, coordination, or balance to do most things that others of their age can do. The professionals involved in early intervention include occupational therapists, physical therapists, speech language pathologists, special education teachers, nurses, doctors, social workers, and service coordinators. Each of these professionals help the child and family learn about ways to improve motor coordination so the child can function more independently.

Types of Motor Skills

Gross Motor Skills

Gross motor skills are the abilities required in order to control the large muscles of the body for walking, running, sitting, crawling, and other activities. Motor skills are actions that involve the movement of muscles in the body. They are divided into two groups: gross motor skills, which are the larger movements of arms, legs, feet, or the entire body (crawling, running, and jumping); and fine motor skills, which are smaller actions, such as grasping an object between the thumb and a finger or using the lips and tongue to taste objects. Motor skills usually develop together since many activities depend on the coordination of gross and fine motor skills. Gross motor skills develop over a relatively short period of time. Most development occurs during childhood. However, soldiers, some athletes, and others who engage in activities requiring high degrees of endurance may spend years improving their level of muscle and body coordination and gross motor skills.

Gross motor skills development is governed by two principles that also control physical growth. Head to toe development refers to the way the upper parts of the body develop, beginning with the head, before the lower ones. The second principle of development is trunk to extremities. Head control is gained first, followed by the shoulders, upper arms, and hands. Upper body control is developed next, followed by the hips, pelvis, and legs.

Encouraging gross motor skills requires a safe, open play space, peers to interact with, and some adult supervision. Promoting the development of gross motor abilities is considerably less complicated than developing fine motor skills. Helping a child succeed in gross motor tasks requires patience and opportunities for a child to practice desired skills. Parents and other persons must understand the child's level of development before helping him or her master gross motor skills.

Children reach developmental milestones at different rates. Pushing a child to perform a task that is impossible due to development status promotes frustration and disappointment. Children should be allowed to acquire motor skills at their own paces.

There are a number of activities parents can have children do to help develop gross motor skills. These include:

- Playing hopscotch and jumping rope; activities that help children learn balance.
- Hitting, catching, kicking, or throwing a ball, such as a baseball, football, or soccer ball; activities that help develop hand-eye or foot-eye coordination.
- Kangaroo hop, in which children hold something, such as a small ball or orange, between their knees and then jump with their feet together frontward, backwards, and sideways.
- Playing wheelbarrow, in which someone holds the children's legs while they walk on their hands along a specific route.
- Walking on a narrow bar or curb, while holding a bulky object in one hand, then the other hand, and then repeating the activity walking backwards and sideways.
- Toss and catch, in which children toss an object, such as a baseball, in the air and then catch it, while sitting or lying down and also while using alternate hands.

Infancy

The first gross motor skill infants learn usually is to lift their heads and shoulders before they can sit up, which, in turn, precedes standing and walking. Lifting the head is usually followed by head control. Although they are born with virtually no head or neck control, most infants can lift their heads to a 45-degree angle by the age of four to six weeks, and they can lift both their head and chest at an average age of eight weeks. Most infants can turn their heads to both sides within 16 to 20 weeks and lift their heads while lying on their backs within 24 to 28 weeks. By about nine to 10 months, most infants can sit up unassisted for substantial periods of time with both hands free for playing.

One of the major tasks in gross motor development is locomotion, the ability to move from one place to another. Infants progress gradually from rolling (eight to 10 weeks) to creeping on their stomachs and dragging their legs behind them (six to nine months) to actual crawling (seven to 12 months). While infants are learning these temporary means of locomotion, they are gradually becoming able to support increasing amounts of weight while in a standing position. In the second half-year of life, babies begin pulling themselves up on furniture and other stationary objects. By the ages of 28 to 54 weeks, on average, they begin navigating a room in an upright position by holding on to the furniture to keep their balance. Eventually, they are able to walk while holding on to an adult with both hands and then with only one. They usually take their first uncertain steps alone between the ages of 36 and 64 weeks and are competent walkers by the ages of 12 to 18 months.

Toddlerhood

Toddlers are usually very active physically. By the age of two years, children have begun to develop a variety of gross motor skills. They can run fairly well and negotiate stairs holding on to a banister with one hand and putting both feet on each step before going on to the next one. Most infants this age climb (some very actively) and have a rudimentary ability to kick and throw a ball. By the age of three, children walk with good posture and without watching their feet. They can also walk backwards and run with enough control for sudden stops or changes of direction. They can hop, stand on one foot, and negotiate the rungs of a jungle gym. They can walk up stairs alternating feet but usually still walk down putting both feet on each step. Other achievements include riding a tricycle and throwing a ball, although they have trouble catching it because they hold their arms out in front of their bodies no matter what direction the ball comes from.

Preschool

Four-year-olds can typically balance or hop on one foot, jump forward and backward over objects, and climb and descend stairs alternating feet. They can bounce and catch balls and throw accurately. Some four-year-olds can also skip. Children this age have gained an increased degree of self-consciousness about their motor activities that leads to increased feelings of pride and success when they master a new skill. However, it can also create feelings of inadequacy when they think they have failed. This concern with success can also lead them to try daring activities beyond their abilities, so they need to be monitored especially carefully.

School Age

School-age children, who are not going through the rapid, unsettling growth spurts of early childhood or adolescence, are quite skilled at controlling their bodies and are generally good at a wide variety of physical activities, although the ability varies according to the level of maturation and the physique of a child. Motor skills are mostly equal in boys and girls at this stage, except that boys have more forearm strength and girls have greater flexibility. Five-year-olds can skip, jump rope, catch a bounced ball, walk on their tiptoes, balance on one foot for over eight seconds, and engage in beginning acrobatics. Many can even ride a small two-wheel bicycle. Eight- and nine-year-olds typically can ride a bicycle, swim, roller skate, ice skate, jump rope, scale fences, use a saw, hammer, and garden tools, and play a variety of sports. However, many of the sports prized by adults, often scaled down for play by children require higher levels of distance judgment and hand-eye coordination, as well as quicker reaction times, than are reasonable for middle childhood. Games that are well suited to the motor skills of elementary school-age children include kick ball, dodge ball, and team relay races.

In adolescence, children develop increasing coordination and motor ability. They also gain greater physical strength and prolonged endurance. Adolescents are able to develop better distance judgment and hand-eye coordination than their younger counterparts. With practice, they can master the skills necessary for adult sports.

Common Problems

There are a range of diseases and disorders that affect gross motor skill development and skills. Among young persons, developmental problems such as genetic disorders, muscular dystrophy, cerebral palsy, and some neurological conditions adversely impact gross motor skill development.

Gross motor skills can become impaired in a variety of ways, including injury, illness, stroke, and congenital deformities. Developmental coordination disorder affects motor skills. A person with this disorder has a hard time with skills such as riding a bike, holding a pencil, and throwing a ball. People with this disorder are often called clumsy. Their movements are slow and awkward. People with developmental coordination disorder may also have a hard time completing tasks that involve movement of muscle groups in sequence. For example, such a person might be unable to do the following in order: open a closet door, get out a jacket, and put it on. It is thought that up to 6 percent of children may have developmental coordination disorder, according to the 2002 issue of the annual journal Clinical Reference Systems. The symptoms usually go unnoticed until the early years of elementary school; the disorder is usually diagnosed in children who are between five and 11 years old.

Gross Motor Skills

Age	Skill
One month	May hold up head momentarily.
Two months	Lifts head when placed on stomach. Holds up head briefly when held in a seated or standing position.
Three months	Holds head and shoulders up when placed on stomach. Puts weight on forearms.
Four months	Holds head up well in sitting position. Can lift head to a 90-degree angle when placed stomach. May start to roll over.
Five months	Has full head control. When pulled by hands to a sitting position, the head stays in line with body.
Six months	Rolls over (front to back first). Bears a large percentage of body weight when held in a standing position.
Seven months	Can stand with support. May sit without support for short periods. Pushes upper part of body up while on stomach.
Eight months	Stands while holding onto furniture. Sits well unsupported. Gets up on hands and knees; may start to crawl backwards.
Nine months	Crawls first by pulling body forward with hands. May move around a room by rolling.
Ten months	Pulls up to standing. Is very steady while sitting; moves from sitting to crawling position and back. Crawls well.
Eleven months	"Cruises," walking while hanging onto furniture. Walks with two hands held.
Twelve months	Walks with one hand held. May walk with hands and feet. Stands unsupported for longer periods of time.
Fifteen months	Walks without help. Crawls up stairs. Gets into a standing position without support.
Eighteen months	Seldom falls while walking. Can walk and pull toy. Runs. Climbs stairs holding railing. May walk backward.
Two years	Kicks a ball. Walks up and down stairs, two feet per step.
Two and a half years	Jumps with both feet. Jumps off step. Can walk on tiptoe.
Three years	Goes upstairs one foot per step. Stands on one foot briefly. Rides tricycle. Runs well.
Four years	Skips on one foot. Throws ball well overhand. Jumps a short distance from standing position.
Five years	Hops and skips. Good balance. Can skate or ride scooter.

Children with any one or combination of developmental coordination disorder symptoms should be seen by a pediatrician who specializes in motor skills development delays. There are many ways to address gross motor skills impairment, such as physical therapy. This type of therapy can include treating the underlying cause, strengthening muscles, and teaching ways to compensate for impaired movements.

Girls using their gross motor skills, large muscle movements, to play soccer.

Parental Concerns

Parents, teachers, and primary caregivers need to have a clear understanding of how young children develop gross motor skills and the timetable for development of the skills. The Lincoln-Oseretsky Motor Development Scale is an individually administered test that assesses the development of motor skills in children and adults. Areas covered include fine and gross motor skills, finger dexterity and speed, and hand-eye coordination. The test consists of 36 tasks arranged in order of increasing difficulty. These include walking backwards, standing on one foot, touching one's nose, jumping over a rope, throwing and catching a ball, putting coins in a box, jumping and clapping, balancing on tiptoe while opening and closing one's hands, and balancing a rod vertically. Norms have been established for each part of the test for children aged six to 14.

When to Call the Doctor

Parents, who suspect that their child has a delay in developments should follow their instincts in having that child evaluated. The earliest intervention possible offers the highest response and success rate among children with special needs. Parents should call the doctor any time they have a concern about their child's motor skill development. Parents should keep in mind that children develop at different rates and try to focus on the skills their children have mastered instead of those they may have yet to master. Still, there are certain signs that may point to a problem, and these should be discussed with a pediatrician or physician. These signs include not walking by 15 months of age, not walking maturely (heel to toe) after walking for several months, walking only on the toes, and not being able to push a toy on wheels by age two. Toddlers may begin to prefer one hand to the other, the first sign of right- or left-handedness, or to use both hands equally. This preference should be allowed to develop naturally. Parents should call a doctor if the child does not seem to use one hand at all or has a strong hand preference before he or she is one year old.

Fine Motor Skill

Fine motor skill (or dexterity) is the coordination of small muscles, in movements—usually involving the synchronisation of hands and fingers—with the eyes. The complex levels of manual dexterity that humans exhibit can be attributed to and demonstrated in tasks controlled by the nervous system. Fine motor skills aid in the growth of intelligence and develop continuously throughout the stages of human development.

Types of Motor Skills

Motor skills are movements and actions of the bone structures. Typically, they are categorised into two groups: gross motor skills and fine motor skills. Gross motor skills are involved in movement and coordination of the arms, legs, and other large body parts. They involve actions such as running, crawling and swimming. Fine motor skills are involved in smaller movements that occur in the wrists, hands, fingers, feet and toes. They involve smaller actions such as picking up objects between the thumb and finger, writing carefully, and even blinking. These two motor skills work together to provide coordination.

Developmental Stages

Through each developmental stage of a child's life and throughout our lifetime motor skills gradually develop. They are first seen during a child's development stages: infancy, toddler-hood, preschool and school age. "Basic" fine motor skills gradually develop and are typically mastered between the ages of 6-12 in children. These skills will keep developing with age, practice and the increased use of muscles while playing sports, playing an instrument, using the computer, and writing. If deemed necessary, occupational therapy can help improve overall fine motor skills.

Infancy

The first motor skills, beginning from birth, are initially characterised by involuntary reflexes. The most notable involuntary reflex is the Darwinian reflex, a primitive reflex displayed in various newborn primates species. These involuntary muscle movements are temporary and often disappear after the first two months. After eight weeks, the infant will begin to voluntarily use their fingers to touch. However, their ability to grab objects is still undeveloped at this point.

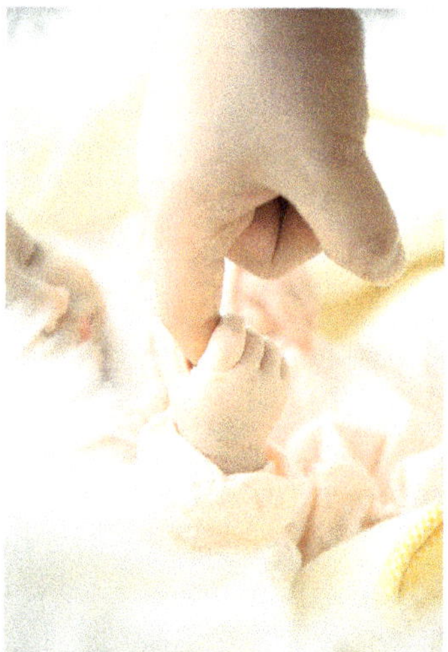

Infant displaying the palmar grasp.

At two to five months the infant will begin to develop hand-eye coordination, and they will start reaching for and grasping objects. In this way, they improve their overall grasping skills.

In 1952, Piaget found that even before infants are able to reach for and successfully grasp objects they see, they demonstrate competent hand-mouth coordination. A study was done by Philippe Rochat at Emory University in 1992, to test the relation between progress in the control of posture and the developmental transition from two handed to one handed engagement in reaching. It was found that the object reached for needed to be controlled. The precision of the reach is potentially maximized when placed centrally. It was also found that the posture needed to be controlled because infants that were not able to sit on their own used bimanual reaches in all postural positions except sitting upright, where they would reach one-handed. As a result, their grasping phases will not have been maximized because of the decrease in body control. On the other hand, if the infant does not have body control, it would be hard for them to get a hold of an object because their reach will be limited. As a result, the infant will just keep falling, stopping them from reaching an object because of no body control. When "nonsitting" infants reached bimanually, while seated upright, they often ended up falling forward which prevented them from reaching toward the target. Regardless of their ability or lack of ability to control self-sitting, infants are able to adjust their two handed engagement in relation to the arrangement of the objects being reached for. Analysis of hand-to-hand distance during reaching indicates that in the prone and supine posture, non-sitting infants moved their hands simultaneously towards the midline of their bodies as they reached which is not observed by stable sitting infants in any position. Non-sitter infants, although showing strong tendencies toward bimanual reaching, tend to reach with one hand only, when placed in the seated posture. Sitter infants show a majority of differentiated reaches in all posture conditions.

A study conducted by Esther Thelen on postural control during infancy used the dynamic systems approach to observe motor development. The findings suggest that early reaching is constrained by head and shoulder instability. The relationship between posture and reaching cannot be disentangled. Thus, head control and body stability are necessary for the emergence of grasping.

The next developmental milestone is between seven and twelve months, when a series of fine motor skills begins to develop. These include, but are not limited to, increase in grip, enhancement of vision, pointing with the index finger, smoothly transferring objects from one hand to the other, as well as using the pincer grip (with the thumb and index fingers) to pick up tiny objects with precision. A lot of factors change in grasping when the infant becomes seven months. The infant will have better chance of grasping due to the fact that the infant can sit up on their own. Therefore, the infant will not fall over. The infant grasping also changes. The infant starts to hold objects more properly when age increases

Toddlerhood

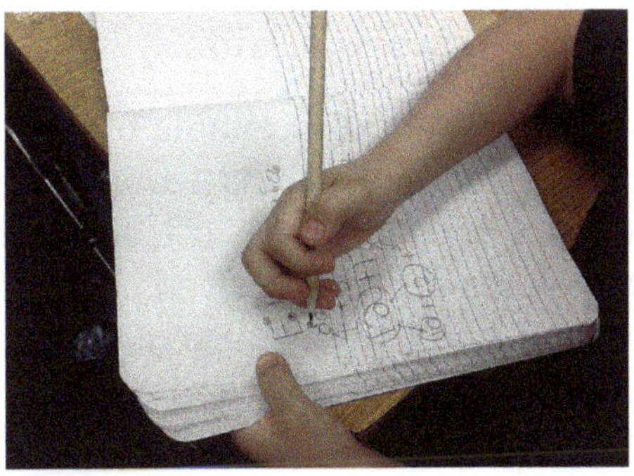

Writing abilities are a major fine motor skill.

By the time a child is one year old, their fine motor skills have developed to allow the manipulation of objects with greater intent.

As children manipulate objects with purpose, they gain experience identifying objects based on their shape, size, and weight. By engaging in hands-on play the child learns that some objects are heavy, requiring more force to move them; that some are small, easily slipping through the fingers; and that other objects come apart and can possibly be put back together again. This type of play is essential for the development of not only the child's fine motor skills, but also for learning how the world works.

It is during this stage in the development of fine motor skills that a toddler will show hand dominance.

Preschool

Children typically attend preschool between the ages of 2 and 5. At this time, the child is capable of grasping objects using the static tripod grasp, which is the combined use of the index, thumb, and middle finger. A preschooler's motor skills are moderate, allowing the child to cut shapes out of paper, draw or trace over vertical lines with crayons, button their clothes, and pick up objects. A preferred hand dominates the majority of their activities. They also develop sensory awareness and interpret their environment by using their senses and coordinate movements based on that.

After the static tripod grasp, the next form is the dynamic tripod grasp. These are shown in a series through Schneck and Henderson's Grip Form chart. Based on the accuracy and form of hold the child will be ranked either from 1-10 or 1-5 of how well they are able to complete the dynamic tripod grasp while properly writing. In conjunction with accuracy and precision the child will be able to properly position a writing utensil in terms of implement diameter as well as form and grip strength. Proper handwriting and drawing fall deeper into a category of graphomotor skills.

The National Center of Teaching and Learning illustrates the abilities that preschoolers should have improved through their fine motor skills in several domains. Children use their motor skills by sorting and manipulating geometric shapes, making patterns, and using measurement tools to build their math skills. By using writing tools and reading books, they build their language and literacy. Arts and crafts activities like cutting and gluing paper, finger painting, and dressing up develops their creativity. Parents can support this development by intervening when the child does not perform the fine motor activity correctly, making use of several senses in a learning activity, and offer activities that the child will be successful with.

Developmental disabilities may render a child incapable of performing certain motor activities, such as drawing or building blocks. Fine motor skills acquired during this stage aids in the later advancement and understanding of subjects such as science and reading. A study by the group which included twenty-six preschoolers who had received occupational therapy on a weekly basis, showed overall advancements in their fine motor skill area. The results showed a link between in-hand manipulation, eye-hand coordination, and grasping strength with the child's motor skills, self-care and social function. In addition, these children were shown to have better mobility and self-sustainment.

School Age

During the ages between 5 and 7 the fine motor skills will have developed to a much higher degree, and are now being refined. As the child interacts with objects the movements of the elbows and shoulders should be less apparent, as should the movements of wrist and fingers. From the ages of 3–5 years old, girls advance their fine motor skills more than boys. Girls develop physically at an earlier age than boys; this is what allows them to advance their motor skills at a faster rate during prepubescent ages. Boys advance in gross motor skills later on at around age 5 and up. Girls are more advanced in balance and motor dexterity.

Children should be able to make precise cuts with scissors, for example, cutting out squares and holding them in a more common and mature manner. The child's movements should become fluid as the arms and hands become more in sync with each other. The child should also be able to write more precisely on lines, and print letters and numbers with greater clarity. In terms of motor development and athletic performance, pediatric boys tend to be much more physically active than pediatric girls by nature and have a harder time staying still for long periods of time. This is due to the early development of motor skills that occurs in boys faster than it does in girls. During the first 2–3 years of elementary school, gross motor skills are similar among girls and boys with basic skills such as being able to run, jump, and toss a ball. However, boys start to develop more gross motor skills that give them an advantage in activities where girls may still be working on the basics. Boys' high energy and choice to be a part of large groups comes from their gross motor skills being developed. In general, pediatric girls tend to fall behind pediatric boys in terms of advancement of gross motor skills toward the end of elementary school.

Common Problems

Fine motor skills can become impaired due to injury, illness, stroke, congenital deformities, cerebral palsy, or developmental disabilities. Problems with the brain, spinal cord, peripheral nerves, muscles, or joints can also have an effect on fine motor skills, and can decrease control. If an infant or child up to age five is not developing their fine motor skills, they will show signs of difficulty controlling coordinated body movements with the hands, fingers, and face. In young children, the delay in the ability to sit up or learn to walk can be an early sign that there will be issues with fine motor skills. Children may also show signs of difficulty with tasks such as cutting with scissors, drawing lines, folding clothes, holding a pencil and writing, and zipping a zipper. These are tasks that involve fine motor skills, and if a child has difficulty with these they might have poor hand eye coordination and could need therapy to improve their skills.

Assessment

Fine motor skills can be assessed with standardized and non-standardized tests in children and adults. Fine-motor assessments can include force matching tasks. Humans exhibit a high degree of accuracy in force matching tasks where an individual is instructed to match a reference force applied to a finger with the same or different finger. Humans also exhibit a high degree of accuracy during grip force matching tasks. These aspects of manual dexterity are apparent in the ability of humans to effectively use tools, and perform challenging manipulation tasks such as handling unstable objects. Other assessments include but are not limited to PDMS "The Peabody Developmental Scales". PDMS is an evaluation done for children from birth till the age seven that examines the child's ability to grasp a variety of objects, the development of eye-hand coordination, and the child's overall finger dexterity. Similar to PDMS, Visual-motor integration assessment, VMI-R, is an assessment that examines the visual motor integration system which demonstrates and points out possible learning disabilities that are often related to delays in visual perception and fine-motor skills such as poor hand-eye coordination. Because additionally advancements in mathematics and language skills are directly corollated to the development of the fine motor system, it is essential that children acquire the fine motor skills that are needed to interact with the environment at an early stage.

Principles of Development

While planning education programmes for young children, the following four major principles of motor development must be kept in mind:

- Motor development depends upon neural maturity and muscular readiness. The development of different forms of motor activity goes on along with the development of different areas of the nervous system.
- A child should be mature enough to learn any skill. Sometimes a child may appear to learn a skill at an early age, but the gain may only be temporary.
- Motor development follows a standard pattern. It shows four general trends or directions:
    - Cephalocaudal Sequence: Growth starts first in the head region and then moves downwards towards the feet.
    - Proximodistal Sequence: Growth progresses from 'central to peripheral' i.e. from' the trunk region to arms and then to fingers and similarly from legs to toes.
    - Differentiation: In this the growth proceeds from 'mass to specific' activities, i.e, when a child practices more and more, he moves towards specific or refined responses in which only the appropriate limbs and muscles are involved. For example, at first a child catches a ball with his fore arms and shoulders later he learns to catch it only with his hands and fingers.
    - Integration: Here, the child starts integrating smaller activities into larger more functional behaviours after gradual refinement of movement.
- The rate of motor development varies in children. Even though motor development does follow a generally predictable pattern, individual differences do occur. The sequence remains the same for all children, but the specific age at which they reach the different stages differ.

Developing of Motor Skill

Another area of development to encourage this year is fine motor skills—or use of the hands. Just as gross motor skills enable your child to perform important everyday tasks, such as getting out of bed and going downstairs for breakfast, fine motor abilities allow for increasing independence in smaller but equally significant matters: opening doors, zipping zippers, brushing teeth, washing hands, and so on.

When combined with increasing hand-eye coordination, fine motor skills also open new doors to exploration, learning, and creative expression. In fact, research shows that emphasis on purely intellectual activities—memorization of letters and numbers, for instance—is far less useful at this stage than pursuits that encourage fine motor abilities and hand-eye coordination. These skills—rather than counting or reciting the alphabet—lay the foundation for academic learning in later years. In order to learn to write or draw, for example, a child's hand must be strong and coordinated enough to hold a pencil steady for a long period of time; in order to participate in school sports, games, and projects, dexterity and coordination must be up to par.

Among the fine motor skills your child will perfect in the preschool years are the abilities to:

- Paste things onto paper.
- Clap hands.
- Touch fingers.
- Button and unbutton.
- Work a zipper.
- Build a tower of 10 blocks.
- Complete puzzles with five or more pieces.
- Manipulate pencils and crayons well enough to color and draw.
- Copy a circle or cross onto a piece of paper.
- Cut out simple shapes with safety scissors.

The best way for you to help promote these and other hand-related skills is to provide your child with a wide range of materials to manipulate as her imagination dictates. Good choices include blocks (especially the interlocking types like magnetic blocks, Legos, bristle blocks, Tinker Toys, and construction straws), crayons, nontoxic and washable markers and paints, paste, glue, modeling clay, an easel, construction paper, safety scissors, a smock to guard against stained clothing, coloring books, and simple sewing cards. This is also a prime time for puzzles, sand and water toys, and musical instruments.

Encourage Fine Motor Skills

1. Teach the pincer grasp: To help your child learn to pick up small items like Cheerios using her thumb and forefinger, stuff an empty baby-wipe container with scarves, and then let her try to pull them out. You can also give her toys that have dials, switches, and knobs.

2. Embrace his filling and dumping obsession: Your toddler will likely load every toy possible into a plastic bin—only to spill it out and start over. While this activity may seem dull, it takes integrated muscle movements, concentration, and cognitive reasoning. Other ways to boost grip and finger strength: squeezing a wet sponge or looking for toys that are buried in sand.

3. Let the stacking begin: Your child needs hand and wrist stability to place blocks with control. Large wooden ones are easiest for toddlers to manipulate. Once she gets the hang of it, you can switch to smaller building materials—but hold off on interlocking bricks until she's at least 2.

4. Facilitate creativity: Most kids can make a mark with a crayon at around 15 months and scribble by age 2. Big crayons are best for little hands, but you can also give him large pieces of chalk and finger-paints to express himself.

5. Be patient with utensils: Have your child start using a fork and spoon at every meal. If she makes a mess or struggles, resist jumping in to help—let her try to figure it out on her own.

6. Build on basic skills: As your toddler's dexterity improves, encourage him to use both hands to do new tasks. Have him try threading big beads or rigatoni pasta with yarn. And play games like "The Itsy-Bitsy Spider" to teach him how to work his hands in tandem.

Encourage your Child's Creativity

Once you've provided your child with the tools that inspire creativity, stand back and let him loose, even if things are likely to get rather messy. Preschoolers tend to focus more on process than on product. They throw themselves into exploring the properties and possibilities of materials like paint, mud, sand, water, and glue without worrying about the results. In fact, when your 3-year-old proudly displays his latest masterpiece, you should try not to ask, "What is it?" That question may have never even occurred to him.

Instead, admire the work for what it is: "That's really wonderful! Tell me just how you did it." Then, encourage him to explain to you in his own words how he felt and what he was thinking about while he was making it.

The less control you try to impose over your child's creativity, the better. This advice especially holds true when it comes to the hand your child favors. One of the milestones of this age is becoming right-handed or left-handed. In fact, handedness is an important sign of increasing brain organization. By age 4, some 90 percent of children have become clearly right-handed, while the rest have become dedicated southpaws.

The main determinant of handedness is heredity, so it's best not to tamper with your child's genetic predisposition. Left-handers are no less socially acceptable than righties. And when pressure from parents or preschool teachers induces a child to switch, doing so usually takes a long-term toll in emotional upset and poor coordination.

So let your child lead the way. And don't be alarmed if her fine motor skills progress more slowly than her gross motor development. Fine motor skills develop more slowly because the kinds of delicate movements that enable children to manipulate objects (stacking and nesting blocks or putting together puzzle pieces, for example) can be learned only over time with a lot of practice. Unfortunately, while most 3-year-olds will run happily for hours on a playground, few really have the patience to sit and copy a drawing of a circle or a cross over and over. And keep in mind that the smaller muscles of the body (like those in the hands and fingers) tire out more easily than the larger muscles in the arms and legs, so endurance and strength must be built up gradually before your child's dexterity can improve.

There's one more reason why your child's fine motor skills progress more slowly: They are closely linked to cognitive development. In order to build a fort with blocks, for instance, a child must be able to think in a three-dimensional manner. Adding limbs, hair, or facial features to an incomplete picture of a person means that your child is capable of understanding that two-dimensional drawings can symbolize real people. Your child must mentally compare the picture with stored images of what people look like to figure out what's missing from the drawing, and he must be able to manipulate a pencil or crayon well enough to fill in the absent features.

The thought process involved in such acts is far more complicated than that for figuring out how to climb a ladder, chase a ball, or walk out a door. So it's important for you to be patient, encouraging, and supportive of your child's efforts. Whatever he masters today will stand him in good stead once he starts more formal learning in kindergarten and beyond.

Physical Motor Development

Patterns of Physical Development

Biologically oriented developmental theorists argue that new behaviour arise from old behaviour owing to district maturational changes in the physical structures and physiological processes of the organism.

The growth of a young child's physical abilities is amazing. You may think of all the physical abilities a child develop to adjust to the world such as, learning to see and recognize others, holding a bottle or cup, crawling around objects, differentiating sounds from one source to another, and so on. All these physical tasks require strength, coordination, perception, and normally developed organs of the body.

Physical development provides children with the abilities they need to explore and interact with the world around them. A child's physical growth first begins as muscles gain strength with use and s/he gradually develops coordination. The development of muscular control is the first step in this process. Physiological growth in human follows standard, orderly pattern. The growth proceeds in two directions: from the top down and from the centre outward.

Growth occurs through approximately the first twenty years of life in humans. Growth is more rapid and more likely to show spurts during both the infancy to early childhood period and the adolescent period. Different parts of the body show different growth patterns. The nervous system is almost fully developed by the age of 6. Body size which includes skeleton, muscles and internal organs shows moderate early growth and then slows down until adolescence, and then increases again. The reproductive system grows very slowly until adolescence, and then grows rapidly. These growth patterns have implications for social and psychological development.

The findings of variety of research works suggest that parents' expectations for a child's physical development depend on culture, family status or the presence of physical limitations.

For example, in a culture where a sport such as soccer is played early and very competitively, a parent's assessment of a child's physical abilities may be linked to performance on the soccer field. But the basic patterns of physical development in children are universal.

The concept of development includes two major categories: normative development and dynamic development:

1. Normative development concerns the typical (normal) capabilities, as well as limitations, of most children of a given age within a given cultural group. It indicates a typical range of what children can and cannot be expected to do and learn at a given time. Normative development is important because it allows parents, teachers and other adults to understand what to expect of a child physically at different ages. For example, expecting a 3-year-old child to zip her own coat would be unrealistic because she still is developing the physical ability to use finger in that way.
2. Dynamic development concerns the sequence and physical changes that occur in all aspects of a child's functioning with the passage of time and increasing experience, how these changes interact.

Development Milestones

Typically, this is referred to developmental milestones to indicate steps in physical ability for a child that should be reflected at different ages. Charts indicating common development milestones in physical abilities have been depicted in section.

Principles of Physical Growth

A number of principles regarding physical growth can be helpful in understanding a child's physical development. We have discussed these principles briefly in the following paragraphs.

Directional Growth

The growth of a child's body follows a directional pattern in three ways. The patterns of development are:

1. Large to small muscle or gross to fine motor development: Large to small muscle development means large muscles develop in the neck, trunk, arms and legs before the small muscles in the fingers, hands, wrists and eyes develop. You have observed that children can walk before they can write or scribble.
2. Head to toe or top to bottom: Children's muscles develop from head to toe. This is why babies can hold up their heads long before they can walk.

3. Inside to outside or center to outside: Muscles develop from the center of the body first and then toward the outside of the body. Muscles around the trunk of the body develop earlier and are stronger than muscles in the hands, feet, etc.

General to Specific Growth

You are aware that large muscle movement begins with waving of the arm and legs of infants, and it then develops into the more specific movements of an older child who can walk and draw a picture. Muscle growth beings with more general abilities and becomes more specific and refined as children get older.

Variations in Growth

You know that children vary in their physical abilities at different ages. Different parts of the body grow at different rates. Physical skills that are expected in gross or fine motor development are different in preschool children than infant.

Optimal Tendency in Growth

If growth in children is slowed for a particular reason, such as malnutrition, the body will try to catch up later when it is able to do so. Because grown in human tries to fulfill its potential in different stages.

Sequential Growth

Development is orderly and occurs is a pattern. Children must be able to stand before they can walk. This pattern is evident in a number of ways, as evident in milestones of development.

Growth During Particular Period

Growth in certain areas of a child's physical development may be more important at particular times during childhood. For example, the first few years of life are very important in the development of the brain's growth. The critical time for the development of motor skills is between 18 and 60 months of age.

Research suggests children go through four physical growth cycles: two of which are slow and two rapid growth cycle. The first period of rapid physical growth goes from conception to the age of 6 months. The rate of growth gradually slows during the toddler and preschool periods. The second period of rapid growth is during puberty in the years of preadolescence and adolescence. Another period leveling off occurs after puberty until adult growth is achieved.

Motor Development in Infancy

Infants grow at a rapid pace over the first two years of their lives. By the age of 5 months, the average infant's birth weight has doubled to around 15 pounds and by the first birth day, the baby's weight has trippled to about 22 pounds. The pace of weight gain slows during the second year, though still continues to increase. By the end of the second year the average child weight around four times as much as he did at birth.

There is a relation between weight gain and increased height. By the end of the first year an average baby grows almost a foot and is about 30 inches tall. By the second birthdays, children become around 3 feet in height. All parts of the human body do not grown in same rate. At the time of birth the head remains around one fourth of the infant's whole body size. By the end of the second year the head of the baby is only one fifth of the body length.

There are gender differences in height and weight. Girls are slightly shorter and weight less than the boys. Similarly, there are ethnic differences too. Asian infants are generally slightly shorter than North American Caucasian infants.

Motor Development

Motor development relies on changes in the neuromuscular system. Motor functions follow a predictable pattern. Infants cannot walk before they sit. Gross motor control involving large areas of the body is achieved more easily than fine motor control involving smaller muscle groups. As the time passes the mass movement becomes specific or differentiated.

Posture and Locomotion

By 13 to 14 month time significant changes in posture and locomotion take place. The nature of these changes and the approximate times at which they are achieved have been reported in the literature. Frankenburg and Dobbs reported the following motor milestones for posture and locomotion of 75% of the babies they tested.

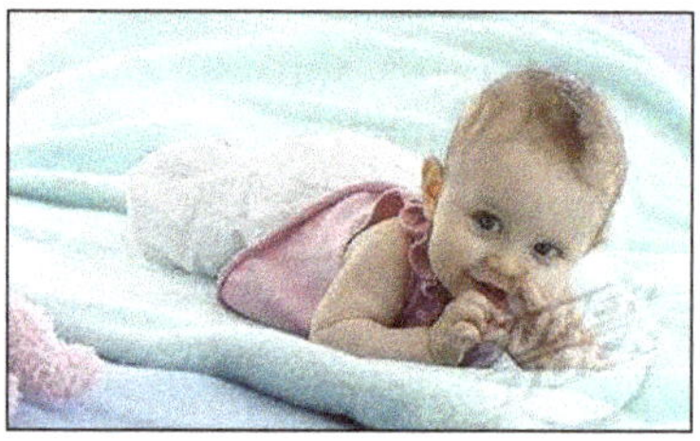

Lift head 450 at 1.9 months

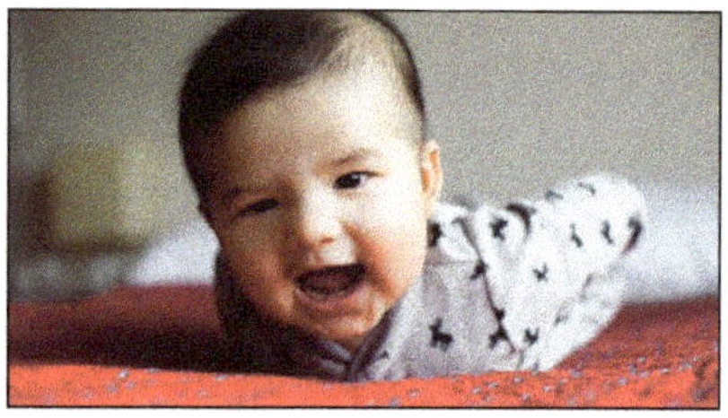

Holds chest up, arm support of 3.5 months

Sits supported, head steady of 3.6 months and Sit without support at 6.5 months

Crawls at 10 months

Stands alone momentarily at 12.1 months

According to Shirley, who studied the growth of upright locomotion, suggested that it occurs in five fundamental stages:

- Stage I: The infant achieves control of the upper body.
- Stage II: The infant achieves control of the entire trunk.
- Stage III: The infant makes an effective effort toward locomotion.

- Stage IV: The infant is able to crawl.
- Stage V: The infant can control posture and coordination for walking.

The infant must first be able to control his or her new body posture in a static position, and then movement concerned with that posture. For example, before the infant start walking, he would have a posture of standing with good control.

Manual Skills

The new born has no control over the arms, hands and fingers. Slowly flailing of the arms begins and gradually it comes under control. By 4 months of age infants are interested in observing the movement of their hands and in touching the objects. As the coordination of the hand and fingers increase, most infants are able to produce precise pincer movement which allows the infants to manipulate objects with greater precision.

By 18 months most of the infants can scribble spontaneously and build a house with few blocks. Before they go to kindergarten, most babies can reasonably copy a circle and square, draw rough human figure and use crayons with confidence.

Fine Motor Skills

While infants develop gross motor skills for example, rolling over, sitting without support etc., they develop some fine motor skills also. For example, by the end of three months, infants show some ability to coordinate movements of their limbs. The motor skills become more sophisticated by the time the infants reach eleven months. They are able to pick up the ground objects as small as marbles. By the end of the two years, children can hold a cup carefully, bring it to their lips and take a drink without spilling a drop.

Nutrition and Motor Development

There is a positive relation between rapid physical growth and nutrition. Infants cannot reach their potential without proper nutrition. Malnourished children show a slower growth rate by the age of six months. Chronically malnourished children score lower on IQ test and perform below average in school.

Factors of Motor Development

To what extent is motor development a function of physical maturation, and to what extent does it rely on experience? Maturation refers to an unfolding of the capacities of the organism that is relatively independent of training or experience.

Motor behaviour is initially controlled by the lower centers of the brain i.e. cerebellum. As the cerebellum and the cortex continue to develop during the first year of life, the cortex starts controlling voluntary movement. Research studies showed that practice facilitate the development of walking.

You must keep in mind that the land mark of motor development of children is based on norms. Norms represent the average performance of a large sample of children of a given age. Norms are useful only to the extent that they are based on data from a large, heterogenous, culturally diverse sample of children. Differences exist in the timing of development in children from different cultural, racial and social groups.

Motor Development in Preschool Children

During the preschool years children rapidly develop physical abilities, their height and weight increase remarkably. However, average differences between boys and girls increase during the preschool years. The boys start becoming taller and heavier, on average, than girls.

During the preschool years, the shape of the body also changes. They become less round and more slender. The arms and legs lengthen, and the head becomes more adult like. The proportions of the body become similar to those of adults. Muscle size increases and children become stronger.

Motor Skills

Gross Motor Skills

Around the age of 3, children mastered a variety of skills like jumping, skipping and running. In between the age of 4 and 5, they gain increasing control over their muscles, so their skills become more refined. For example, at the age of 3, children can throw a ball but with less accuracy. At the age of 4 to 5, they can throw a ball with more accuracy, so that their father can catch it. They can learn how to ride bicycles, climb ladder and so on.

Due to differences in muscle strength boys and girls differ in certain aspects of motor coordination. Boys can jump higher and throw a ball greater than girls. Girls generally do better in balancing act.

Fine Motor Skills

You know that of the age of 3, children can draw a circle and square, can fit blocks of different shapes into matching holes without much precision. By ages 4 to 5 they can do these activities better with more precision.

Fine motor skills mean the skills which involve more delicate and smaller body movements such as using a spoon, cutting with scissors, tying shoelaces etc. These skills require practice.

Importance of Play

You must know play is very important for child development. At about 12 months babies begin to play with objects in ways that are increasingly similar to the ways these objects are conventionally used by adults. Between the ages of 15 and 18 months, babies investigate objects before doing anything with them. Between the ages of 18 and 24 months, babies begin to treat an object as if it were another. They comb the doll's hair with a scale or something else. This kind of behaviour is called symbolic play. During the second year, symbolic play becomes more complex and elaborate. Malcom, Watson and Kurt Fischer observed four kinds of pretending that differed with respect to how the action was carried out.

Table: four steps in the developing of agent use in pretending.

Type of Agent use	Example
1. Self an agent	The baby puts his head on a pillow to pretend to sleep.
2. Passive other agent	The baby puts a doll on a pillow to pretend that it goes to sleep.
3. Passive substitute agent	The baby puts a block on pillow to pretend that it goes to sleep.
4. Active other agent	The baby has the doll lie down, on the pillow and go to sleep, as if the doll were actually carrying out the action itself.

Developmental psychologists believe that play serves important function for the developing organism. Early forms of infant play provide practice in activities that will become important later. Play allows exploration and invention without the possible negative consequences of the "real thing".

Smith reported four major types of play that provide practice for later functions:

1. Locomoter play e.g., action that involve running, jumping etc.
2. Object play, which includes pulling, shaking things etc.
3. Social play which can be divided into two types:
   (a) Play that involves physical contact, such as chasing and wrestling and
   (b) Play that does not involve physical contact, such as building with blocks.

4. Fantasy play, in which the meanings of objects and action are transformed to fit an imaginary situation.

Vygotsky opined that social nature of symbolic play is important to development. Play is very important as it helps the children develop physically, mentally and socially. At the beginning of the preschool years, children engage in functional play. This kind of play is simple and repetitive activities e.g., pushing an object or can on the floor, jumping etc.

By age of 4, children like more sophisticated and constructive form of play. In this kind of play children manipulate objects to build something, e.g. building a house using wooden blocks. Constructive play given children a chance to practice their physical and cognitive skills and fine muscle movements.

Many a time children are engaged in parallel play, that is, the two or more children are engaged in play with similar kind of toys or objects. For examples, they may be engaged in building houses using similar wooden blocks, but there is no interaction between them. Children may be engaged another type of play i.e. onlooker play, in which a child simply watch other children at play, but do not participate actively.

In another type of play, children may interact with one another by sharing toys, although they do not perform the same act. This type of play is called associative play. While children play with one another, it is called cooperative play.

Role of Parents and Teachers

It has been observed that normally significant physical growth and motor development occur in the preschool years. Children become taller, stronger, and their muscles become more coordinated. They acquire gross motor skills, i.e. develop abilities to use the large muscles and fine motor skills i.e. small-muscles abilities in a predictable sequence.

Teachers, parents and others have important role to play. They should provide opportunities for children to exercise large muscles every day. They should create areas or space in the house and in the school. These might include low climbers, tossing games, a balance beam, and so on. Preschool children should be engaged in games that involve running and walking, such as open-ended chasing on the playground, follow-the leader, and giant steps. Preschool children should be given small balls and toys for catching and throwing, such as soft, large balls, and other objects, both in the classroom and on the playground.

Balance materials should be available for preschool age children. Low balance beams, tires, and line on the sidewalk or classroom floor are some of the important materials that help developing motor skills. You should appreciate the importance of rough-and-tumble play. Safe areas for rough play, such as soft mats and grassy hills, can be identified. Rules for rough-and-tumble play, such as taking your shoes off when wresting on the mat, can be instituted. If you monitor carefully rough play will not lead to injury.

You can offer a range of activities like drawing painting, sculpting, cutting and making collages and materials such as blocks, puzzles, books, stringing beads etc. which promote fine motor development in children.

Children's motor development varies from culture to culture children in some cultural group acquire certain abilities quickly, others more slowly. How newly learned motor behaviors are used also differs significantly across cultures. Some children play tag, others fly kites, and still others chase cows or chickens. However, all these activities promote the same basic motor abilities. You must understand and appreciate cultural differences in motor development. You must recognize that some children will be more rough or active and that other will be quieter or less advanced in terms of motor developing. You should always keep in mind that you should not compare the development of the children in one culture with the children of another culture and think their slow development is a deficit. You can create a multicultural motor curriculum in the classroom by interviewing families about motor activities and games played in the home. This information can be used to integrate traditional games of diverse cultural groups into classroom play activities. Children will gain motor skills as well as cultural understanding when playing such games.

You should integrate the arts – including drawing, painting, and sculpture – into all learning activities and projects.

Girls and boys show different pattern of physical growth motor activity. Some of these differences are related to genetics, others to You must understand and appreciate gender diversity in motor play. Difference in activity level, accuracy or strength in movement, and play preference must not be construed as deficits that need to be remediated.

Advancements in motor development allow preschoolers to perform self-help skills and family chores. The kinds of family tasks young children will be assigned vary by culture. Children in same culture are often given tasks, such as cleaning their own rooms or helping wash dishes. In some culture they may be asked to garden, heard livestock, and care for younger siblings. You can plan classroom activities around caring for oneself and helping family members with chores. Children can be encouraged to reflect on ways they assist their family and friends. Such activities will inspire a desire to contribute to family life and the classroom community.

You can plan daily chores to be assigned to all children in the classroom. Caring for plants and animals, cleaning up after snack, putting away blocks, or helping a friends with a puzzle with give children a sense of responsibility and belonging.

You must be aware of the characteristics of children who have physical challenging conditions and who suffer from malnutrition. Early identification of exceptionalities is one of the most important responsibilities of professionals working with young children.

You can support the motor play of children with special needs. You can adapt classroom, equipment, and materials so that all children have access to games and activities. You can guide children with physical challenges in exercising small and large muscles.

You must ensure that children get exercise every day. It is an incorrect assumption that children will get all the exercise they need after school at home or at child care.

You should redesign organized games so that all children should move all the time while playing them. Again, you can also modify some games in which less competent children are quickly eliminated and have to sit out e.g., musical chairs. Select games in which all can take part continuously for reasonable period of time.

Embodied Movement

Movements occur in a body, and the morphology of the body determines the range of possible movements. Thus, developmental changes in body morphology change the possibilities for action. Jumping in grasshoppers provides a remarkable example of the developmental relations between body and movement. If grasshoppers' growth were linear, we might expect a continuous upward developmental trajectory in jumping ability; but neither is the case. Grasshoppers jump farther when their exoskeleton is more rigid because part of their jumping power comes from releasing energy temporarily stored in the exoskeleton. However, while the exoskeleton is rigid, insects cannot grow. Juvenile grasshoppers and other arthropods must periodically molt—shed their exoskeleton—to increase in size. Between molts, grasshoppers double in mass, but the new soft exoskeleton is less able to store elastic energy and, as the exoskeleton hardens, the increase in muscle mass does not keep pace with the increase in overall body mass. The result is a scalloped developmental trajectory: Jumping distance doubles from juvenile to adult, but within each molt period, jumping distance begins low, increases sharply as the exoskeleton hardens, then decreases again because body grows faster than muscle.

Vertebrates have skeletons on the inside of the body and do not molt. But like growth in grasshoppers, human growth is not equivalent to simply scaling up the current form. Put a different way, infants are not Lilliputians with miniature adult bodies. Indeed, mere stretching would have disastrous outcomes. In Gulliver's Travels, Jonathan Swift simply scaled up the 60-foot Brobdingnagians relative to Gulliver's typical adult size, but these 90-ton giants could not have walked on dry land because, with Gulliver's dimensions, their bones would have broken under their great weight. Similarly, if a 2-meter-tall man falls, he will hit the ground with 20-100 times more kinetic energy than a toddler. This is why toddlers can fall dozens of times per day with no untoward consequence, whereas adults occasionally break a bone. Perhaps Haldane said it best: "To the mouse and any smaller animal, [gravity] presents practically no dangers. You can drop a mouse down a thousand-yard mine shaft; and, on arriving at the bottom, it gets a slight shock and walks away. A rat is killed, a man is broken, a horse splashes".

Clearly, the body matters for motor behavior. We consider the developmental function of incidental activity, the problem of continuity between earlier and later behavior, the role of variability in development, the treatment of time in developmental research, and the ways that children must adapt behavior to the short- and long-term status of their bodies.

Incidental Activity and Consequential Function

Motor behavior is ubiquitous. Movement begins as soon as fetal muscles are innervated. It occurs during waking and sleep. It happens incidentally as well as on purpose. And it includes actions not typically considered motor behavior—eating, speaking, and facial expressions.

Why so much movement and to what end? Some activities (breathing) support life and some activities (reaching) accomplish immediate goals. But even those activities that to casual observation appear to be random and purposeless—incidental by-products of some physiological process—may reveal exquisite real-time structure, change over development, and serve important developmental functions.

Moving Before Birth

Birth is not ground zero for behavior. Fetal movements appear at 5-6 weeks after conception, shortly after nerves from the spinal cord establish functional synapses with muscle fibers. Fetuses in the first trimester—while still resembling a Kewpie doll with foreshortened limbs and a disproportionately large head—exhibit a variety of movements and postures: generalized movements that ripple through the entire body, sideways bending of head and trunk, startles, hiccups, twitches, isolated head, limb, and finger movements, "breathing" movements, "stepping" movements, somersaults, and facial movements such as mouth openings, tongue protrusions, and yawns. They bring hand to face and suck their fingers and thumb; they touch the umbilical cord and uterine wall. They move freely through the amniotic fluid with their bodies oriented in every direction relative to gravity. By the second trimester, fetuses produce smiles, grimaces, and the distinct assemblage of facial movements that comprise adult-like expressions of laughter, crying, and pain. Hand-to-face contacts, kicks, hiccups, and other movements occur in bouts of activity separated by 2-5 minute periods of quiescence. Over development, body and limb movements generally increase in frequency—up to 30% of each day is spent actively moving—until the fetus's growing body becomes cramped by lack of space; then movements decrease until birth.

Why do fetuses move? Spontaneous motility is a product of the central nervous system. Thus, a primary motivation for studying fetal movements is to gain insight into the developing nervous system. An in vitro spinal cord, lacking both body and brain, generates spontaneous neural activity and patterned muscle activity when the nerves are attached to isolated muscles. But fetal movements can reveal more sophisticated behaviors than a spinal cord in a dish. Fetuses open their mouths in anticipation of, not in reaction to, the hand arriving at the mouth. On some level, the fetus must perceive that the hand is approaching the mouth and not another part of the face or head.

Moreover, causality can go in the other direction. The act of moving can influence the developing nervous system. A tiny flexible tether linking two legs together in a rat fetus changes the pattern of interlimb coordination from alternation, one leg at a time, to synchrony, two legs moving together. When the tether is cut and leg movements are again unconstrained, the new pattern of synchronous leg movements continues, indicating that real-time feedback from movement is detected and learned by the fetus. Thus, spontaneous movements generated by the fetal nervous system create sensory experiences that, in turn, generate neural activity that helps to shape neural development.

Incidental fetal activity has other consequences for development, seemingly far afield. For example, moving before birth is necessary for proper physical development. Fetal movement exercises muscles, flexes joints, stretches skin, and circulates amniotic fluid. Without these consequences of movement, physical development does not proceed normally. Rat fetuses immobilized with curare do not develop normal facial features, skin, muscles, bones, connective tissue, mouth, gut, and lungs. The developmental functions of incidental activity span a variety of time frames. Some fetal movements are adaptations to life in the womb (e.g., swallowing amniotic fluid regulates water balance in utero and may stimulate neural activity), some are preparation for birth ("version" turns the fetus into a cephalic head-down presentation for birth), and others presage functions for postnatal life (fetal "breathing" of amniotic fluid promotes normal lung development) and lay the groundwork for intentional action (fetal self-directed movements, such as hand-to-mouth, may be the earliest goal-directed actions). Indeed, most movements in the repertoire of the neonate have been practiced for months by the fetus.

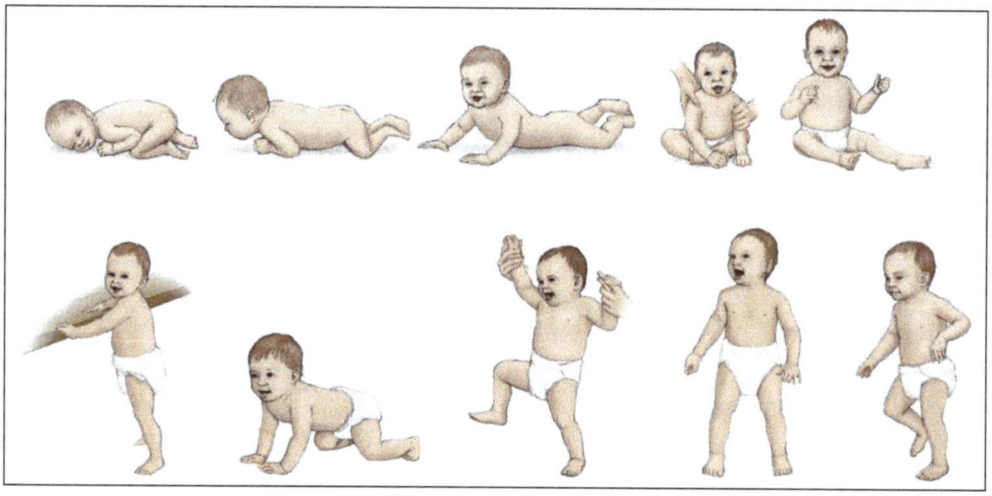

The examples of spontaneous movements involving arms, legs, or torso in 6- to 12-month-old infants. From left to right: alternate-leg kicking while supine, single-leg kicking supine, arm-waving with object, lateral arm sway, sit-bouncing of the torso, handsand-knees rocking, bouncing while standing with support.

Stereotypies and Flails

Spontaneous motility is a signature feature of infant movement. Over the first year, infants display a smorgasbord of kicks, stomps, sways, flaps, flails, rocks, rubs, nods, shakes, bounces, bangs, waves, and wiggles —totaling 67 documented forms of movement of every body part, from tongue to toes. Spontaneous movements occur in isolation (e.g., a single leg kick) and in bouts of rhythmic activity (e.g., repetitively flexing and extending the leg). They are frequent, up to several hundred movements per hour, and are frequently coordinated across the two sides of the body. Simultaneous kicks with both legs are more frequent than step-like alternation or single-leg kicks; movements are more correlated between right and left arms and between right and left legs than between an arm and a leg; and an infant's free hand is likely to produce spontaneous "overflow" movements while the other hand manipulates an object, sometimes exactly mirroring the rotating, shaking, and dropping movements of the object-oriented hand.

What is the purpose of so much kicking, rocking, and waving? Flails, stereotypies, and overflow movements are more frequent when infants are mildly aroused, while engaged in social interactions, playing with toys, or fussing, but they do not immediately accomplish anything. Spontaneous movements appear to be performed for their own sake: When infants get excited, the nervous system produces movements. But this motility still can serve useful developmental functions. The same movements that infants display spontaneously can be harnessed for intentional action. For example, over the course of a few minutes, spontaneous kicks or arm flaps become seamlessly instrumental—what Piaget termed "secondary circular reactions"—when the previously inconsequential movements now cause an overhead mobile to jiggle. (Infants lay on their backs and limb movement is linked to the mobile by a tether or electronic sensor such that every kick or arm flap results in a satisfying jiggle of the mobile elements.) At first, infants increase movement in all their limbs, but by 3-4 months of age, infants discern which limb is jiggling the mobile, they move the contingent limb more than non-contingent ones, and they remember the contingency for up to a week. Infants can even alter the form of their kicks if the contingency is specific to particular limb configurations or, if needed, kick with two legs instead of one.

Thus, spontaneous motility ensures practice for many soon-to-be intentional movements and provides the raw material from which goal-directed actions are selected. Arm flapping and reaching provide another apt example. Months before they can bring their hand to a target, infants flap their arms when offered a toy. They also flap without the eliciting stimulus of a toy. Over several weeks, flaps gradually bring the hand closer to the toy and eventually result in consistent toy contact. As infants spontaneously flap with no toy, flap in the presence of a toy, and actually succeed in contacting the toy, many important aspects of goal-directed reaching improve simultaneously in all three contexts. For example, coordination at the shoulder and elbow becomes more adult-like, suggesting that the movements required for reaching are carved out from the spontaneous flaps.

Twitching during Sleep

We ordinarily think of sleep as the absence of behavior. But while fast asleep, mammals exhibit a peculiar type of involuntary motor behavior: twitching. Think of a sleeping dog twitching its nose, paws, and tail. The movements are brief, discrete, jerky, and isolated to one part of the body at a time. All of the skeletal muscles of the body twitch during sleep, and human infants sleep for 16 hours a day, adding up to hundreds of thousands of twitches.

Like fetal and neonatal movements, seemingly random twitches mask intricate temporal and spatial organization. In infant rats, twitches are dispersed in lightning fast 50-ms bouts nested within longer bouts lasting about 500 ms, which in turn are nested within bouts lasting 1-2 seconds. Twitches in one arm are followed by twitches in the matching muscle of the other arm: shoulder abduction on the left followed by shoulder abduction on the right, elbow flexion in one arm by elbow flexion in the other. Since the pattern occurs across the limbs in a girdle, the temporal links between joints cannot be the result of passive forces pulling the arm. And since the pattern evolves sequentially across limbs and muscles, it is not the result of simultaneous commands from a central controller.

Apparently, the brain takes notice. More frequent patterns of limb twitching in 2-day-old rats result in more organization in those patterns at 8 days of age; reciprocally, more organized patterns at 2 days result in more frequent expression of those patterns at 8 days. Twitches in the whiskers and limbs of infant rats trigger sensory feedback that drives activity in the brain and spinal cord. So spontaneous activity of the sleeping nervous system generates twitches, which in turn relay information about the limb back to the developing nervous system. Infants may learn some of the most critical information about the workings of their bodies by moving while they are asleep.

Moreover, twitches during sleep are uniquely well suited for mapping muscle-to-brain relations because one muscle twitches while the others are completely quiet. Feedback from the twitch stands out against a background of atonic silence, like a bright light in a dark room. In contrast, waking movements in one part of the body typically are coordinated with other parts of the body within a context of postural compensations and anticipatory postural adjustments. It is like trying to make yourself heard at a loud cocktail party.

Gross Motor Play

Children, like the young of other placental mammals, devote an inordinate amount of their waking lives to spontaneous, seemingly pointless, repetitive, voluntary activity—play. Across species, gross motor play involves large movements of the body and appears in varied forms: exaggerated locomotion (e.g., foals gamboling), object-directed actions (kittens pawing a ball of yarn), and rough-and-tumble social play (young macaques slapping, biting, and chasing each other). Gross motor play typically involves modifications in form or timing compared to similar behavior in a functional context—think of the exaggerated jumps and bursts of speed in a puppy or young lamb. Movements are repeated, typically with novel variations. Social play often involves rapid role reversals, with the chaser becoming the chasee, and self-handicapping, as when an older juvenile monkey exercises restraint when play fighting with a younger sibling.

Play also is common among birds (crows repeatedly dropping and catching a stick in mid-air; parakeets ringing the bell in their cage) and is exhibited by reptiles (Komodo dragons pushing and shaking objects to make noise) and fish (leaping over turtles or floating objects). Even invertebrates, including insects, play: Captive octopuses grab floating objects, pull them down to the bottom of the tank, release them to watch the object shoot up to the surface; newly emerged worker honeybees engage in 'play flight' by leaping into the air, flapping wings, drifting to the ground, then climbing up to repeat. Children's gross motor play is comparable to these examples and more. They engage in spinning, rolling, handholding, and mock fighting; incorporate objects, surfaces, substances, and other people into their activities; and their play frequently involves sophisticated symbolic functions and rules.

Within and across species, playful activities do not reflect a common function or generative mechanism. The common thread is that they are voluntary, evidently pleasurable, and not immediately useful. Although gross motor play has fascinated developmental and comparative psychologists for over a century, researchers still do not agree about how to define it, what it is good for, how it originated, or how it evolved. From an evolutionary perspective, play poses a serious puzzle. In the wild and in captivity, play can take up to 20% of animals' time and 10% of their energy that otherwise could be channeled into growth. Juveniles at play are conspicuous and less vigilant, exposing themselves to greater risk from predators and accidents. And play may depend on the availability of abundant nutrition and protective parents to create "surplus resources" that can be expended on "useless" behavior with little cost.

So why do young animals play? Play provides a source of physical activity that can promote development of bones and muscles, a mechanism for generating variable neural activity and proprioceptive feedback to promote neural plasticity, opportunities to discover new skills, and consequence-free practice for hazardous behaviors such as hunting and fighting. Moreover, young animals reared without opportunities for normal social play show long-term deficits. Isolation-reared polecats are incompetent at mating and predatory killing and rhesus monkeys reared in same-sex groups show aberrant sexual behavior as adults.

Juvenile social play may even provide the basis for skilled performance under stressful conditions. When first encountering sunflower seeds, adult rats shred the shell, rendering the kernel inedible. After a few days, they learn to nip the ends and split the shell in half to remove the kernel. If reared with social play, rats easily open sunflower seeds in the presence of another rat, regardless of whether the interloper is dominant or subordinate. But subordinate adults reared in isolation revert to shredding in the presence of a dominant rat, suggesting that early social play provides the developmental basis for managing stress.

Developmental Continuity: Ontogenetic Adaptations, Historical Antecedents and Primitives

Some behavior that appears early in infants' repertoire shares striking similarities with adult-like behavior. How shall we consider the relations between the two? One possibility is that the earlier appearing behavior has no direct relation to the later behavior; instead it is an ontogenetic adaptation, an alternative way of accomplishing a general function. A second possibility is that early and later appearing behaviors are related historically, but aspects of their form or function differ; the earlier behavior is a historical antecedent. A third possibility is that the behaviors are identical; the earlier appearing behavior is a primitive that shares some critical feature of later behavior.

Striking Similarities

A remarkable feature of some behaviors that appear early in development is their similarity to mature, adult-like behaviors. Fetal rats exhibit facial wiping behavior that bears striking resemblance to adult grooming: The animals bring one or both paws to their ears and stroke downward. While still in the egg, chick embryos produce motions with their legs that—like a record spinning slowly beneath the needle on a turntable—turn the chick's body in a circle as the egg tooth cracks the shell for hatching. Once out, chicks use similar flexion and extension movements of their legs for walking. Newly hatched loggerhead sea turtles make their way into the ocean using the same trot-like crawling gait that they will exhibit years later when they return to nest on the beach of their birth, and the hatchlings swim away using the same "power stroke" gait—a sort of turtle breast stroke with front limbs sweeping backward simultaneously—that they will use for the rest of their aquatic lives.

Human infants also show an assortment of movements that foreshadow later ones. Fetuses and neonates bring hand to mouth using the same movements they will use months later for mouthing objects and eating. Three- to five-month-olds spontaneously produce "vacuous" precision grips, bringing thumb to index finger with nothing in hand—the same movements that they will use months later to grasp a small object. Banging a toy against the table at earlier ages uses the same up-and-down movements as hammering at later ages. Most celebrated are the "newborn reflexes"—sucking, palmar grasping, swimming (yes, underwater), upright stepping, and so on—which bear striking resemblance to intentional sucking, grasping, swimming, and walking months later.

Relations between Earlier and Later Behaviors

The similarities are indeed striking. But are the behaviors really the same? Movements at different points in development likely differ in details—banging in a toddler is less straight and controlled than hammering in an older child, just as hammering in a 3-year-old is less accurate and consistent than hammering in an adult. However, exact replication is not the issue in considering developmental continuity. The issue concerns which aspects of the earlier and later behaviors are similar and how they are related developmentally.

Despite similarity in form or function, some earlier and later appearing behaviors are not developmentally continuous. The earlier behavior is merely a temporary solution for the problems facing the animal during a limited period of development. The placenta and umbilical cord provide an apt anatomical analogy of such an "ontogenetic adaptation" to a particular developmental niche. Mammalian fetuses develop in the womb, where the placenta and umbilical cord transport all the necessary nutrients, fluids, oxygen, and other vital resources from mother to fetus and remove waste products in the other direction. These structures develop from embryonic (not maternal) tissues and serve essential physiological functions until birth. After birth they become afterbirth. The placenta and umbilical cord are no longer needed for ingestion and breathing and are discarded.

Suckling is another example of an ontogenetic adaptation that involves ingestion. Suckling, an essential activity expressed by all infant mammals, comprises a suite of behaviors that includes orienting toward the mother, finding and attaching the mouth to the nipple, rhythmic sucking which stimulates the mother to let down milk and extracts milk from the nipple, and finally disengaging from the nipple. Because the function of suckling is ingestion of nutrients and its form involves movements of the lips, tongue, and jaw, we might expect developmental continuity between suckling and feeding. However, suckling is not an early form of feeding. The sensory cues (odor and touch) to elicit suckling are qualitatively different from the factors that prompt feeding in adults (hunger and associations with particular foods and contexts). Moreover, adults stop eating when they are full, but infant rats continue to ingest milk as long as it is available. In some experiments, pups suckle until they are so filled with milk that they stop breathing! Even the patterns of muscle activation in the tongue and jaw differ when sucking a nipple versus eating or drinking. Despite similarities in form and function (i.e., providing nutrition and fluids), suckling and feeding are distinct ingestive systems that develop independently, are controlled by different stimuli, and are regulated by different neural systems.

In contrast to ontogenetic adaptations, earlier and later appearing behaviors can be related historically. The two behaviors can have different forms or functions, but the earlier behavior, like a movie prequel, lays the foundation for the later one. It is a historical antecedent. Embryology provides a clear analogy: The limb bud of a 4-week embryo is not yet an arm; it lacks bones, joints, and fingers. But it becomes an arm and is essential for the existence of the arm. The evidence is not merely circumstantial. Teratogenic drugs that disrupt the development of limb buds (e.g., thalidomide) result in malformation or complete absence of limbs. The earlier structure is necessary for development of the later structure.

Similarly, the clearest way to distinguish a typical precursor from a mandatory antecedent in behavioral development is to knock out the earlier behavior and observe whether the later behavior develops. For example, crawling typically precedes walking and babbling typically precedes speaking. However, despite the traditional lore that infants must crawl before they walk, some infants do not crawl and nonetheless walk normally. Crawling is not a true historical antecedent. In contrast, without the earlier period of babbling, infants do not learn to speak. If prelinguistic infants are prevented from producing vocal sounds due to the medical necessity of a tracheostomy, they do not produce communicative sounds once the tube is removed from their throat. Babbling is not the same thing as speaking, but it is a necessary historical antecedent for speaking. The two behaviors are developmentally contingent.

A third conception of developmental continuity is an isomorphism between critical components of infant and adult behaviors. Early behaviors are "primitives," "proto-somethings," or forms of "core knowledge"; later behaviors are the mature endpoint. In fact, some researchers tackle the question of "what develops?" by assuming such isomorphic continuity unless proven otherwise: "the null hypothesis in developmental psychology is that the cognitive mechanisms of children and adults are identical; hence it is a hypothesis that should not be rejected until the data leave us no other choice".

In motor development, a popular candidate for a primitive is the alternating leg movements so characteristic of mature walking. Neonates and pre-locomotor infants display alternating leg movements under a variety of conditions: while held in the air; supported on the ground; under water; facing forward, backward, and sideways on a treadmill moving at varied speeds; on a split-belt treadmill; wearing weights on one leg; when one leg is pulled out from under them; and while viewing simulated optic flow. In motor development, a popular candidate for a primitive is the alternating leg movements so characteristic of mature walking. Neonates and pre-locomotor infants display alternating leg movements under a variety of conditions: while held in the air; supported on the ground; under water; facing forward, backward, and sideways on a treadmill moving at varied speeds; on a split-belt treadmill; wearing weights on one leg; when one leg is pulled out from under them; and while viewing simulated optic flow.

The developmental isomorphism between infant and adult leg movements also holds at a neural level. Despite different muscle actions for each type of alternating leg movement, the same neural circuitry that is responsible for forward, backward, and sideways treadmill stepping in newborns is operating during walking in adults. Similarly, despite different muscle actions for different leg movements, the same neural circuitry produces leg movements during hatching and walking in chicks. And the same neural circuitry underlies trotting and swimming movements in turtles. Like the gears and axle in a car that produce forward and backward rotation by turning the wheels in different directions at different speeds, an identifiable system of neural circuitry can produce varied patterns of coordination in the legs.

So what are the developmental implications of striking similarities between earlier and later behaviors? Although some neural elements that will play key roles in adult walking can be active during newborn stepping, the two behaviors are not isomorphic. Newborns cannot support their own weight or keep balance without help. Successive steps are not consistently timed to ensure that one foot is always on the ground. And one foot may step while the other is passively dragged. Stepping is not walking.

The problem with the continuity assumption is that rejecting the null hypothesis is a matter of interpretation, not a matter of "the data leaving us no other choice." For example, "cruising" (moving sideways in an upright position while holding onto furniture for support) is traditional ly considered an early form of walking, although everyone knows that cruising involves sideways not forward movement and infants do not support their full weight on their feet. Moreover, cruising serves the same general function as walking (upright locomotion), it is temporally contiguous with walking (infants cruise for several weeks before they walk), and it shares structural similarities with walking (upright, alternating legs). However, there is a critical functional discontinuity between cruising and walking: Experience cruising does not teach infants that they need a floor to support their body. In this sense, cruising does not prepare infants to walk and is not "proto-walking."

Similarly, leg movements in the fetus may simultaneously be considered to have different continuity relations. Fetal leg movements may be an ontogenetic adaptation to the uterine environment that functions to orient the body or free the umbilical cord. Or they may be a historical antecedent that ultimately will allow moving in a gravitational environment. Or they may be a primitive continuous with adult walking. But there is no foolproof way to resolve the question of developmental continuity, because behavior, unlike anatomy, does not have a continuous existence. Any behavior is interrupted by other activities, including sleep, meaning that identical elements and functional relations are in the researcher's mind, not in the data.

Variability: Problem and Promise

Like most areas of psychology, developmental research is typically geared toward assessing differences in average performance between groups or individuals. As a consequence, most developmental researchers consider intra-individual variability to be a nuisance, like variance in the error term of an ANOVA. Historically, research on motor development followed a different path. Change in intra-individual variability was always considered an important outcome and a window into developmental process. Yet despite widespread appreciation that variability is a meaningful measure, researchers disagree about how to measure it and what it means.

Consistency and Control

A basic fact of motor development is that motor skills become increasingly consistent, smooth, and precise with age and experience. A common interpretation of this fact is that variability decreases as control increases. Variability in this sense is measured by quantifying the magnitude of variation around a central point. Infant reaching provides a good illustration: Intra-individual variability between reaches decreases, but what really characterizes improvement in infant reaching is a decrease in the variability of the movements within a reach.

Goal-directed reaching first appears at 11-24 weeks of age. The spread in onset age reflects the fact that getting a hand to a target is difficult. At first, infants reduce the number of limb segments to control by co-contracting their elbow muscles to lock it in place; their reaches have inefficient, jerky, curved paths, with changes in course direction and multiple speed bursts. After several weeks, elbow movement gets thrown back into the mix, allowing the hand to move on a straighter path to the target. Over the next 1-2 years, reaching gets smoother and more adult-like. Jerk (change in rate of acceleration) decreases; straightness (path relative to straight-line distance) increases; and changes in course direction decrease. Eventually, reaches coalesce into two adult-like phases: an early phase in which the hand rapidly accelerates toward the target, and a terminal phase in which the hand slows and adjusts for grasping before contacting the target.

Learning to sit follows a similar developmental trajectory of improved proficiency and decreased intra-individual variability. The key to sitting is to control the segmented, eminently bendable, spinal column so that head and trunk stay securely inside the base of support provided by the baby's bottom and legs. "Wobble" (variability in the location of spinal segments and the speed of trunk movements) and falling decrease as infants learn to anticipate and counteract effects of gravity on the head and torso.

Dynamic Stability

Linear measures of variability— as exemplified by jerk and wobble in infant reaching and sitting— do not reflect the sequence of values in a time series. Thus, based on linear measures, two very different time series, say a sine wave versus white noise, can have an identical magnitude of variation (e.g., the same range in values or the same standard deviation). In contrast, nonlinear measures of variability reflect the order of data points in a time series and are designed to reveal different underlying structures: A sine wave has a predictable, periodic structure whereas white noise has an unpredictable, random structure; and both signals show low mathematical complexity. Other time series such as "chaotic" attractors show intermediate levels of predictability and much more complexity compared to sine waves and white noise.

Thus, nonlinear measures of variability, such as approximate entropy (which quantifies predictability in the signal) and the Lyapunov exponent (which quantifies stable patterns and complexity in the signal), can reveal patterns of change not revealed by standard linear methods. Infants, for example, show greater predictability (smaller entropy values) and a compression of movement strategies (smaller Lyapunov values) as they acquire independent sitting, regardless of change in linear measures of variability. Nonlinear measures also reveal structure in the variability of postural sway beyond infancy. Approximate entropy values show an inverted U shape in the variability of standing sway, increasing from 3 to 5 years of age (indicating less predictable sway) and decreasing from young to older adults (indicating more predictable, stereotyped sway). In contrast, linear measures of variability (total area traced by the center of pressure) yield a U-shaped progression in standing postural sway, with variability decreasing from 3 to 5 years of age and increasing from young to elderly adults. Opposite patterns in nonlinear and linear measures of sway suggest that postural development in childhood involves increasing control over more degrees of freedom, which is then lost during aging.

A general conclusion from studies on dynamic stability is that too much variability leads to lack of stability and control, as in early stages of sitting and standing. But too little variability reflects inadequate complexity and fewer strategies for controlling posture, as in infants with developmental disorders and elderly adults. Nonlinear approaches thus suggest the Goldilocks Principle: Variability should not be too little or too much, but just right.

Variation, Exploration and Selection

"Just right" variability can support adaptation by providing the raw material for selection and refinement. Darwinian selection (propagation of successful variants, elimination of unsuccessful variants) can operate with reference to evolution, tuning of the nervous system, or behavior. In motor development, variability creates new forms that feed selective processes to make movements more adaptive.

A selection process requires variants to act upon. When variation runs out, selection grinds to a halt. In evolution, new variants are replenished with each generation. In motor development, a renewable supply of variants arises through spontaneous activity and the practical impossibility of repeating actions in exactly the same way. We call it exploration and see it most clearly when infants face a novel task. When suspended for the first time in a baby bouncer (a seat held by springs to the top of a doorway), infants have no idea how to behave, or even what the task is. Initially, spontaneous activity results in minimal bouncing, but this evokes more activity and—here is the crucial point—variable leg movements. Some jumps work against the natural periodicity of the springs, but some accentuate the bounce. Gradually infants converge on a solution in which the timing and magnitude of vertical jumps matches the stiffness and elasticity of the springs.

A bouncing biped robot provides converging evidence of a variability-exploration-selection process. The robot was designed to produce a wide variety of variable jumps. Like infants, the robot initially generated small jumps in short, irregular bursts. As random jumping became more effective at producing a single bounce, the robot produced longer bouts of periodic jumping. Bouts that produced longer, stable periods of bouncing were selectively favored. Eventually the robot, like the infants, converged on behavior that matched the resonance of the spring system. Variation and selection among motor variants was sufficient to support motor learning.

Overlapping Waves and Variety of Means

Selection implies that less desirable strategies are eliminated from the motor repertoire. Similarly, stage theories of development imply that more advanced behaviors replace less advanced ones. An alternative possibility is that older, less optimal strategies co-exist with newer, more optimal ones. On this view, development is like a series of overlapping waves. Existing strategies change in the frequency of expression, new strategies arise on the scene, and interactions among old and new strategies create more richness and variety of behavior. In fact, using a variety of means to solve a problem may be a hallmark of adaptive behavior.

In cognitive development, strategy choice is generally adaptive. But children often discover new strategies despite successful performance with existing ones, they typically use a variety of means rather than only one strategy to solve a problem, and they often do not switch from old to new strategies even when new is clearly better. Likewise, in motor development, infants generally select a locomotor strategy to suit the task. For example, toddlers walk down shallow slopes and slide down steep ones. But they discover new sliding strategies such as backing feet-first, despite already knowing how to slide headfirst and in a sitting position, and although any single sliding strategy would work, infants use all of them within a single session. Infants persist using a variety of belly crawls and inchworm crawls despite inefficiency in particular movements, and less efficient movements co-exist with more efficient ones for pulling to a stand.

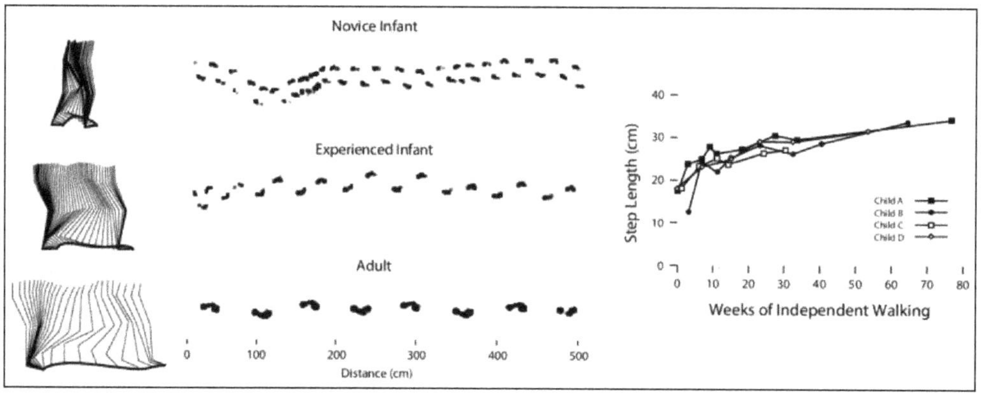

Developmental changes in walking in the standard "straight-line" paradigm over different time scales. The left column of stick figures depict the movement of the leg (gray line segments) and path of the foot (dark smooth line) during a single step in a 12-month-old novice walker (top), a toddler with 5 months of walking experience (middle), and an adult (bottom). Note that new walkers display exaggerated elevation of the foot relative to leg length and they drop the foot in place at the onset of stance, in contrast to the low trajectory of foot motion in adult walkers. Second column shows an example of footfalls during walking on a pressure-sensitive gait carpet, revealing the shorter, wider, more variable steps of an infant walker with only 2 weeks of walking experience (top), an infant with 2 months of walking experience (middle), and an adult (bottom). Graph at right shows the time course of improvement in step length (distance between consecutive steps) for four infants over the first 80 weeks of independent walking. Note the characteristic rapid increase during the first 10 weeks and slower, steady improvement over the subsequent 70 weeks.

Likewise, in other animals, various movement strategies may emerge as overlapping waves. In rat pups, various righting responses (strategies for returning to a right-side up position if turned upside down) emerge at different points in development and change in frequency depending on the mélange of other movements in their repertoire, the availability of eliciting sensory information (e.g., pups are blind at birth), initial posture, and interactions between motor and sensory systems. As a consequence, righting performance gets better, and then worse, then better again. It improves initially as newborns learn to bend into a "U" and flop to one side. Then corkscrewing dominates, with the shoulders turning one direction while the hips turn the other, like a body battling itself. Finally, the mature strategy emerges in which the head turns and the body follows.

The Passage of Time and Development

Behavior unfolds over multiple time scales, from milliseconds to millennia. Figure illustrates the idea of multiple, nested time scales in walking: A single step occurs over the course of milliseconds, a sequence of steps over seconds, dramatic changes in sequences over months, and changes from infant to adult-like over years. Each time scale has its own trajectory, and in the case of walking, it has its own spatial trajectory as well.

Time as Maturation, Test Age, Onset Age and Experiences

Developmental scientists are uniquely positioned to think about change over multiple, nested time scales, but we generally do a very poor job of it. Researchers in cognitive development typically consider "developmental time" in terms of chronological age and ignore other time scales. This gambit is far worse than it sounds. Treating age as a predictor or independent variable confuses the passage of time with the factors actually responsible for creating developmental change; slotting children into age groups overlooks the fact that age groupings are transient and fictions of convenience. Although motor development lends itself beautifully to deep analysis of time-based behaviors, research in this area is no better when it comes to analyses of developmental time. Like researchers in other areas, we typically put chronological age on the x-axis. Maturation, always a popular explanatory principle in motor development, represents only time passing and has no explanatory value beyond neural-hand waving as an agent of change. Onset age, a long-favored measure in motor development, represents only the number of days between birth and the first appearance of a motor behavior. Experience performing the skill is no better. As normally indexed, experience is only the number of days between onset and test dates; essentially, we replace chronological age on the x-axis with "walking age" or "sitting age."

The development of walking is a good example of behavioral descriptions at different ages, in this case, different walking ages. In the standard test, infants are encouraged to walk repeatedly over a straight, flat path. After a century of increasingly sophisticated recording technologies, what have we learned from the standard test? To the naked eye, infants' first steps look wobbly, choppy, unbalanced, and idiosyncratic; after a few months, walking looks relatively smooth, rapid, stable, and uniform. Recordings from gait carpets, force plates, high-speed motion trackers, and electromyography confirm these impressions. Simply put, infants get better.

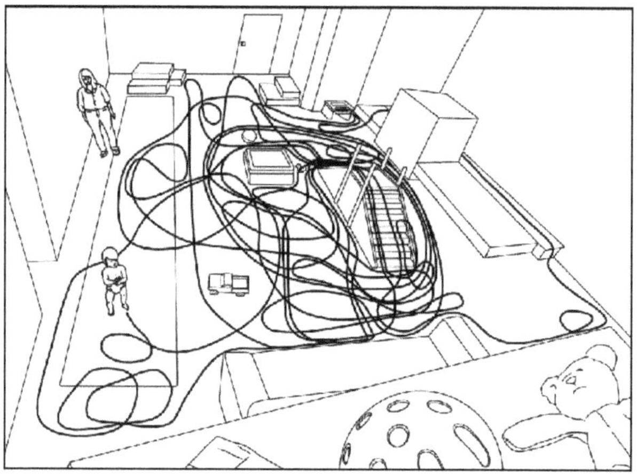

Natural infant walking in a large laboratory playroom containing a long gait carpet (left), couch (bottom), padded pedestal, slide and stairs, narrow catwalk, carpeted and wooden steps, an activity table, and a wall lined with shelves of toys. The superimposed line shows the walking path of one typical 13-month-old during 10 minutes of spontaneous activity.

New walkers suffer from poor balance control. Their initially slow, asymmetrical, short, wide steps become faster, more symmetrical, longer, and narrower, and they spend less time with both feet on the ground. Abrupt flat-footed or toe-first landings transition into cushioned heel-toe landings and toe-off progression. Some new walkers hold their arms up like balance poles, creating variable forces on the trunk; over several weeks, their arms lower and eventually swing. New walkers' knees and hips are flexed in the stance leg, causing the torso to lean forward; the hip is elevated as the leg swings forward, so the pelvis tilts from side to side. The overall consequence is inefficiency. Relatively little kinetic energy from forward movement is recaptured as potential energy. As knee and hip become more extended instance, the pelvis stays level, the torso is more erect, and more of the energy expended in forward movement is recovered. New walkers show more co-contraction of their leg muscles and poorly timed bursts of muscle activity. Over ensuing weeks, the idiosyncrasies of new walkers transform into more uniform solutions. Across measures, the rate of improvement is initially rapid over the first 4-6 months of walking and then slows over the next several years.

Despite the elegant technologies and gorgeous descriptions of change within steps and across sequences, research on infant walking is still lacking fundamental information about developmental time. After all these years, we still put walking age on the x-axis and call it "experience." But what do infants experience during natural walking? The actual facts are astounding yet obvious. Each hour, infants spontaneously take 2300 steps, travel the length of 8 football fields, and fall 17 times; over the course of a waking day, toddlers accumulate over 14,000 steps, travel the length of 45 football fields, and fall 100 times. They do not do this, however, by traipsing back and forth in straight lines as in the standard walking task. They turn! Natural walking is omnidirectional. Infants' paths meander wildly and half of their walking bouts have only 1-3 steps—too short for standard gait analyses. Human infants are not unique in this. For all animals at every point in development, steady straight locomotion is the exception, not the rule. In fact, training robots to walk like infants—with omnidirectional gait on variable paths instead of periodic gait in straight lines—was sufficient to win all 24 games in the 2011 RoboCup, scoring 136 goals and conceding none. Other teams have now caught on: The actual experiences matter, not the empty passage of time.

Sampling and Stages

Ironically, with so much time on the x-axis, developmental research has few guidelines for how to space observations over time. Generally, sampling intervals are quite large. In cross-sectional studies, we compare newborns, toddlers, preschoolers, and adults. In longitudinal studies, we observe infants at walking onset and three months later. Under more heroic regimes, we test infants weekly or monthly. Such decisions about sampling intervals are based on tradition, convenience, or intuition. But, overly large sampling intervals compromise our ability to discern the true shape of the developmental trajectory.

For example, the standard growth charts showing smooth, continuous increase in children's height derive from quarterly or yearly measurements. Daily measurements reveal that growth is actually episodic, with dramatic spurts within a single day followed by no growth for days or weeks. The same problem holds for binary data such as infants' ability to walk, produce words, or demonstrate object permanence. The widespread practice of attributing an onset age to the first appearance of a skill relies on the assumption that skill acquisition is stage-like— before this day, infants cannot walk; after this day, they can. Daily sampling, however, reveals variable trajectories. Most motor skills sputter in and out of infants' repertoires— they walk on one day, but not again until a few days later. Infants can exhibit dozens of vacillations between "pass and fail" before the skill stabilizes. Simulations of sampling at different rates (every other day, every third day, every fourth day, and so on) show that the ability to detect a variable trajectory decreases precipitously with each day of widening the sampling interval. With weekly samples, half of the variable skill onsets appear stage-like; at a monthly sampling rate, nearly all variable skill onsets appear stage-like. Infrequent sampling can mistake the date of first appearance by weeks—a virtual lifetime in infant motor development. Regardless, first appearance is an arbitrary choice given variable patterns of onset.

What, then, is the take-home message from so much depressing news about the (mal) treatment of time in developmental science? Developmental research has the tools and concepts for describing and explaining change over time. We just need to do it.

Adaptation and Developmental Diversity

Behavior is movement of the body. Changing the body experimentally or during everyday activity alters the real-time biomechanical constraints on movement. Similarly, developmental changes in the body alter the biomechanics of movement. With normal physical growth comes increases in overall body size and also changes in body proportions. Thus, learning to move entails learning to adapt behavior to short-term changes in the body, and acquiring new motor skills entails learning to move in your particular body.

Coordinated movement is a continual dialogue between body and brain. Consider the celebrated case of the Hensel twins, conjoined mid-thorax. Each sister's brain controls the limbs on one side of the body in continual dialogue with her sister's brain so that the girls learned to walk, bicycle, play basketball, swim, drive, and most other typical skills. The central nervous system cannot contain motor programs— either hardwired or learned—to control the necessary body parts for movement because it cannot know the relevant body specifications ahead of time. Without foreknowledge of the "hardware specs," the central nervous system cannot generate the appropriate muscle forces to move the appropriate body parts. Addressing this calibration problem's one of the central challenges in developmental science. Nonetheless, researchers have scarcely begun to examine the changing relations between the growing body and motor development.

Short-term Effects of Changing Biomechanics

A simple way to experimentally manipulate body dimensions is to add weight to the body. An external load, like a backpack, adds mass and shifts the location of the center of mass; this requires modifications in posture and gait to solve the new balance problem. Older children and adults adjust smoothly, leaning away from the load to maintain their center of mass over the base of support. Adults also adapt to loads on the limbs. Adding weights to the thighs, shanks, or ankles increases the energy cost of walking, but does not cause significant gait disruptions. Infant walkers alter arm position while carrying objects, but paradoxically they do not compensate for packs on their backs, fronts, or sides. They lean into the load, allowing their center of mass to creep dangerously close to the edge of the base of support. Infants also fall more frequently while carrying loads, despite strategies to improve balance such as shorter, wider steps, slower speeds, and longer periods with both feet on the ground.

Another way to experimentally manipulate body dimensions is to alter limb lengths. For example, leg length was ingeniously altered in Saharan desert ants by clipping the distal segment of the leg ('stumps') or gluing a bristle to the end of the leg ('stilts'). The altered ants moved their legs as before such that stilt steps were 14% longer and stump steps were 33% shorter than normal ant steps. Because changes in leg length systematically altered step length, stilts traveled greater distances and stumps shorter distances in the same number of steps, resulting in systematic navigation errors. In contrast to ants, children with elongated legs do not immediately move their legs as before. Boys walking on stilts and a boy with achondroplastic dwarfism after surgical lengthening of his lower legs shortened their steps and reduced their walking speed, presumably to cope with the new balance constraints of their unfamiliar, longer legs.

Long-term Adaptation to Body Changes

People come in all shapes and sizes, and for motor control, size matters. Atypical bodies are common in sport performance. The average height of players in the National Basketball Association is > 2 meters (79 in); the average weight of a lineman in the National Football League is 142 kg (313 lbs.); the average height and weight of an Olympic female gymnast is 1.5 m (61 in), 47 kg (103 lbs.). However, researchers know surprisingly little about motor skill acquisition in people with such atypical body morphology.

Atypical bodies are also common in everyday life: Overweight and obesity are epidemic among American children—in fact, so prevalent that overweight may soon become the norm. Overweight and obesity are associated with decreased motor coordination in childhood and delayed development in infants. Obese children walk with shorter, wider steps, at slower speeds, and spend more time supported by both feet and less time supported by just one foot. Differences in the timing of hip and knee muscle activation result in longer stance, greater lateral movement of the leg during swing, and reduced extension of the hip.

As one would predict from moving heavier legs, widening stance, and reducing the pendular efficiency of swinging the legs, energy utilization is less efficient and the mechanical cost of locomotion is greater for obese children. However, the increase in energy expended during walking (about 10-25% more per kilogram in obese adults) is less than one might expect— much less, for instance, than the 80% increase experienced by a lean person wearing external leg weights walking in a similar pattern. This counter-intuitive fact implies that obese children and adults adapt to their bodies by walking in a more energy-efficient manner. One possible explanation is that obese people expend more energy moving heavy legs, but less energy supporting their weight on straight knees. Reciprocally, massive (33%) weight loss results in reduced time in stance, longer and narrower steps, increased preferred walking speed, greater range of hip motion, and greater knee flexion—effects that reflect the opposite adaptation as obesity gives way to a leaner body.

The effects of growing up with different body dimensions are particularly evident when expanding the range of human variation. Achondroplastic dwarfism, for instance, alters bone growth and results in short stature with short arms and legs relative to the trunk and head. Although this condition does not directly affect the nervous system, it results in motor delays. Infants sit at 12 months (compared to 6 in typical infants) and walk at 18 months (compared to 12). Locomotor development includes unusual behaviors such as "logrolling" and "snowplowing" on legs and head. Because their arms are about the same length as their legs, achondroplastic infants crawl on hands and feet instead of hands and knees. Due to hypermobility at knees and hips, achondroplastic infants transition from crawling or lying to sitting by pushing themselves straight back through a "straddle split" so they are facing their original orientation. Typically developing infants, in contrast, roll one hip over the ipsilateral leg, turning the body 90° away from the original direction of crawling. Both methods appear biomechanically favored for infants' respective body proportions. Developmental plasticity ensures that children who grow up with atypical bodies can produce adaptive motor behaviors.

Movement is Embodied

Most research on motor development is of the embodied type—studies of infants' movements that implicitly acknowledge the body in the form of the measurements (limb trajectories, forces, muscle actions, etc.) or explicitly examine the effects of the body on motor outcomes (e.g., obesity). The literature shares a deeper theme of embodiment, however. These are studies of the morphology of movement—its form and shape—and the evolution of behavioral morphology over space and time. As Gesell wrote in an earlier chapter of this Handbook, motor behaviors "have shape". In fact, the early pioneers represented infants' bodies in isolation so as to highlight the changing morphology—the body so to speak—of infants' movements.

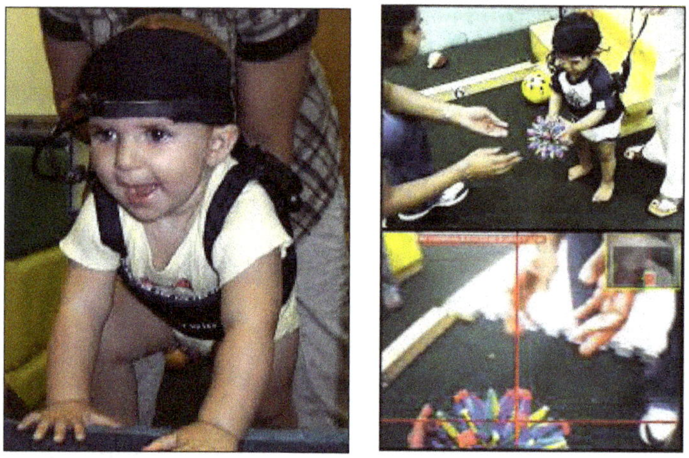

Head-mounted eye-tracker worn by a 14-monthold infant (top), objective camera view of the activity of the infant in the laboratory playroom (middle), and child's view and point of gaze, shown by crosshairs, provided by the head-mounted scene camera (bottom). The small inset in the bottom photo shows picture-in-picture from the eye camera.

Embedded Action

Animals are always situated in a physical environment that constrains, shapes, and invites motor action. Some factors are omnipresent—gravity, temperature, air, and ground. But most environmental factors are continually in flux—the layout and the objects and surfaces therein. All of it affects motor development. Rats reared in microgravity on a space shuttle do not show surface righting and never achieve normal righting responses back on earth. If the room is too hot or too cold, sleeping rat pups do not twitch normally and awake movements also differ in hot and cold.

The variable nature of the environment requires that actions be flexible and adaptive. Even a simple creature like the worm C. elegans (302 neurons) adapts to the environment by swimming in water and crawling on land. More sophisticated animals rely on perceptual information to guide actions adaptively. Perception does not just happen to a passive perceiver, like a patron waiting for the server to arrive with a meal. Instead, we do things to make perception happen; we sample and select from a buffet of potential information. Perception does not occur only in the brain; it is a whole body activity. Animals generate perceptual information through action. Human vision is a clear example. Although the fovea is very small, we have an illusion of seeing equally well over the entire visual field because we turn our eyes and head to where our attention is directed. In the language of the new robotics, animals "self-structure" perceptual information.

The focus is on perception-action development and how infants learn to cope with novelty and variability in the environment. We describe how infants extract information from the environment by exploring from a distance and through direct contact, how this information is used to plan actions in advance and during execution of a skill, and how children learn the limits of their motor abilities in specific situations.

Learning by Doing: Exploration of the Environment

From the very beginning, infants are motivated to explore the environment and all that it affords for action. Motor development—postural control, mobility, and manual dexterity—initially limits access to the environment and then expands the effective environment. In this sense, infants' environments, like their bodies and skills, develop. No body part is universally privileged for exploration. Animals have evolved different anatomical and sensory solutions for exploring the environment from a distance and for getting to know it up close. What all exploratory systems have in common is an active search for information that involves putting the right body part in the right place and moving it.

Exploration from a Distance

For humans, vision is a primary means of exploring the world from a distance. Until recently, research on infants' visual exploration of the layout relied on third-person camera views and intuition. A popular (and eminently reasonable) idea was that locomotion and visual exploration are developmentally related: Spying a distant object gives infants incentive to move and seeing obstacles a few steps ahead spurs gait modifications and changes in path. Now researchers can measure visual exploration directly with head cameras and head-mounted eye trackers.

In the natural environment, adults and infants look at an object just before their hand moves to reach for it. While walking, adults, children, and toddlers direct gaze mostly at objects they are moving toward, not at obstacles in the path. Obstacle fixations are always brief and are more frequent in toddlers (72% of obstacle encounters) than in children (59%) or adults (32%). Otherwise, navigation is guided by information from the periphery. One reason for the developmental shift from foveal to peripheral control is differences in eye height: Shorter observers naturally see more of the ground near their feet.

Postural development constrains looking in other ways. While prone or crawling, infants mostly see the floor; while supine they see the ceiling; but when infants sit or stand up, the whole room swoops into view. What do they look at? Freely mobile infants look surprisingly little at faces, which are typically too high, and infants seldom tilt their heads up. As Frank et al. put it, toddlers "spend much of their time in a world primarily populated by knees". Even while sitting across the table from each other, mothers typically look at their infants, but infants rarely look at their mothers. Mothers see infants' face and the whole table top. Infants see mostly objects and hands.

Although visual exploration dominates research, other perceptual systems can serve as long-distance probes. Owls use sound to find a scampering mouse in the dark. Rat dams find lost pups from ultrasonic cries. Salmon smell their way upstream to the place they were spawned. Fish use pressure-sensitive pits along their bodies to detect vibrations produced by other fish. Whales navigate by listening to breakers crashing against a distant shore. Pigeons and sea turtles orient by detecting Earth's magnetic field. Bats and dolphins echolocate by bouncing sound from their cries off objects. Electric eels and fish electrolocate by generating electrical fields that are distorted by the bodies of other fish. In all cases, perception guides locomotion via information generated, reflected, or distorted by distant features of the environment.

Exploration through Direct Contact

Information from a distance can prompt exploration by direct contact. Sight of an obstacle in the path—albeit in mostly brief, incidental glances from the periphery—prompts infants to pause at the edge of the obstacle and probe its surface with hands or feet. Some ground properties are emergent—friction and rigidity—and must be explored through direct contact. Infants explore the slip of their shoes against a sloping surface by rocking their feet at the brink. They explore the compliance of a waterbed or foam pit by pressing their hands into the surface. Over weeks of crawling and walking, exploration becomes faster, more efficient, and supports more error-free navigation.

Likewise for objects: The sight or sound of a nearby object prompts prehension and manual exploration. Sighted infants reach for objects sounding in the dark and blind infants reach for continually sounding objects. Some objects characteristics are revealed only through touch—texture, rigidity, weight, and temperature. At first, infants use mouth, lips, and tongue to explore objects. Then, as posture improves and infants can sit up, hands predominate and eventually work in tandem with mouthing and visual inspection.

On one view, haptic perception piggybacks on developments in manual dexterity. Some exploratory procedures identified in adults (lateral finger motions to discover texture, contour following to reveal shape, etc.) are too difficult for very young infants, so haptic perception suffers. However, simple exploratory procedures are available early. By 3 months of age, infants differentiate object weight based on unsupported holding and by 4-6 months they differentiate object rigidity based on squeezing and tapping. Between 6 and 10 months, infants explore object-surface relations differently by pressing a spongy cube but banging a rigid one. By 3 years of age, children show the full adult-like repertoire of exploratory procedures and by 4 years they exhibit adult like procedures to explore the rigidity of a mixing stick. On a second view, adult-like exploratory procedures are unnecessary. Newborns exhibit rhythmic changes in finger pressure that yield information about object texture, shape, and weight long before more complex manual actions are available.

Mouths and hands are not the only way to "feel out" the environment, especially for animals. Whisking is an example. At birth, rats' whiskers are sensitive to touch, but movement is largely passive. Over the next three weeks as pups develop postural and locomotor skills, their whiskers fan out, sweep to and fro in waves, and move individually like fingers to explore the layout. Whiskers are like fingers in another sense. Each whisker has its own representation in somatosensory cortex. If a whisker is clipped, barrel fields in somatosensory cortex reorganize; ditto as the whisker grows back.

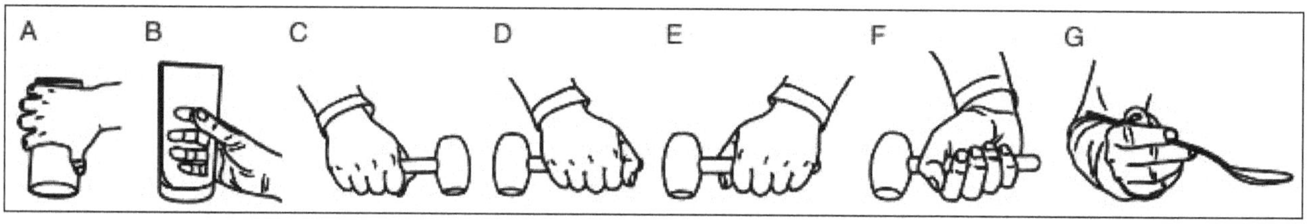

Various grip configurations for grasping a tool with one hand. (A) Side view of initial grasp of upside-down glass with power grip of right hand, thumb down. (B) End state grip of glass right-side up with right hand, thumb up. (C-F) Overhead views of initial grasps of the handle of a hammer. (C) Adult-like overhand grip with preferred (right) hand using hammer, thumb to working end. (D) Inappropriate overhand grip with right hand, pinky to working end. (E) Overhand grip with non-preferred (left) hand, thumb to working end. (F) "End-state comfort" underhand grip with right hand, thumb to working end. When the wrist rotates, the hammer will be in the most comfortable and efficient position to pound a peg. (G) Adult-like precision grip with fingertips of right hand holding a spoon.

Planning and Innovating: Prospective Control

In a variable world, actions must be planned and prospective. Children must lift their foot to avoid tripping on an obstacle and lower their foot to go down stairs; turn their bodies to steer through narrow openings or circumvent an obstacle in the path; retract their heads to dodge a looming object; move their hand to catch a ball; and avoid getting hit by a car when crossing the road. Actions must be selected, timed, and shaped prospectively to adapt to the changing environment.

Infants show evidence of prospective control from the start. Fetal mouth opening in anticipation of the thumb may be the first inkling of prospective control. The fact that 10-month-olds adjust their reach depending on whether they intend to throw a ball into a tub or push it down a tube provides exquisite evidence of prospective control. Similarly, older infants alter the speed of their initial reach for a block depending on whether the block is placed on a tower or thrown into a tub. Preschoolers plan their initial step onto a target so that their next step lands on a nearby target, like using stepping-stones to cross a river. Prospective control improves with age and experiences by bringing action into closer alignment with what children intend to do and what the situation requires. For example, 4- to 11-year-olds show age-related refinements in reaching depending on subsequent demands for precision after grasping the object—holding the object, fitting it into a tight hole, placing it in a loose hole, or tossing it into a bin.

Intuitively, prospective control may seem simple. It is not. We are used to thinking about time in terms of dichotomies: prospective-reactive, feed forward-feedback. But time runs irreversibly in one direction. What has just happened is only relevant for what will come next. Actions are always prospective, just more or less accurate more or less sensitive to current constraints, more or less attuned to the animal's goals, and planned more or less far into the future. In biological systems, the delays in neural control pathways may be substantial—greater than 200 ms for visual-motor control in adults and longer for infants. Waiting for feedback is not always viable. Imagine the delay waiting for feedback from sensor to brain to muscle in a blue whale. It is more adaptive to adopt a succession of motor control strategies: formulate a plan before acting, modify ongoing movements as needed, and discover new means on the fly.

Formulate a Plan

For an old-fashioned industrial robot to grasp an object, it brings the "hand" to the right location, stops, swivels the effector into the correct orientation, adjusts the aperture of its "grip," and then clamps on. But this clunky, discrete sequencing works only for grasping the same objects in the same location and only for transport actions that can be halted mid-stream. No bird stops mid-flight to open its feet to perch on a branch, no shark stops mid-pursuit to open its mouth to bite its prey, and no person stops mid-reach to spread the fingers to grasp. It is all one fluid motion. In the course of moving their hand to an object, adults form a grip based on its intended use and visual information about its size, shape, and orientation; transport and grasp are flexibly integrated and geared prospectively to object properties.

Although infants exhibit visually guided grasping by 4 months, coordination between transport and grip formation is not fully adult-like until 12 years of age. At first, infants' hands are closed into fists at object contact. Then they reach with the hand wide open and adjust their grip after object contact. Then the fingers begin to close during transport in anticipation of grasping the object.

Eventually, infants use visual information to conform thumb-finger grip aperture and hand orientation to object properties— smooth balls and fluffy pompoms, straight and tilted rods, regular and irregular shaped objects—even when the object translates or rotates. Adjusting grip aperture and hand orientation simultaneously is more difficult than dealing with only one dimension, but infants solve this by 12 months of age.

Generally, infants pre-shape the hand for a power grip (all fingers wrap around the object), but for tiny objects or toys with protuberances, they switch to a precision grip with thumb and forefinger. Between 5 and 13 months, reaching with one hand for small objects and two hands for large objects becomes more reliable; infants scale the space between their two hands to object size; and they aim their two hands closer to the center of mass of an irregularly shaped object. By 3 years of age, children switch from one- to two-handed grasping when object size exceeds finger-thumb aperture size.

Sometimes prospective control of grasping stretches farther into the future than simply preparing the fingers to latch on. The intended use may require an initially awkward grasp so that subsequent movements are comfortable and efficient—dubbed the "end-state comfort" effect. Adults, for example, grasp an object to be inverted with the thumb awkwardly pointing down so that the grip is comfortable when the object is rotated; you flip an upside down glass before filling it with water. Prospective control in this case entails a second step that is not immediately accessible to visual guidance. Transport and grip formation are still in play for the initial grasp, but planning for the end state determines whether to grasp thumb up or down, over- or underhand.

Do infants exhibit two-step action planning? At 9-14 months of age, infants grasp a spoon laid horizontally with their preferred (right) hand. When the handle points right, they use an overhand, power grip and bring spoon to mouth with the thumb near the bowl. They do exactly the same thing, however, when the handle points left, only now the overhand power grip causes them to bring spoon to mouth with the pinky finger near the bowl—an unwieldy end state that causes the food to spill. At 19-24 months of age, infants use the same overhand grip, but when the handle points left, they use their left hand to grasp and the food arrives intact. The same grip strategies hold for other tools such as hammers. Is this evidence of two-step planning? Yes, but infants switch hands rather than switching grips, presumably with some cost for manual control in the second part of the action sequence. By 4 years of age, children show the first evidence of adult-like end-state planning, sometimes using their dominant hand with an underhand power grip, thus bringing spoon to mouth with the thumb near the bowl. By 8 years, awkward pinky-to-bowl grips have completely disappeared and children primarily use underhand power grips or adult-like fingertip grips with the dominant hand.

Hand choice can show stronger evidence of end-state planning when the tool-target relation requires bringing the hand toward the chest. Two-year-olds grasp a stick laid horizontally with their preferred (right) hand to sweep a toy toward a goal on either side of the table, whereas 3-year-olds grasp with the hand opposite the goal to make the sweeping motion more comfortable and efficient. However, 2-year-olds can select the grasping hand with the end state in mind when raking rather than sweeping the object.

Two-step planning of manual actions is clearly more difficult when only the preferred hand is allowed, and children do not consistently display end-state planning with their dominant hand until 10-12 years of age. Thus, children would make lousy waiters: Four- to 6-year-olds show end-state comfort when inverting a water glass on fewer than 50% of trials. They would also make lousy fencers: Ten-year-olds display end-state planning when grasping a sword on only 61% of trials. Adult monkeys are about on par with children: Rhesus monkeys use whichever hand allows for a thumb-to-bowl overhand power grip on a spoon. Tamarins invert a cup using a thumb down grip on 83% of trials. Lemurs use the thumb down grip on 38% of trials.

Is the cognitive dimension (representing the end state and sequencing of actions) what makes two-step planning with the dominant hand so hard? Perhaps it is not so hard. One difference between children and adults is consistency of grip choice. Many children show the end-state effect only on a subset of trials whereas adults show it on every trial. Consistency may have more to do with task compliance and cost assessment than children's ability to form a plan.

Modify the Plan

Once the hand is positioned on the object, it is a simple matter to grasp. Or is it? Robots designed with traditional notions of action feedback are notoriously poor at grasping. Too little pressure causes the robot hand to drop the coffee cup; too much pressure crushes it. Think of picking a ripe raspberry. Grip force should be just above the level needed to keep the object from slipping out of the fingers. To lift an object by grasping requires coordinating the grip forces used to squeeze the object between the fingers and the load forces used to lift the object off the table. Adjusting grip to object compliance, weight, and slip requires continual modifications of the action plan, as these properties cannot be seen in advance like object shape. They must be felt—at least on the first encounter. Online modification of finger forces and position requires rapid tactile feedback from the object and efficient activation of finger muscles.

Development of control over finger forces for grasping (squeeze and lift) takes years. Protracted development is less about strength and more about coordination. Long before infants show visually guided grasping, they close their fingers around an object placed in their hand. But the grip forces are typically excessive. Neonates can grasp an experimenter's fingers so tightly that the experimenter can lift them from the examining table. Likewise, newborn monkeys can cling so tightly to their mothers' fur that they can hang on as mothers walk and climb. In Halverson's words, "Infants from birth to 6 months exhibit a grasp of a force entirely disproportionate with the pressure necessary to hold and lift the seized object. Whether the object be heavy or light, it is driven hard against the palm in a vicelike palm grip, which is purely an expediency for procuring and holding the object".

At 2-3 months of age, infants' index and middle fingers exert most of the grip force. Between 4 and 7 months, power grip forces increase. When picking up a narrow object, infants grip first (sometimes generating negative load force by pushing down) and then lift upward; the grip force is excessive for preventing slip, even when lifting an object covered with sandpaper, not slippery silk. Over the next few years, children show increasing coordination between grip and load forces until their timing and amplitude are smoothly coordinated. Moreover, from infancy to adulthood, children show improvements in their ability to learn over trials about the appropriate forces for lifting objects varying in slip, weight, and size, and show faster, more appropriate responses to unexpected perturbations, as when the experimenter drops a weight onto the object mid-lift.

A "spring" task yields an elegant model of rapid online adjustment. When holding a spring between index finger and thumb, exerting more force in the fingers compresses the coils of the spring, but also causes the spring to become more unstable. To keep the spring from buckling while maintaining tight compression requires the fingers to exert faster and faster tiny adjustments. Children's manual dexterity continually improves in this task between 4 and 16 years of age, alongside age-related decreases in muscle contraction time, increases in motor speed, and improvements in tactile spatial resolution. Manual dexterity, muscle contraction time, motor speed, and tactile spatial resolution depend on cortical sensory and motor mechanisms that are not adult-like until 12-18 years of age or later. Thus, online modification of precision grip develops gradually over nearly two decades as experience with objects and neural control of finger musculature work hand-in-hand.

Make a New Plan

Sometimes the original plan is unworkable or there is no ready-made plan. Flexibility—the ability to transfer existing means to a new situation or to concoct a new plan—is a cornerstone of adaptive behavior. True motor skill involves problem solving and creativity. Improvisation and innovation are key. Lack of flexibility is a primary impediment in designing freewheeling, adaptive robots. Current robots cannot use old strategies in new ways or discover new solutions on the fly.

Infants, in contrast, repurpose old movement strategies, recombine existing skills in new ways, and invent utterly new solutions. For example, the short, wide immature steps of the novice walker enjoy new life as adaptive gait modifications in experienced toddlers and adults—to brake forward momentum while walking down slopes or to keep balance on the rolling deck of a ship. Crawling infants recombine existing strategies to carry objects: They crawl while holding objects in their mouth or pushing them on the floor; they bum shuffle while holding the object in hand or under an arm. Walking infants, like adult hikers crossing a log over a stream, revert to crawling to cross a deformable waterbed or squishy foam pit. When toddlers face a slope too steep to manage by braking, long discarded forms of belly crawling and bum shuffling reappear as descent strategies to slide down headfirst or in a sitting position.

Examples of strategy discovery abound: Infants "cruise" over a low handrail by hunching over at their waist or cruising on their knees instead of feet. Infants turn around (detouring) and back feet-first to descend pedestals, drop-offs, stairs, and steep slopes. McGraw's description of how infants acquire the backing strategy to descend 70-inch pedestals without banging their chins or crashing at the bottom still makes for a gripping read. Moreover, detouring adds challenging cognitive demands for infant humans and other animals. The backing strategy, including the detour, emerges in various ways: constructed out of whole cloth, discovered serendipitously in the course of doing something else, piecemeal, or all at once.

Tool use is emblematic of strategic planning and innovation. In tool use, infants use an object or part of the environment as a means to augment their body capabilities to attain a goal. For example, toddlers use handrails to augment their balance while climbing stairs or crossing bridges; moreover, they distinguish the utility of the handrail based on its distance from the bridge and whether it is composed of sturdy wood or wobbly rubber. Like Köhler's chimps, toddlers rearrange the environment to create new means by relocating or stacking boxes to reach lures hanging from the ceiling. However, the most sensible solutions, such as stacking boxes smaller upon larger, emerge only after weeks of practice.

Handheld tool use is considered the epitome of flexibility and problem solving, perhaps because innovation, manufacture, and use of stone tools was a turning point in human evolution. Children's play with objects seems to entail limitless variety of manual, creative actions. But making tools is not child's play. When a tool must be invented, manufactured, or used for a particular (adult-defined) purpose, young children show protracted development and many limitations in planning the actions. Three- to 7-year-olds, for example, bend and straighten a pipe cleaner during play, and they choose a bent pipe cleaner to hook an out-of-reach object. But they do not spontaneously bend the pipe cleaner to use as a hook without prior demonstration.

Of course, the motor components of manual tool use are important. Infants' first adult tool, the spoon, requires a host of skills to load the spoon with food and transport it to mouth: unimanual grips, hand position on the handle, spoon angle positions to keep the bowl upright, arm positions while loading and transporting, anticipatory mouth opening, visual monitoring, and inhibition of movements in the other hand. The process is still incomplete by two years of age. However, problem solving and innovating new plans requires something more cognitive. The familiarity of the spoon leads to "functional fixity"; toddlers are loath to treat the handle as the business end even when the bowl is clearly unsuitable. Three-year-olds perseverate by pulling a cane toward an object that needs pushing if they did the pulling motions first. Two year-olds fail to use a rake if the target sits slightly outside the protruding edge of the tool. Perhaps most astounding, 1- to 3-year-olds make scale errors by trying to use a doll-sized tool on a person-sized object and vice versa. The grips are appropriate, two-step planning is evident, but children bring the wrong tools to the job.

Tool manufacture and use is widespread throughout the animal kingdom, from bug to bird, fish to octopus, rat to elephant, and monkey to ape. But two species rise above the rest as flexible and effective tool makers/tool users in the wild, chimpanzees and New Caledonian crows. Chimps strip a slender branch to use as a "fishing lure" for termites or ants. They often begin by using a stouter stick to break a hole in the nest and then delicately insert the probe into the tunnel to extract insects clutching onto the twig. Chimps may bite the end of the probe to create a frayed, brush tip better able to secure insects. Crows fabricate equally elaborate tools by carefully crafting hooks at the end of stripped-down twigs or by fashioning probes by cutting the barbed leaves of pandanus trees into slender shapes. The probes then are inserted into crevices to prize grubs.

Chimps attend to functional properties of food extractors. For example, they choose longer sticks to retrieve rewards from deeper tubes. Crows likewise recognize the functional properties of stick tools. When presented with a hooked stick with a non-functional end, crows grasp the tool in their beak so as to hold the hooked-end downward. If the tool is presented upside-down, the crow flips it or even inverts its head 180° to grasp it in the functional direction, consistent with end-state comfort. Thus, both chimps and crows adopt successive strategies when facing motor challenges. They both pre-shape their grip to grasp a tool (Formulate a Plan). They modify tools as needed by reducing the length, trimming parts, or fine-tuning the business end of the tool (Modify the Plan). They also alter the means-ends relations by flipping a stick to reverse its orientation, dropping or manipulating it to change grips, exchanging it for another tool, or abandoning the stick to manufacture an entirely new tool (Make a New Plan).

Learning the nuances of making, using, modifying, and switching tools takes a long time. Young chimps require up to two years to become proficient at selecting and using stones as hammers to smash nuts against an anvil stone. Juvenile crows require more than a year to achieve adult levels of grub fishing. Moreover, tools are manufactured following consistent, detailed procedures that are standardized in a local area. Although neither chimp nor crow parents actively teach offspring about tool manufacture and use, infant chimps and juvenile crows spend much of their time hanging out with skilled adults and gaining access to discarded tools. In this regard, they are very like human children that grow up in a material culture.

Perceiving and Generalizing: Affordances for Action

Selecting (or guiding, modifying, or creating) actions from the set of all possible actions presupposes that animals can tell which actions are possible and which are not. Distinguishing possible from impossible actions is what Gibson termed "perceiving affordances." An affodance is the fit between an animal's capabilities and features of the environment that make a particular action possible. A drop-off is navigable if the obstacle is suitably small relative to the animal's leg length, limb strength, and balance control. An aperture is passable if the opening is sufficiently large relative to the size, deformability, and slip of the body parts. Actions are possible or not, regardless of whether the affordance is perceived. But perceiving affordances is what we must do for actions to be prospective and adaptive.

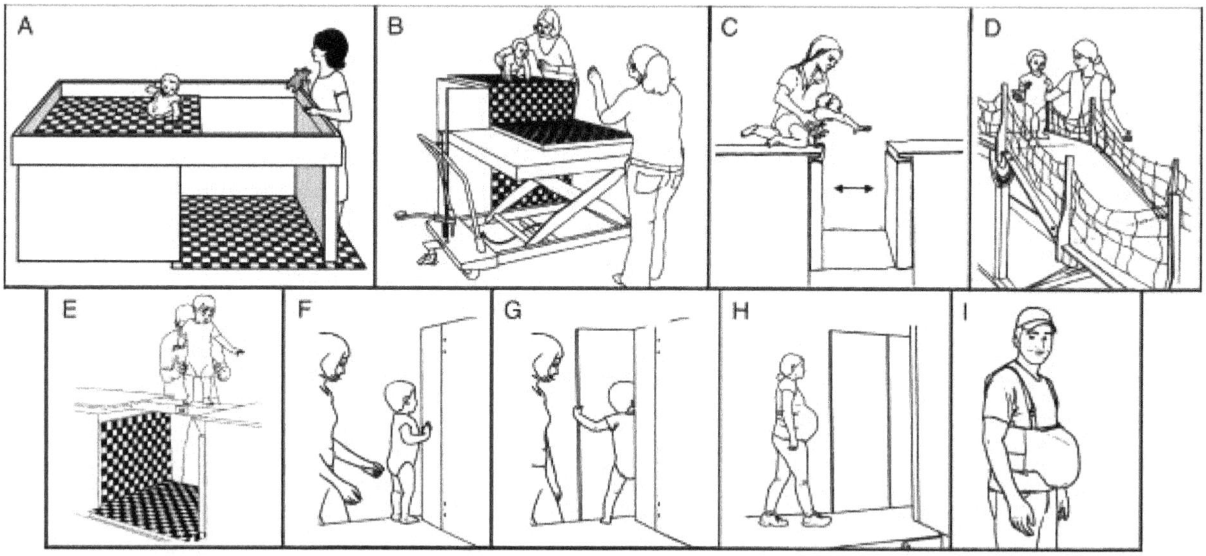

Various apparatuses used to test infants' perception of affordances as they encounter novel and variable challenges to balance and locomotion. (A) Crawling infant facing a visual cliff. The surface on the deep side is 102 cm below the edge. (B) Crawling infant facing a real cliff, with an adjustable drop-off of 0-90 cm. (C) Crawling infant facing a gap (0-90 cm) in a horizontal walkway. (D) Toddler preparing to descend an adjustable slope (0°-90°). (E) Toddler crossing a bridge over a gap. The width of the bridge adjusts from 2-60 cm. (F) Toddler negotiating a narrow ledge above a cliff. The ledge width adjusts from 0-70 cm. (G) Toddler squeezing through an aperture (0-70 cm) between vertical walls. (H) Adult pregnant woman preparing to walk through a narrow aperture. (I) Adult man wearing a "pregnancy pack" before testing with a narrow aperture. In each of the experiments involving infants (A-F), an experimenter followed alongside infants to ensure their safety. Caregivers (shown only in B) encouraged infants from the far side of the obstacle.

The affordance concept is inherently comparative and profoundly developmental. The distinction between possible and impossible drop-offs is meaningless for animals that walk down vertical walls (e.g., geckos, houseflies). Passable aperture size means something entirely different to an animal with a skeleton than to an octopus. Different species have different bodies, skills, ecological niches, and life tasks, and so different affordances for action. For every animal, affordances develop. What is impossible earlier in development can become possible later, and vice versa. For children, developmental changes are rapid and dramatic. A crawler last week is a walker this week. A poor walker this week will be better next week. Physical growth and new postural, locomotor, and manual skills expand the effective environment and invite new opportunities to take advantage of what the environment affords. Learning to perceive affordances happens concurrently with the development of new affordance relations. Learning occurs in the context of continual development.

Learning in Development

Learning in the context of development has two important implications. One implication concerns information overload. Only a subset of possible actions is relevant for the task at hand and only part of the available information is relevant for perceiving those affordances. Animals never use all the information reaching their receptors; they never perceive every option for action. Instead, animals sample from this vast pool so that only some of the potential information for affordances becomes effective.

Earlier periods of development create a smaller set of action possibilities than later periods, thereby reducing the maelstrom of perceptual information for affordances. Fetuses can perform innumerable actions, but the set of affordance relations between fetal body and uterine environment is smaller than the set of relations between toddlers' bodies and their environments, which in turn is smaller than that of adolescents. In this sense, immaturity of infants' perceptual-motor systems is an advantage because it effectively decreases information overload, and thereby constrains learning. As learning progresses, so does development. Infants are born with the perceptual-motor skills they practiced prenatally, which now can be used to discover new affordances in the more complex extra-uterine environment. Bootstrapping between learning and development continues throughout the lifespan.

The second implication concerns flexibility. Learning in the midst of development results in learning that is sufficiently flexible to scale up to the novelty and variability that characterize everyday activity in the natural environment. A compendium of fixed solutions (or for robots, preprogrammed routines) is not viable long-term because yesterday's solution may no longer work with today's body and environment. Infants do not really learn to move. Instead, infants acquire something like learning sets; to use Harlow's phrase, they are "learning to learn" to move. They learn to generate and detect information for affordances at each moment— what they can do right now with this body and these skills in this environment for this task. The flux of a changing body in a variable world ensures that infants learn to perceive affordance relations (my current leg length and level of balance control relative to the features of that particular drop-off) rather than static facts (big drop-offs are dangerous, or my balance is shaky).

As in acquiring simple learning sets, learning to learn entails immense amounts of variable experiences over a very long time. But this presents no real limitation for motor development. By 3.5 months of age, infants have performed 3-6 million eye movements; at 11-13 months, they spend half of each waking hour interacting with objects; at 12-19 months, they take 14,000 steps per day.

Development also puts limits on the flexibility of learning. New action systems create entirely new affordance relations. Thus, learning to perceive affordance relations does not transfer from one perception-action system to another. Why should it? Affordance relations for crawling and walking, for example, are completely different. Exploratory movements to generate information for affordances are different. Thus, crawling experience teaches infants to perceive affordances for crawling; walking experience provides opportunities for learning about affordances for walking.

Variations in the Environment

For many animals, the size of a drop-off affects affordances for locomotion. In the classic "visual cliff" paradigm, animals approach an apparent drop-off on a glass-covered precipice. When they first learn to crawl, human infants (and other animals that do not locomote at birth) cross right over the safety glass; avoidance requires several weeks of self-produced locomotor experience. Experience is also necessary in paradigms where the information for the drop-off is veridical. On real cliffs, gaps, slopes, bridges, and ledges, novice crawlers and walkers repeatedly fall over the brink of impossibly large drop-offs, whereas experienced infants precisely scale attempts to cross to the affordance relations.

Is this evidence of learning to learn or learning something else? A popular interpretation is that locomotor experience teaches infants a general rule: fear of heights. In line with this view, infants show accelerated heart rate, an index of fear, if placed on the glass covering the deep side of the visual cliff, and animals show stereotyped fear responses such as freezing and backing up. However, being placed on the glass is more like being thrown off a cliff than exploring affordances from the edge. When infants are cajoled by their caregivers to cross, they do not show outward signs of fear (e.g., crying, backing away from the brink). Rather, they happily explore at the edge, but do not cross. Moreover, when deciding whether to cross bridges varying in width, experienced crawlers and walkers scale attempts to bridge width, meaning they attend to affordances for crossing, but they treat large and small drop-offs under the bridge as equivalent, which indicates they do not respond based on the severity of a potential fall. Thus, the evidence does not support an explanation based on fear of heights.

A second interpretation is that locomotor experience teaches infants facts about drop-offs. This is not the case. Although infants' everyday experience does not include locomotion over cliffs, gaps, steep slopes, bridges, or ledges, experienced infants respond adaptively on their first encounter with these situations in the lab. Infants do not exhibit within-session learning either within or across tasks. When tested weekly, infants behave the same way as those tested only once). And infants instantly update their perception of affordances to take changes in their bodies and skills into account, whether those changes occur naturally or are induced experimentally.

Moreover, if infants were learning general rules, such as "large drop-offs are dangerous" or "be afraid", they should avoid large drop-offs regardless of the posture in which they are tested. But they do not. Despite achieving accurate perception of affordances after 10-20 weeks of experience, learning does not transfer from earlier- to later-developing action systems. In an experienced sitting posture, infants correctly gauge how far they can lean over the edge of a gap; but in a novice crawling posture, they fall into the gap repeatedly. Experienced crawlers avoid crawling over impossibly high cliffs and steep slopes, but novice walkers walk over the brink. Experienced cruisers perceive affordances for cruising over gaps in a handrail, but novice walkers do not; and both groups step into impossibly large gaps in the floor.

Variations in Both Body and Environment

Changes in the body or environment alter affordance relations. It is typically not a matter of simple geometric scaling: leg length to drop-off height, shoulder width to aperture size. Rather, affordances typically involve dynamic aspects of body and skills such as balance, strength, coordination, stretch, and deformability. Infants' ability to walk over gaps, barriers, bridges, and drop-offs depends more on their locomotor experience than their leg length. For infants, the head is the widest dimension and does not compress, so passage depends on head size. But torsos are widest in adults, and squeezing through apertures also depends on deformability of the torso.

Perceiving affordances under changing body conditions requires generating and detecting information about the dynamic status of the body. Four- to 10-year-olds lift their feet to clear an obstacle based on both leg length and the variability of their movements relative to obstacle height. Eight- to 10-year-olds rotate their shoulders to fit through apertures based on both shoulder width and side-to-side sway relative to aperture width. Infants and children rotate their hands to fit them through apertures based on both absolute and scrunched hand size relative to opening size. Infants attempt to walk along a narrow ledge based on both body size and balance control relative to ledge width.

Bodies can change from day to day or even faster, so perception of affordances must be continually updated. Pregnant women update their perception of affordances for squeezing through narrow doorways based on changes in the size and compressibility of their growing torsos. Nonpregnant college students, female and male, update their perception of affordances for passage after a brief period of experience wearing a "pregnancy pack". Experienced walking infants update their perception of affordances from trial to trial, depending on whether they are wearing lead- or feather-weight shoulder packs, or rubber or Teflon-soled shoes. They treat the same degree of slope as safe while wearing the feather-weight or rubber shoes, and as risky while wearing the lead-weight or slippery-soled shoes.

Animal Life at the Edge

Whether young animals have rudimentary motor skills, like humans, or are more adult-like and walk soon after birth, perceiving affordances requires continual updating of body-environment relations. Tree snakes decide whether to crawl, lunge, or avoid crossing gaps between branches based on their body length relative to gap size and the width of the destination branch. Smaller snakes attempt larger gaps relative to body length because they have relatively more muscle to support the part of their body suspended midair. Tree snakes explore affordances by extending their heads, viewing the drop-off, and tentatively "feeling out" the space between branches.

Unlike most crabs, hermit crabs do not form a protective shell of their own, so they have to find housing in the shells of deceased snails. As a young crab grows over a series of molts, it outgrows its home and has to find a suitable replacement (too small or too large makes it vulnerable to predators). So hermit crabs are almost always on the market. When a crab comes across an empty shell, it has to assess whether it is a suitable step up in housing. It does this by a series of measuring operations. It faces the aperture, rotates the shell, runs its major claws over the exterior, then inserts each claw into the aperture. Switching is risky business, so if the shell is found suitable, the crab quickly exits its old shell and backs into the new one. The intertidal housing market is always tight, so crabs often resort to trading or stealing shells. Trades occur after crabs measure each other's shell. If it is a better fit, one crab raps the other (by banging its shell down on the other one). If the exchange is a good fit for both, then rapper and rappee swap. If the rappee declines, a shell fight may ensue.

Does all the measuring and rapping imply that lowly hermit crabs perceive affordances? They do, not only for shell selection, but also for passing through cracks and crevices in rocky tide pools. In an experimental setting, large hermit crabs avoid an aperture that is too narrow for passage in favour of a wide aperture, but small crabs make no distinction. However, after small shells are glued to the exterior of their homes, small crabs also avoid the narrow aperture, suggesting that they quickly adjust to the wider dimensions and altered dynamics of their shell. Moreover, crabs can perceive affordances for passage based on visual information alone, without touching the aperture.

Actions are Embedded

The specifics of perceiving and acting necessarily differ among different types of animals. But for human infants, snakes, monkeys, crows, robots, or any creature that must act adaptively in a changeable world, motor behavior cannot be stereotyped or preprogrammed. Learning cannot entail general rules or fixed solutions. The process of learning to learn may differ between human infants with very immature abilities (and altricial animals, such as rats and cats) and animals that can perform seemingly adult-like behavior soon after birth (precocial, like snakes and goats). But in all cases, the outcome is the same: Animals learn to explore the environment, guide actions prospectively, and select actions based on body-environment relations.

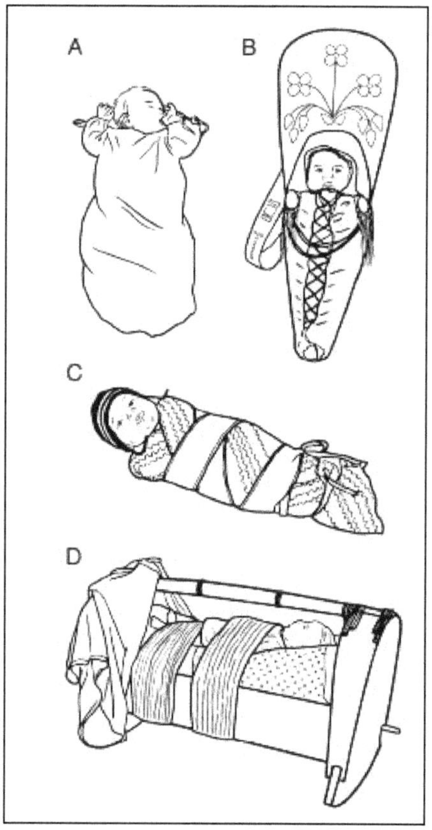

The above figure shows the examples of clothing and swaddling practices used for sleeping infants in various cultures.

(A) Sleep sack or "nightie" in widespread use in the United States and Western Europe. (B) Infant strapped to traditional Nez Percé cradle board, once used by many Native American tribes throughout western North America. (C) Tightly swaddled Quechua infant from Peru. (D) Infant from Tajikistan in a gahvora cradle with binding straps, a common practice through much of central Asia.

Enculturated Interaction

Infants' world is inherently social. It is a world populated by other people. Caregivers, siblings, and peers offer opportunities for social interaction and social information for guiding motor action. Research conducted from the embodied and embedded approaches routinely exploits the persuasive power of social information to convince infants to reach for objects, use tools, crawl and walk down straight paths, and navigate obstacles. But social influences are treated as a constant, like temperature or ambient lighting. When social information is explicitly considered, it turns out to be an important factor—at least in some conditions. In a classic study, 12-montholds crawled over an apparent "ambiguous" drop-off on the visual cliff when mothers posed frozen facial expressions of joy or interest; infants avoided when mothers posed fear or anger. By 18 months of age, infants are sophisticated consumers of social information. They defer to unsolicited advice—with mothers using their natural repertoire of dynamic facial expressions, vocalizations, and gestures—only at the point of true ambiguity. Infants ignore encouragement to walk down steep slopes beyond their ability and ignore discouraging messages to avoid shallow slopes within their ability. But at borderline slopes just at the limit of their individual ability, infants walk if mothers say "go" and stay put if mothers say "no."

The path between motor behavior and social interaction is bidirectional. Social information can guide and facilitate motor action, and infants' motor actions elicit social behaviors from others. Bidirectional influences operate at every time scale. A parent's open arms may be the impetus for an infant's first walking steps; the advent of walking changes the nature of infants' social interactions with parents.

Infants' world is social in a broader sense as well. Motor development is not just embodied and embedded; it is enculturated. Infants' physical environment has been shaped, designed, and constructed by people, sometimes with infants specifically in mind. Caregivers play a central role in structuring the environment for action. Caregivers decide where infants are, what positions they are in, when they are held or carried, what features of the environment are accessible, what infants wear, and what they eat. Such basic, everyday childrearing decisions are so culturally ingrained and pervasive that we ignore their potential influence on development—that is, until we learn about childrearing practices from a different culture.

We show that cultural differences in everyday childrearing practices have profound effects on motor development. And within a culture, motor development can instigate a cascade of developmental events in domains far afield from motor behavior.

Cultures and Paths

Research on human motor development, like every other area of psychology, represents less than 5% of the world's population. Most participants in psychological research are American or from

English-speaking or Western European countries. Worse, the American participants do not even represent the diversity of America's population. Most adult participants are students in psychology courses, meaning they are of college age, educated, affluent, and white. Most child participants are drawn from an even smaller sliver of the population: families with the time, resources, and interest to bring children to participate in laboratory studies. The typical participant is from a Western, Educated, Industrialized, Rich, Democratic society, or as Heinrich et al. dubbed it, WEIRD.

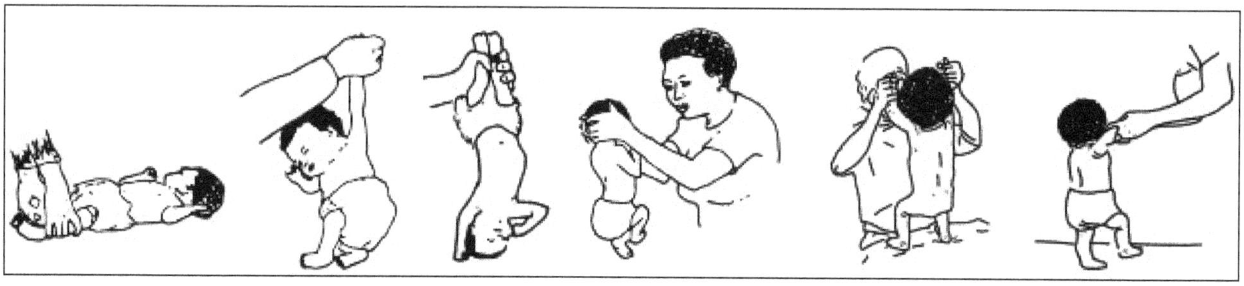

Examples of formal massage and exercise practices used by caregivers in Africa, India, and the Caribbean to facilitate infants' motor development. Left to right: passive stretching of infants' limbs; suspension and shaking by both arms, one arm, or ankles; encouragement to bear weight while standing upright and to take steps with support.

The fact that developmental research is conducted nearly exclusively with hyper-WEIRD children has several troubling implications. First, because weird children share a more homogeneous childrearing environment, researchers cannot fully assess social and cultural effects on development. Second, conclusions about what children at various ages can and cannot do (or should and should not do) are at best unproven and at worst incorrect. Without considering the rest of the world, norms for motor development are not likely to reflect the true human distribution. The statistics on screening tests and milestone charts reflect the populations from which the sampled data are drawn. Even the selection of test items (e.g., "grasps cube," "crawls on hands and knees") is biased by the cultural lens of the researchers who devise the screening tests.

Third, there is something intellectually perverse about cross-cultural comparisons showing that infants in some "far-away land" are accelerated or delayed relative to WEIRD norms since the norms are likely not "normal" at all. Minimally, the World Health Organization developmental standards recommend norms based on a geographically diverse sample. Fourth, as Lancy points out, enthnocentrism in developmental research has caused some researchers to confuse nurture with nature by attributing cultural differences to biological differences. Indeed, motor development boasts an ignominious tradition of interpreting group differences in terms of racial differences, without considering effects of childrearing practices. For example, in contrast to WEIRD norms, Chinese infants reared in Hong Kong roll supine-to-prone before prone-to supine. This cultural difference disappears for Chinese infants growing up in Canada.

Finally, assuming biologically based, culture-free universals in motor development—a domain of development where such universals are typically assumed—is currently unwarranted. The prime candidates for universal status are the postural, manual, and locomotor skills (sitting, standing, reaching, walking) that are most valued across cultures. Ironically, some scholars who have argued for a more culturally contextualized psychology also assume that motor control is somehow impervious to cultural influences. It is not. Childrearing practices have a profound influence on which motor skills children acquire, the age and sequence in which children acquire them, and the subsequent developmental trajectory.

Sleeping, Swaddling, Cradling and Toileting

As illustrated in figure above caregivers around the world adopt very different solutions for managing infants' sleep, containment, transport, and toileting—including sleep sacks, swaddles, cradleboards, and cradles. For example, mothers in rural areas of northeastern China use sandbags to toilet their infants and to keep them safely in one location. For most of the day until they are 12-24 months of age, infants lay on their backs inside a bag of fine sand, with only their arms free to move. Infants buried in sand stay clean and dry (like kitty litter) and safely contained while mothers work (like a horizontal, immobilizing play pen). But restricted movement (coupled with social deprivation) retards motor development: Sandbag-reared infants sit and walk at later ages compared to infants not reared in sandbags. In central Asia, mothers use a "gavorah" cradle for toileting, sleeping, and transporting infants. Infants are swaddled and bound into the cradle so that mothers can safely transport them around the house and keep them out of harm's way. Infants stay clean and dry via external catheters that carry waste through a hole in the bottom of the cradle. They eat, sleep, and rest in the gavorah for up to 20 hours a day, until they outgrow its confines at about 24 months of age.

Researchers need not travel to exotic locations to study effects of toileting and sleep position on infant motor development. In fact, the WEIRD research community is witness to a kind of grand "experiment" on the effects of sleep position. To reduce the incidence of sudden infant death syndrome (SIDS), the American Academy of Pediatrics advised parents to place infants on their backs to sleep. The "Back to Sleep" campaign succeeded in reducing the incidence of SIDS, but resulted in unanticipated, less positive effects on infants' skulls and skills. Back-sleepers incur more plagiocephaly (skull flattening) than belly-sleepers, and they achieve skills such as head-lifting, rolling, belly crawling, hands-knees crawling, and tripod-sitting at later ages. In response, parents were advised to give infants "tummy time" when they are awake. More time in a prone position each day predicts earlier onset ages for prone skills. Even something as seemingly mundane as a diaper exerts effects on motor development. Infants exhibit less mature walking patterns while wearing a cloth or disposable diaper compared with walking naked.

Infant Exercise

Caregivers in parts of Africa, the Caribbean, and India perform customary exercise, stretching, and massage as part of infants' daily routine. As illustrated in Figure, infants' arms and legs are repeatedly extended and flexed, knees pulled to the chest and toes to the chin. The body is vigorously rubbed and anointed, suspended by the head or one limb, shaken, and tossed. Starting from the newborn period, infants are encouraged to hold their head up, support their body weight, sit, stand, and take steps. To an observer from a WEIRD society, such practices seem rough and abusive. WEIRD people are taught that newborns must be handled like a fragile carton of eggs, with the head always carefully supported. Mothers from cultures that practice infant exercise and massage are just as appalled by WEIRD mothers' lack of vigorous motor handling and deliberate exercise; they are taught that infants must be trained to resist gravity, sit, and walk.

Rituals of infant exercise and stimulation affect motor development. Infants who receive deliberate training in sitting, standing, and stepping as part of daily childrearing routines sit and walk at earlier ages than infants who do not. Such "natural experiments" point to cultural, not ethnic differences. Infants of the same ethnic origin do not show accelerated development if reared with traditional WEIRD practices. Moreover, WEIRD infants show the same facilitative effects of training in true experiments with random assignment to exercise and control groups. Infants given a few minutes of daily stepping practice for a few weeks retain upright stepping movements for longer durations and begin walking at earlier ages than infants who receive only passive exercise. A few minutes of gentle postural training from 2-3 months of age leads to accelerated postural, manual, and locomotor skills over the next 12 months.

To Infinity and Beyond

If humans have any species-typical behavior, it is surely bipedal walking. Although other species stand, hop, or bound on two legs, no other mammals habitually walk like humans. The anatomy of our hips and feet distinguish us from other primates. But after a century of research on walking, researchers still consider the endpoint of development in terms of the WEIRD students who populate our courses. We know relatively little about what people around the world can make their bodies do.

Carrying loads is a necessary function in most of the world. In many places, children and adults carry water, firewood, and other burdens in buckets, parcels, or baskets balanced on the head—often more than their body weight. Remarkably, African women and Nepalese porters who routinely carry head loads can transport up to 30% of their body weight with no extra energy expenditure. In contrast, obese Westerners maintain the same rate of energy use per kilogram as lean walkers, but still use twice as many calories to walk as someone half their size. African load-carriers accomplish this extraordinary feat by altering the kinematics and kinetics of walking. The pendular motion so well described in WEIRD walkers is perfected in African load-carriers; they recover up to 80% of energy by transferring forward kinetic energy into vertical potential energy.

Long-distance running is practiced around the world and celebrated in international competition. But the performance of Olympic marathoners is eclipsed by the customary practices of rank-and-file Tarahumaran Indians of north-central Mexico and Kung bushmen in Botswana. Unarmed Tarahumaran hunters pursue deer through the harsh mountains of the Sierra Madre Occidentale for days until their prey drop from physical exhaustion. Bushmen do the same to hunt antelope in the Kalahari Desert until the animals succumb to fatigue or heat stress. Running for sport is even more remarkable. Tarahumarans' kickball races cover 150-300 km. Their extraordinary abilities are not due to unusual anatomy, but to intense cradle-to-grave physical conditioning that produces extremely lean bodies and highly efficient cardiovascular systems. In fact, the human foot may be engineered for long-distance running. Because Tarahumarans and Bushmen run barefoot or in light sandals instead of in sneakers, they land on the ball of their foot instead of the heel. As a consequence, they experience less force at foot contact and develop fewer running-related injuries.

Developmental Cascades

The developmental story does not end with motor skill acquisition. Rather, the story is just beginning. Motor development can instigate a cascade of events that leads to learning and development in areas seemingly far afield from motor behavior and at time points far removed from the initiating event. For a long time, the idea of developmental cascades was largely unsubstantiated, but central nonetheless to prominent developmental theories. Now researchers are inundated with evidence that motor experience can facilitate developmental change in perceptual, cognitive, and social domains. The evidence has awaited a change in zeitgeist from considering only single domains of development at a time to considering development of the whole baby in context.

For example, postural skill and manual exploration at 5 months of age is a catalyst for academic achievement at 14 years of age. How can this be? Developmental relations between such distant time points may seem like the spurious magic of statistics. But a tighter zoom reveals developmental and real-time relations between infants' posture, manual skills, object exploration, and perception, cognition, and social understanding. Specifically, the development of sitting facilitates improvements in reaching and visual-manual object exploration. Improvements in manual skills, in turn, facilitate shifts in attention to object form, changes in object appearance, object size, and other people's intentions to grasp objects.

Several lines of evidence support a causal developmental cascade rather than general maturation. Artificial motor experience instigates the same stream of developmental events. Pre-reaching infants who get a few weeks of self-generated experience retrieving objects with the help of "sticky mittens," Velcro-covered mittens that attach to objects without grasping, show short and long-term advances in reaching, grasping, and visual exploration of objects and people. A few weeks of training with posture and object interaction improves reaching, object exploration, and means-ends problem solving.

Simply performing a manual action (whether natural or with sticky mittens) for a few minutes prior to viewing a display leads to increased mental rotation abilities, visual anticipation of the outcomes of other people's actions and enhanced attention to other people's intentions during goal-directed manual actions, other people's actions on the same objects, features that distinguish one object from another, and causal relations between objects. Finally, motor development can both impede and enhance perception and cognition. Pre-sitters and experienced sitters process faces holistically, but the acquisition of sitting appears to interfere with face processing.

New locomotor skills similarly instigate a cascade of developmental changes. Crawling experience is related to increased anger when infants' goals are thwarted, sensitivity to optic flow information for balance, differentiation of self-propelled versus externally-caused object motion, mental rotation abilities, more flexible memory, more efficient use of distal and proximal landmarks, preferential looking to point light displays of crawlers compared with walkers, and greater activation in motor cortex while watching displays of infants crawling compared to walking.

Walking experience leads to more contacts with distal objects, more object carrying, more carrying objects to interact with mother, and more action directives from mother in response to moving bids. Walking experience also promotes more frequent and sophisticated social interactions with mother and more social looking. And walking is associated with a significant increase in both receptive and productive language.

Artificially enhanced locomotor experience provides corroboration of a causal developmental cascade. Pre-crawling infants who get a few weeks of experience moving themselves around in a powered mobility cart (sitting up and operating a joy stick) show more postural compensation when exposed to peripheral optic flow and earlier avoidance of a visual cliff than pre-crawlers who received no practice.

How should we interpret these cascades of development? Causal developmental links do not imply a linear causal chain: For "want of a nail, the kingdom was lost" or for want of self-generated object exploration, object cognition is lost. The developmental pathways are more reticulate, more redundant, more context specific, and more plastic than that. Developmental researchers must gather all of the usual suspects together and then figure out who done it, case by case. But we are still several chapters away from the end of that story. In 1927, anthropologist Ales Hrdlicka proclaimed his "discovery" that infants from exotic cultures "run on all fours" like monkeys. He considered crawling on hands and feet to be "anomalous," "animal-like," and "atavistic", although a torrent of letters from WEIRD parents and contemporary descriptions of "bear crawling" by Gesell and McGraw argued otherwise. Hrdlicka's comments were strangely prophetic of the recent discovery of 5 adult siblings in a remote area of Turkey who crawl on hands and feet. Early reports suggested that the Turkish crawlers were "atavistic throwbacks" to a more "apelike" stage in human evolution, the cause of this "reverse evolution" being a genetic defect that resulted in incomplete development of the cerebellum. Such rash conclusions ignored the details of the case. The siblings crawl on their palms, as do typical human infants, not on their knuckles as do great apes. Many (perhaps most) WEIRD infants exhibit bear crawling prior to walking. People with cerebellar agenesis can walk on two legs and lead relatively normal lives. The other 14 siblings in the family crawled on hands and feet, providing models for their younger siblings. The parents accepted crawling in their adult children as a "gift sent by God". And the Turkish crawlers began walking upright after their isolation was broken by researchers and physical therapists.

The case of the Turkish crawlers is clearly a missed opportunity to examine developmental relations between brain, body, environment, childrearing, and behavior. It is also a missed opportunity to investigate how this unusual way of navigating and viewing the world might cascade into other areas of development. Rather than considering this case as a weird, isolated phenomenon, we should consider it as a natural experiment that could shed light on relations among developmental domains. More generally, research on motor development in non-WEIRD societies can challenge our assumptions about the plasticity of development by illustrating possibilities not previously imagined.

References

- Motor-development, applied-and-social-sciences-magazines, children: encyclopedia.com, Retrieved 2 April, 2019
- Gross-Motor-Skills: healthofchildren.com, Retrieved 10 July, 2019
- Grissmer, David (2010). "Fine motor skills and early comprehension of the world: Two new school readiness indicators". Developmental Psychology. 46 (5): 1008–17. doi:10.1037/a0020104. PMID 20822219, Retrieved 15 February, 2019
- Child-developing-motor-skills, physical, development: parents.com, Retrieved 5 May, 2019
- AdolphRobinson-inpress-MussenMotorDev: psych.nyu.edu, Retrieved 19 March, 2019

Cognitive Development

The branch of psychology which seeks to understand how children think, explore and figure things out is termed as cognitive development. There are a number of important theories within this field of study such as Jean Piaget theory, Lev Vygotsky theory and dual coding theory. This chapter discusses in detail these theories related to cognitive development.

Cognitive development is the construction of thought processes, including remembering, problem solving, and decision-making, from childhood through adolescence to adulthood.

It was once believed that infants lacked the ability to think or form complex ideas and remained without cognition until they learned language. It is now known that babies are aware of their surroundings and interested in exploration from the time they are born. From birth, babies begin to actively learn. They gather, sort, and process information from around them, using the data to develop perception and thinking skills.

Cognitive development refers to how a person perceives, thinks, and gains understanding of his or her world through the interaction of genetic and learned factors. Among the areas of cognitive development are information processing, intelligence, reasoning, language development, and memory.

Historically, the cognitive development of children has been studied in a variety of ways. The oldest is through intelligence tests, such as the widely used Stanford Binet Intelligence Quotient (IQ) test first adopted for use in the United States by psychologist Lewis Terman in 1916 from a French model pioneered in 1905. IQ scoring is based on the concept of "mental age," according to which the scores of a child of average intelligence match his or her age, while a gifted child's performance is comparable to that of an older child, and a slow learner's scores are similar to those of a younger child. IQ tests are widely used in the United States, but they have come under increasing criticism for defining intelligence too narrowly and for being biased with regard to race and gender.

In contrast to the emphasis placed on a child's native abilities by intelligence testing, learning theory grew out of work by behaviorist researchers such as John Watson and B. F. Skinner, who argued that children are completely malleable. Learning theory focuses on the role of environmental factors in shaping the intelligence of children, especially on a child's ability to learn by having certain behaviors rewarded and others discouraged.

Infancy

As soon as they are born, infants begin learning to use their senses to explore the world around them. Most newborns can focus on and follow moving objects, distinguish the pitch and volume of sound, see all colors and distinguish their hue and brightness, and start anticipating events, such as sucking at the sight of a nipple. By three months old, infants can recognize faces; imitate the facial expressions of others, such as smiling and frowning; and respond to familiar sounds.

At six months of age, babies are just beginning to understand how the world around them works. They imitate sounds, enjoy hearing their own voice, recognize parents, fear strangers, distinguish between animate and inanimate objects, and base distance on the size of an object. They also realize that if they drop an object, they can pick it up again. At four to seven months, babies can recognize their names.

By nine months, infants can imitate gestures and actions, experiment with the physical properties of objects, understand simple words such as "no," and understand that an object still exists even when they cannot see it. They also begin to test parental responses to their behavior, such as throwing food on the floor. They remember the reaction and test the parents again to see if they get the same reaction.

At 12 months of age, babies can follow a fast moving object; can speak two to four words, including "mama" and "papa"; imitate animal sounds; associate names with objects; develop attachments to objects, such as a toy or blanket; and experience separation anxiety when away from their parents. By 18 months of age, babies are able to understand about 10–50 words; identify body parts; feel a sense of ownership by using the word "my" with certain people or objects; and can follow directions that involve two different tasks, such as picking up toys and putting them in a box.

Toddlerhood

Between 18 months to three years of age, toddlers have reached the "sensorimotor" stage of Piaget's theory of cognitive development that involves rudimentary thought. For instance, they understand the permanence of objects and people, visually follow the displacement of objects, and begin to use instruments and tools. Toddlers start to strive for more independence, which can present challenges to parents concerned for their safety. They also understand discipline and what behavior is appropriate and inappropriate, and they understand the concepts of words like "please" and "thank you."

Two-year-olds should be able to understand 100 to 150 words and start adding about ten new words per day. Toddlers also have a better understanding of emotions, such as love, trust, and fear. They begin to understand some of the ordinary aspects of everyday life, such as shopping for food, telling time, and being read to.

Preschool

Preschoolers, ages three to six, should be at the "preoperational" stage of Piaget's cognitive development theory, meaning they are using their imagery and memory skills. They should be conditioned to learning and memorizing, and their view of the world is normally very self-centered. Preschoolers usually have also developed their social interaction skills, such as playing and cooperating with other children their own age. It is normal for preschoolers to test the limits of their cognitive abilities, and they learn negative concepts and actions, such as talking back to adults, lying, and bullying. Other cognitive development in preschoolers are developing an increased attention span, learning to read, and developing structured routines, such as doing household chores.

School Age

Younger school-age children, six to 12 years old, should be at the "concrete operations" stage of Piaget's cognitive development theory, characterized by the ability to use logical and coherent actions in thinking and solving problems. They understand the concepts of permanence and conservation by learning that volume, weight, and numbers may remain constant despite changes in outward appearance. These children should be able to build on past experiences, using them to explain why some things happen. Their attention span should increase with age, from being able to focus on a task for about 15 minutes at age six to an hour by age nine.

Adolescents, ages 12 through 18, should be at the "formal operations" stage of Piaget's cognitive development theory. It is characterized by an increased independence for thinking through problems and situations. Adolescents should be able to understand pure abstractions, such as philosophy and higher math concepts. During this age, children should be able to learn and apply general information needed to adapt to specific situations. They should also be able to learn specific information and skills necessary for an occupation. A major component of the passage through adolescence is a cognitive transition. Compared to children, adolescents think in ways that are more advanced, more efficient, and generally more complex. This ability can be seen in five ways.

First, during adolescence individuals become better able than children to think about what is possible, instead of limiting their thought to what is real. Whereas children's thinking is oriented to the here and now—that is, to things and events that they can observe directly—adolescents are able to consider what they observe against a backdrop of what is possible; they can think hypothetically.

Second, during the passage into adolescence, individuals become better able to think about abstract ideas. For example, adolescents find it easier than children to comprehend the sorts of higher-order, abstract logic inherent in puns, proverbs, metaphors, and analogies. The adolescent's greater facility with abstract thinking also permits the application of advanced reasoning and logical processes to social and ideological matters. This is clearly seen in the adolescent's increased facility and interest in thinking about interpersonal relationships, politics, philosophy, religion, and morality.

Third, during adolescence individuals begin thinking more often about the process of thinking itself, or metacognition. As a result, adolescents may display increased introspection and self-consciousness. Although improvements in metacognitive abilities provide important intellectual advantages, one potentially negative by product of these advances is the tendency for adolescents to develop a sort of egocentrism, or intense preoccupation with the self.

A fourth change in cognition is that thinking tends to become multidimensional, rather than limited to a single issue. Whereas children tend to think about things one aspect at a time, adolescents can see things through more complicated lenses. Adolescents describe themselves and others in more differentiated and complicated terms and find it easier to look at problems from multiple perspectives. Being able to understand that people's personalities are not one-sided or that social situations can have different interpretations depending on one's point of view permits the adolescent to have far more sophisticated and complicated relationships with other people.

Cognitive development	
Age	Activity
One month	Watches person when spoken to.
Two months	Smiles at familiar person talking. Begins to follow moving person with eyes.

Four months	Shows interest in bottle, breast, familiar toy, or new surroundings.
Five months	Smiles at own image in mirror. Looks for fallen objects.
Six months	May stick out tongue in imitation. Laughs at peekaboo game. Vocalizes at mirror image. May act shy around strangers.
Seven months	Responds to own name. Tries to establish contact with a person by cough or other noise.
Eight months	Reaches for toys out of reach. Responds to "no."
Nine months	Show likes and dislikes. May try to prevent face-washing or other activity that is disliked. Shows excitement and interest in foods or toys that are well-liked.
Ten months	Starts to understand some words. Waves bye-bye. Holds out arm or leg for dressing.
Eleven months	Repeats performance that is laughed at. Likes repetitive play. Shows interest in books.
Twelve months	May understand some "where is?" questions. May kiss on request.
Fifteen months	Asks for objects by pointing. Starting to feed self. Negativism begins.
Eighteen months	Points to familiar objects when asked "where is?" Mimics familiar adult activities. Know some body parts. Obeys two or three simple orders.
Two years	Names a few familiar objects. Draws with crayons. Obeys found simple orders. Participates in parallel play.
Two-and-a-half years	Names several common objects. Begins to take interest in sex organs. Gives full names. Helps to put things away. Peak of negativism.
Three years	Constantly asks questions. May count to 10. Begins to draw specific objects. Dresses and undresses doll. Participates in cooperative play. Talks about things that have happened.
Four years	May make up silly words and stories. Beginning to draw pictures that represent familiar things. Pretends to read and write. May recognize a few common words, such as own name.
Five years	Can recognize and reproduce many shapes, letters, and numbers. Tells long stories. Begins to understand the difference between real events and make-believe ones. Asks meaning of words.

Finally, adolescents are more likely than children to see things as relative, rather than absolute. Children tend to see things in absolute terms—in black and white. Adolescents, in contrast, tend to see things as relative. They are more likely to question others' assertions and less likely to accept facts as absolute truths. This increase in relativism can be particularly exasperating to parents, who may feel that their adolescent children question everything just for the sake of argument. Difficulties often arise, for example, when adolescents begin seeing their parents' values as excessively relative.

Common Problems

Cognitive impairment is the general loss or lack of development of cognitive abilities, particularly autism and learning disabilities. The National Institutes of Mental Health (NIMH) describes learning disabilities as a disorder that affects people's ability to either interpret what they see and hear or to link information from different parts of the brain. These limitations can show up in many ways, such as specific difficulties with spoken and written language, coordination, self-control, or attention. Such difficulties extend to schoolwork and can impede learning to read or write or to do math. A child who has a learning disability may have other conditions, such as hearing problems or serious emotional disturbance. However, learning disabilities are not caused by these conditions, nor are they caused by environmental influences such as cultural differences or inappropriate instruction.

Parental Concerns

As of 2004 it is widely accepted that a child's intellectual ability is determined by a combination of heredity and environment. Thus, although a child's genetic inheritance is unchangeable, there are definite ways that parents can enhance their child's intellectual development through environmental factors. They can provide stimulating learning materials and experiences from an early age, read to and talk with their children, and help children explore the world around them. As children mature, parents can both challenge and support the child's talents. Although a supportive environment in early childhood provides a clear advantage for children, it is possible to make up for early losses in cognitive development if a supportive environment is provided at some later period, in contrast to early disruptions in physical development, which are often irreversible.

Jean Piaget Theory

Piaget's theory of cognitive development explains how a child constructs a mental model of the world. He disagreed with the idea that intelligence was a fixed trait, and regarded cognitive development as a process which occurs due to biological maturation and interaction with the environment.

Piaget was employed at the Binet Institute in the 1920s, where his job was to develop French versions of questions on English intelligence tests. He became intrigued with the reasons children gave for their wrong answers to the questions that required logical thinking. He believed that these incorrect answers revealed important differences between the thinking of adults and children.

Piaget was the first psychologist to make a systematic study of cognitive development. His contributions include a stage theory of child cognitive development, detailed observational studies of cognition in children, and a series of simple but ingenious tests to reveal different cognitive abilities.

What Piaget wanted to do was not to measure how well children could count, spell or solve problems as a way of grading their I.Q. What he was more interested in was the way in which fundamental concepts like the very idea of number, time, quantity, causality, justice and so on emerged.

Before Piaget's work, the common assumption in psychology was that children are merely less competent thinkers than adults. Piaget showed that young children think in strikingly different ways compared to adults.

According to Piaget, children are born with a very basic mental structure (genetically inherited and evolved) on which all subsequent learning and knowledge are based.

Piaget's Theory Differs from others in Several Ways

- It is concerned with children, rather than all learners.
- It focuses on development, rather than learning per se, so it does not address learning of information or specific behaviors.
- It proposes discrete stages of development, marked by qualitative differences, rather than a gradual increase in number and complexity of behaviors, concepts, ideas, etc.

The goal of the theory is to explain the mechanisms and processes by which the infant, and then the child, develops into an individual who can reason and think using hypotheses. To Piaget, cognitive development was a progressive reorganization of mental processes as a result of biological maturation and environmental experience.

Children construct an understanding of the world around them, then experience discrepancies between what they already know and what they discover in their environment.

Schemas

Imagine what it would be like if you did not have a mental model of your world. It would mean that you would not be able to make so much use of information from your past experience or to plan future actions. Schemas are the basic building blocks of such cognitive models, and enable us to form a mental representation of the world. Piaget defined a schema as: "a cohesive, repeatable action sequence possessing component actions that are tightly interconnected and governed by a core meaning."

In more simple terms Piaget called the schema the basic building block of intelligent behavior – a way of organizing knowledge. Indeed, it is useful to think of schemas as "units" of knowledge, each relating to one aspect of the world, including objects, actions, and abstract (i.e., theoretical) concepts.

Wadsworth suggests that schemata (the plural of schema) be thought of as 'index cards' filed in the brain, each one telling an individual how to react to incoming stimuli or information. When Piaget talked about the development of a person's mental processes, he was referring to increases in the number and complexity of the schemata that a person had learned. When a child's existing schemas are capable of explaining what it can perceive around it, it is said to be in a state of equilibrium, i.e., a state of cognitive (i.e., mental) balance.

Piaget emphasized the importance of schemas in cognitive development and described how they were developed or acquired. A schema can be defined as a set of linked mental representations of the world, which we use both to understand and to respond to situations. The assumption is that we store these mental representations and apply them when needed. For example, a person might have a schema about buying a meal in a restaurant. The schema is a stored form of the pattern of behavior which includes looking at a menu, ordering food, eating it and paying the bill. This is an example of a type of schema called a 'script.' Whenever they are in a restaurant, they retrieve this schema from memory and apply it to the situation.

The schemas Piaget described tend to be simpler than this - especially those used by infants. He described how - as a child gets older - his or her schemas become more numerous and elaborate.

Piaget believed that newborn babies have a small number of innate schemas - even before they have had many opportunities to experience the world. These neonatal schemas are the cognitive structures underlying innate reflexes. These reflexes are genetically programmed into us.

For example, babies have a sucking reflex, which is triggered by something touching the baby's lips. A baby will suck a nipple, a comforter (dummy), or a person's finger. Piaget, therefore, assumed that the baby has a 'sucking schema.'

Similarly, the grasping reflex which is elicited when something touches the palm of a baby's hand, or the rooting reflex, in which a baby will turn its head towards something which touches its cheek, are innate schemas. Shaking a rattle would be the combination of two schemas, grasping and shaking.

Assimilation and Accommodation

Jean Piaget viewed intellectual growth as a process of adaptation (adjustment) to the world. This happens through:

- Assimilation: Which is using an existing schema to deal with a new object or situation.
- Accommodation: This happens when the existing schema (knowledge) does not work, and needs to be changed to deal with a new object or situation.
- Equilibration: This is the force which moves development along. Piaget believed that cognitive development did not progress at a steady rate, but rather in leaps and bounds. Equilibrium occurs when a child's schemas can deal with most new information through assimilation. However, an unpleasant state of disequilibrium occurs when new information cannot be fitted into existing schemas (assimilation). Equilibration is the force which drives the learning process as we do not like to be frustrated and will seek to restore balance by mastering the new challenge (accommodation). Once the new information is acquired the process of assimilation with the new schema will continue until the next time we need to make an adjustment to it.

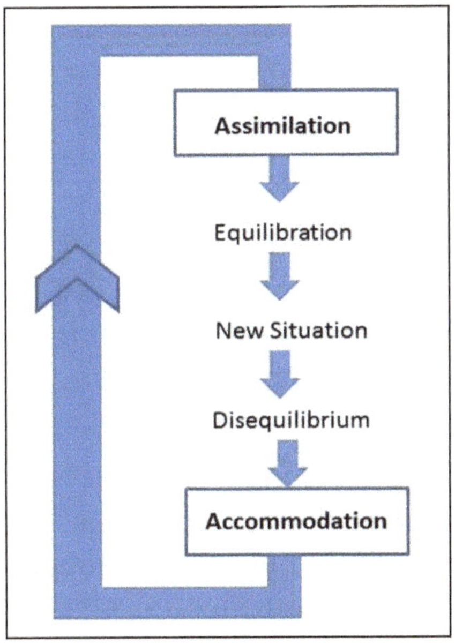

Example of Assimilation- A 2-year-old child sees a man who is bald on top of his head and has long frizzy hair on the sides. To his father's horror, the toddler shouts "Clown, clown".

Example of Accommodation- In the "clown" incident, the boy's father explained to his son that the man was not a clown and that even though his hair was like a clown's, he wasn't wearing a funny costume and wasn't doing silly things to make people laugh.

With this new knowledge, the boy was able to change his schema of "clown" and make this idea fit better to a standard concept of "clown".

Piaget's 4 Stages of Cognitive Development

Piaget proposed four stages of cognitive development which reflect the increasing sophistication of children's thought:

1. Sensorimotor stage (birth to age 2)
2. Preoperational stage (from age 2 to age 7)
3. Concrete operational stage (from age 7 to age 11)
4. Formal operational stage (age 11+ - adolescence and adulthood).

Each child goes through the stages in the same order, and child development is determined by biological maturation and interaction with the environment. Although no stage can be missed out, there are individual differences in the rate at which children progress through stages, and some individuals may never attain the later stages.

Piaget did not claim that a particular stage was reached at a certain age - although descriptions of the stages often include an indication of the age at which the average child would reach each stage.

Sensorimotor Stage (Birth-2 Years)

The main achievement during this stage is Object Permanence - knowing that an object still exists, even if it is hidden. It requires the ability to form a mental representation (i.e., a schema) of the object.

Preoperational Stage (2-7 Years)

During this stage, young children can think about things symbolically. This is the ability to make one thing - a word or an object - stand for something other than itself. Thinking is still egocentric, and the infant has difficulty taking the viewpoint of others.

Concrete Operational Stage (7-11 Years)

Piaget considered the concrete stage a major turning point in the child's cognitive development because it marks the beginning of logical or operational thought. This means the child can work things out internally in their head (rather than physically try things out in the real world).

Children can conserve number (age 6), mass (age 7), and weight (age 9). Conservation is the understanding that something stays the same in quantity even though its appearance changes.

Formal Operational Stage (11 Years and Over)

The formal operational stage begins at approximately age eleven and lasts into adulthood.

During this time, people develop the ability to think about abstract concepts, and logically test hypotheses.

Educational Implications

Piaget did not explicitly relate his theory to education, although later researchers have explained how features of Piaget's theory can be applied to teaching and learning. Piaget has been extremely influential in developing educational policy and teaching practice. For example, a review of primary education by the UK government in 1966 was based strongly on Piaget's theory. The result of this review led to the publication of the Plowden report.

Discovery learning – the idea that children learn best through doing and actively exploring - was seen as central to the transformation of the primary school curriculum.

'The report's recurring themes are individual learning, flexibility in the curriculum, the centrality of play in children's learning, the use of the environment, learning by discovery and the importance of the evaluation of children's progress - teachers should 'not assume that only what is measurable is valuable.'

Because Piaget's theory is based upon biological maturation and stages, the notion of 'readiness' is important. Readiness concerns when certain information or concepts should be taught. According to Piaget's theory children should not be taught certain concepts until they have reached the appropriate stage of cognitive development. According to Piaget, assimilation and accommodation require an active learner, not a passive one, because problem-solving skills cannot be taught, they must be discovered.

Within the classroom learning should be student-centered and accomplished through active discovery learning. The role of the teacher is to facilitate learning, rather than direct tuition. Therefore, teachers should encourage the following within the classroom:

- Focus on the process of learning, rather than the end product of it.
- Using active methods that require rediscovering or reconstructing "truths."
- Using collaborative, as well as individual activities (so children can learn from each other).
- Devising situations that present useful problems, and create disequilibrium in the child.
- Evaluate the level of the child's development so suitable tasks can be set.

Critical Evaluation

Support

- The influence of Piaget's ideas in developmental psychology has been enormous. He changed how people viewed the child's world and their methods of studying children.
- He was an inspiration to many who came after and took up his ideas. Piaget's ideas have generated a huge amount of research which has increased our understanding of cognitive development.

- His ideas have been of practical use in understanding and communicating with children, particularly in the field of education (re: Discovery Learning).

Criticisms

- Are the stages real? Vygotsky and Bruner would rather not talk about stages at all, preferring to see development as a continuous process. Others have queried the age ranges of the stages. Some studies have shown that progress to the formal operational stage is not guaranteed.

  For example, Keating reported that 40-60% of college students fail at formal operation tasks, and Dasen states that only one-third of adults ever reach the formal operational stage.

- Because Piaget concentrated on the universal stages of cognitive development and biological maturation, he failed to consider the effect that the social setting and culture may have on cognitive development.

  Dasen cites studies he conducted in remote parts of the central Australian desert with 8-14 year old Aborigines. He gave them conservation of liquid tasks and spatial awareness tasks. He found that the ability to conserve came later in the aboriginal children, between aged 10 and 13 (as opposed to between 5 and 7, with Piaget's Swiss sample).

  However, he found that spatial awareness abilities developed earlier amongst the Aboriginal children than the Swiss children. Such a study demonstrates cognitive development is not purely dependent on maturation but on cultural factors too – spatial awareness is crucial for nomadic groups of people.

  Vygotsky, a contemporary of Piaget, argued that social interaction is crucial for cognitive development. According to Vygotsky the child's learning always occurs in a social context in co-operation with someone more skillful (MKO). This social interaction provides language opportunities and language is the foundation of thought.

- Piaget's methods (observation and clinical interviews) are more open to biased interpretation than other methods. Piaget made careful, detailed naturalistic observations of children, and from these he wrote diary descriptions charting their development. He also used clinical interviews and observations of older children who were able to understand questions and hold conversations.

  Because Piaget conducted the observations alone the data collected are based on his own subjective interpretation of events. It would have been more reliable if Piaget conducted the observations with another researcher and compared the results afterward to check if they are similar (i.e., have inter-rater reliability).

  Although clinical interviews allow the researcher to explore data in more depth, the interpretation of the interviewer may be biased. For example, children may not understand the question/s, they have short attention spans, they cannot express themselves very well and may be trying to please the experimenter. Such methods meant that Piaget may have formed inaccurate conclusions.

- As several studies have shown Piaget underestimated the abilities of children because his tests were sometimes confusing or difficult to understand.

  Piaget failed to distinguish between competence (what a child is capable of doing) and performance (what a child can show when given a particular task). When tasks were altered, performance (and therefore competence) was affected. Therefore, Piaget might have underestimated children's cognitive abilities.

  For example, a child might have object permanence (competence) but still not be able to search for objects (performance). When Piaget hid objects from babies he found that it wasn't till after nine months that they looked for it. However, Piaget relied on manual search methods – whether the child was looking for the object or not.

  Later, research such as Baillargeon and Devos reported that infants as young as four months looked longer at a moving carrot that didn't do what it expected, suggesting they had some sense of permanence, otherwise they wouldn't have had any expectation of what it should or shouldn't do:

- The concept of schema is incompatible with the theories of Bruner and Vygotsky. Behaviorism would also refute Piaget's schema theory because is cannot be directly observed as it is an internal process. Therefore, they would claim it cannot be objectively measured.

- Piaget studied his own children and the children of his colleagues in Geneva in order to deduce general principles about the intellectual development of all children. Not only was his sample very small, but it was composed solely of European children from families of high socio-economic status. Researchers have therefore questioned the generalisability of his data.

- For Piaget, language is seen as secondary to action, i.e., thought precedes language. The Russian psychologist Lev Vygotsky argues that the development of language and thought go together and that the origin of reasoning is more to do with our ability to communicate with others than with our interaction with the material world.

Stages of Intellectual Development

The intellectual development of early childhood is divided into phases by the famous psychologist, Piaget. Intellectual development in children happens quickly using the kind of experiences that they gain. With time and experience, their memory, problem-solving skills, reasoning and thinking abilities get honed and developed.

This is the period of 0 to 2 years of age where certain activities are observed in a child that marks his or her growth of mental faculties.

- The first two months are marked by very elementary motor movements such as sucking and grasping. This is the reflexive stage.

- The next two months are marked by repetitive motions. This is the stage of primary circular reactions.

- The 4 to 8 months phase sees the child repeating movements with consequence like making a hanging toy over the crib move by touching or kicking it. This is the stage of secondary circular reactions.
- By the time the child is one year old, you will see his or her movements become more complex. This stage is the coordination of secondary reactions.
- The next six months will see the child discover new ways to do the same task. You may find your child pulling a pillow to take a toy kept on it without directly taking it.This comprises the tertiary circular reactions.
- At the age of two years, the child starts to show signs of solving simple activity related problems mentally before executing the actions. This is the invention of new means through mental combination.

Pre-Operational Period

This early childhood intellectual development phase lasts from 2 to 7 years of age and is marked by the following developments in the child:

- From the age of 2 to 4 years, language skills of the child develop. His or her speech, however, is not highly logical. The child can recall and talk about objects that are not presently in sight. This is the pre-operational phase.
- The age from four to seven years sees the child develop his speaking skills. The talk makes more sense and the child is able to recognize and use simple logic.
- Games with simple rules are comprehensible to the child now. This is the intuitive phase.

Period of Concrete Operations

This intellectual child development stage comprises of the mental growth taking place in the child from the age of 7 to 12 years:

- The child is now able to understand logical patterns and also use them. The mental faculties are now taking a turn towards solid understanding and cognition of what is to be done for what.
- The child is able to understand categories now and can also solve problems logically and correctly.

Period of Formal Operations

This is the period of development that takes place from the age of 12 years and above:

- It is in this final stage of intellectual development that the child is able to start understanding and thinking about abstract concepts.
- Logic and deductive reasoning becomes comprehensible to the child. Complex logical and abstract sequences becomes easy for the child to think about and apply in problem-solving.

A child's mental as well as physical growth is highly accelerated in the initial years of his or her life. You need to remember that every child is different in his own way. Do not put unnecessary pressure on your darling. Let your child develop his skills on his own and enjoy the stages of growth.

Lev Vygotsky Theory

The work of Lev Vygotsky has become the foundation of much research and theory in cognitive development over the past several decades, particularly of what has become known as Social Development Theory. Vygotsky's theories stress the fundamental role of social interaction in the development of cognition, as he believed strongly that community plays a central role in the process of "making meaning."

Unlike Piaget's notion that childrens' development must necessarily precede their learning, Vygotsky argued, "learning is a necessary and universal aspect of the process of developing culturally organized, specifically human psychological function". In other words, social learning tends to precede (i.e., come before) development.

Vygotsky has developed a sociocultural approach to cognitive development. He developed his theories at around the same time as Jean Piaget was starting to develop his ideas, but he died at the age of 38, and so his theories are incomplete - although some of his writings are still being translated from Russian.

No single principle (such as Piaget's equilibration) can account for development. Individual development cannot be understood without reference to the social and cultural context within which it is embedded. Higher mental processes in the individual have their origin in social processes.

Vygotsky's theory differs from that of Piaget in a number of important ways:

- Vygotsky places more emphasis on culture affecting cognitive development: This contradicts Piaget's view of universal stages and content of development (Vygotsky does not refer to stages in the way that Piaget does). Hence Vygotsky assumes cognitive development varies across cultures, whereas Piaget states cognitive development is mostly universal across cultures.
- Vygotsky places considerably more emphasis on social factors contributing to cognitive development:
    - Vygotsky states cognitive development stems from social interactions from guided learning within the zone of proximal development as children and their partner's co-construct knowledge. In contrast, Piaget maintains that cognitive development stems largely from independent explorations in which children construct knowledge of their own.
    - For Vygotsky, the environment in which children grow up will influence how they think and what they think about.
- Vygotsky places more (and different) emphasis on the role of language in cognitive

development: According to Piaget, language depends on thought for its development (i.e., thought comes before language). For Vygotsky, thought and language are initially separate systems from the beginning of life, merging at around three years of age, producing verbal thought (inner speech). For Vygotsky, cognitive development results from an internalization of language.

- According to Vygotsky adults are an important source of cognitive development: Adults transmit their culture's tools of intellectual adaptation that children internalize. In contrast, Piaget emphasizes the importance of peers as peer interaction promotes social perspective taking.

Casual Reasoning

Causal reasoning is the idea that any cause leads to a certain effect, and is an example of inductive reasoning. It is based around a process of elimination, with many scientific processes using this method as a valuable tool for evaluating potential hypotheses.

Medical practitioners, as an example, will try to establish and deduce what is causing a certain symptom. By isolating and treating this cause, through eliminating others, the symptom can be alleviated. It is based around a process of elimination, with many scientific processes using this method as a valuable tool for evaluating potential hypotheses.

Medical practitioners, as an example, will try to establish and deduce what is causing a certain symptom. By isolating and treating this cause, through eliminating others, the symptom can be alleviated.

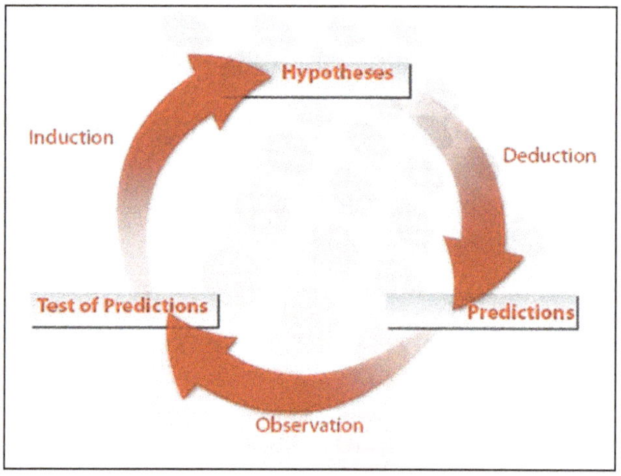

Causal reasoning may be used to direct scientific research and eliminate unlikely hypotheses for understanding certain phenomena. As an example, we are certain that global warming is happening but are unsure exactly what factors are contributing to the phenomenon.

There are five methods of using causal reasoning to determine what causes a certain effect, as set down by the philosopher John Stuart Mill.

The Method of Agreement

For this, the researcher must try to find the conditions under which a certain effect occurs and try to isolate the causes that underpin and occur in every case. This method shows that a certain cause or causes must be present for the effect to occur. In addition, this process is reversible and can show that the effect occurs only without the specified cause.

The Method of Difference

By contrast, this method determines which potential causes existed when an effect happened, and were not present when the effect did not happen. For example, causal reasoning is used to suggest that humanity is contributing to Global Warming. The earth's atmosphere, although it has gone through historical periods of warming, has never warmed up this quickly. Therefore, we assume that humanity adding greenhouse gases is causing this accelerated rate of change.

This cause was not present during historical warm periods in the earth's history but is present during this unique period of rapid warming. We can assume that this is a sound basis for a testable hypothesis.

Agreement and Difference

In many circumstances, both agreement and difference will be present and provide reinforcement to the causal reasoning process. Increased CO_2 levels appear to have caused the atmosphere to warm throughout the long history of our planet, an example of agreement.

This process is now occurring more rapidly, with modern society pumping greenhouse gases into the atmosphere. This cause was not present in antiquity, a notable difference. Therefore, this method would suggest that humanity is contributing to the rapid warming of the atmosphere.

Concomitant Variation

This is an even more powerful causal relationship where a cause of increasing intensity leads to an increasing magnitude of effect. If we look at the historical composition of the atmosphere, via ice cores, and find that high carbon dioxide levels coincide with high global temperatures, this reinforces the causal link.

The Method of Residues

This is a process of building up and amalgamating likely causes. For example, assume that the link between carbon dioxide emissions is established. We find that temperatures are increasingly more rapidly than they should, at the same time that the levels of methane in the atmosphere are increasing. Using the same methods, we can deduce that methane may also contribute to global warming.

Causal Reasoning is not Proof

It cannot be assumed that a causal relationship constitutes proof as there may be other unknown factors and processes involved. For example, the dynamics of the atmosphere and their interaction with oceanic temperatures are too complicated to be explained by a single factor.

The Mills methods can be useful as a process of elimination but scientific proof is always needed to back up the findings. Causal reasoning may aid in uncovering useful lines of research but is not accepted as verification. The method's strength is in uncovering plausible and realistic lines of research. For example, another method, such as abductive reasoning, may have generated a few likely hypotheses.

Causal reasoning can help to eliminate a few and strengthen the case for researching others, focusing research and targeting resources.

Learning and Memory

Human learning and memory is often conceived as having three stages: encoding, storage, and retrieval. Encoding refers to the acquisition and initial processing of information; storage refers to the maintenance of the encoded information over time; and retrieval refers to the processes by which the stored information is accessed and used. Historically, the scientific study of human memory can be seen as progressing through four phases, the first three of which correspond to an emphasis on encoding, storage, and retrieval, respectively. The fourth phase, which reflects the current state of the field, emphasizes the dynamic interaction among the stages.

The earliest influential concept of memory, derived from Aristotle, was that of an association, a connection between two ideas, thoughts, or events. Associations are formed when two items occur close together in time or space, when two items are very similar, or when two items are very different. The presence of one of these, the cue, brings the other to mind. One point of disagreement was whether associations could be formed only between adjacent items (direct associations) or whether an association could be formed between items that were further removed (a remote association). For example, for three events that occur in a series, not only could there be a direct association between the first and second and between the second and third, but there could also be a remote association between the first and third. Although many early theorists devoted much thought and speculation to the nature of memory, their enthusiasm and insight were hampered by a lack of appropriate tools, methods, and procedures.

Convincing evidence on this issue was not available until 1885, when Hermann Ebbinghaus published the first scientific study on memory. Ebbinghaus was the first scientist to design, conduct, and report an experiment to distinguish between two competing theories of memory. In a series of studies, he reported evidence not only for direct and remote associations, but also for backward associations. Ebbinghaus is also noted for being among the first to use statistical procedures to analyze his data.

Until the 1950S, the verbal learning tradition dominated research on memory in the United States. Following the lead of Ebbinghaus, the emphasis was on the encoding stage, especially on how associations were formed and acquired. One particularly influential line of research, for example, focused on measuring how well learning transferred to new situations. Of course, some emphasis was placed on retrieval; in particular, the dominant theory of forgetting, interference theory, included both unlearning and response competition as factors. Nonetheless, even within this framework, principles of acquisition, such as the differential effectiveness of massed versus distributed rehearsal, dominated.

Beginning in the 1950s, the so-called cognitive revolution ushered in a change of emphasis to storage. The dominant metaphor was the computer, with various buffers, registers, and other forms of storage that were linked to different hypothetical memory structures. The most common view of memory, called the modal model (after a statistical measure, the mode) had three such hypothetical memory structures: sensory register, short-term store, and long-term store. Information was first briefly registered in a sensory buffer before being converted from its raw physical form into a more durable (usually verbal) code and deposited into short-term store. Short-term store had a limited capacity, around five to nine items, or "chunks," and was intended mainly as a buffer where information could be temporarily stored. Rehearsal was the process whereby an item was either maintained or copied into long-term store.

Despite the considerable success of this type of model, empirical and logical problems quickly became apparent. The most significant of these was trying to separate the contributions of short- and long-term store in a given situation. Two reactions followed. One was the development of the idea of working memory, an update of the short-term memory concept. Working memory viewed memory in a broader context, including an attentional and visuospatial system, and was fundamentally a place where cognitive work was performed. The other reaction was an increasing emphasis on processes rather than structures; this emphasis on processing also followed an intensive study of the retrieval stage in the late 1960s and early 1970s. Indeed, working memory can be seen as a hybrid model, containing both a structure (the phonological store) and a process (the articulatory loop).

According to the levels of processing framework, memory is the result of a successive series of analyses, each one at a deeper, more conceptual level than the previous, that are performed on the information. The deeper the level of analysis the better the memory. Memory is therefore more of a by-product than anything else; it is the residue of the processing that was performed. This view offered an explanation for why intent to learn is not an important factor in subsequent tests of memory: if a person tries to memorize something but uses an inappropriate process, performance is poor. Indeed, most of the information that people do remember is not learned intentionally; rather, it is the residue of their processing of the original experience.

Levels of processing focused almost exclusively on encoding and said relatively little about retrieval. The second major processing view of the 1970S was developed as a way of rectifying this omission. The primary difference between levels of processing and transfer-appropriate processing is that the latter explicitly includes retrieval as a factor. According to this view, a particular encoding process leads to better performance not because it is necessarily deeper but rather because it is appropriate given the kind of processing that the test requires.

Currently, memory research is in the fourth phase, where the interaction between encoding and retrieval is emphasized. A good example is Tulving's encoding specificity principle. According to this principle, the recollection of an event, or a certain aspect of it, depends on the interaction between the properties of the encoded event and the properties of the encoded cues available at retrieval. Note that there is an explicit acknowledgment of two possible distortions: the representation of the original information may or may not be veridical, and the representation of the retrieval cues may or may not be veridical. Memory is the interaction of these two potentially distorted representations.

It follows from this type of interactive view that memory is inherently cue driven: Information cannot be recollected or otherwise used in processing unless an appropriate cue is present. A second implication is that slight changes in the cue constellation can easily disrupt memory performance. Even a good cue can lose its effectiveness if it is used too often, a phenomenon known as cue overload. A third implication is that memory is a dynamic process, including the potential for multiple ongoing distortions of the event, both from processing that occurs at study and processing that occurs at test. These implications are inherent in most current theories.

The intention of learning is not necessarily an important factor in subsequent memory performance. One topic that has been of considerable interest in recent years concerns situations where both acquisition and retrieval of information is performed without conscious awareness. This area is typically referred to as implicit memory, although the terminology is quite confusing. The more clear terms separate the type of learning situation (intentional or incidental) and the type of test. Traditional memory research focused on intentional learning and direct tests. Implicit memory research uses incidental learning and indirect tests. The interesting finding is that the information processed at study facilitates performance on a variety of tests even though the subject is unaware of this influence.

One ongoing controversy concerns how best to view memory, as either a set of multiple memory systems or a set of processes. The multiple memory systems view attributes memory performance to the underlying memory system. Although there is some disagreement about the number of memory systems, the most popular conception lists five. The procedural memory system is responsible for performance on tasks that involve motor skills (typing, bicycle riding), simple conditioning, and simple associative learning. The perceptual representation system is responsible for identifying and processing visual forms and in speech recognition. Primary memory (also known as working memory) is responsible for storing information that is to be held briefly, such as a telephone number for the time between looking it up and dialing. Semantic memory processes knowledge, and episodic memory is concerned with autobiographical information and events that have been personally experienced.

The major advantage of this view is that it is able to explain a large number of dissociations. A dissociation occurs when one variable, such as delay between study and test, affects one memory task differently than a second. Thus a typical explicit memory task shows worse performance after a long delay, whereas the typical implicit memory task shows almost no detrimental effect of delay. According to the multiple systems view, implicit memory is supported by the procedural representation system, whereas explicit memory depends on episodic memory. Because two different systems are used, two different results are seen. Similar explanations are offered to account for amnesia and the effects of normal aging: different systems can be affected and selectively impair some types of memory performance while leaving other memory abilities unimpaired.

The two major weaknesses of this approach are the lack of consensus on the number and type of systems and the lack of predictive dissociations. Although most multiple-system theorists subscribe to the divisions presented above, many offer additional systems (such as sensory memory systems reminiscent of the modal model), whereas others prefer fewer systems (such as combining episodic and semantic memory).

The inability of this view to formulate predictive dissociations is more problematical. For example, there is a phenomenon known as the fan effect: the time to respond to a given sentence increases as the number of facts known about the components in the sentence increases. The fact that this is true only for episodic tasks and not for semantic tasks is taken as evidence supporting the distinction between these two systems. However, the exact opposite finding-if the fan effect were seen only in semantic tasks and not episodic tasks-would also be taken as support for a distinction between the two systems. The problem is that the multiple-systems view cannot yet predict a priori the nature of the dissociations. Many researchers are currently working on addressing this problem.

The other major theoretical orientation is the processing (or proceduralist) view. Sometimes known as the monolithic view (due to the unwillingness to fractionate memory into multiple systems), this view arose out of and is related to the levels of processing and transfer-appropriate processing views. The main idea is that memory resides in the same neural units that originally processed the experience. When an event is initially experienced, it is processed by certain neural assemblies. Memory is what happens when the same or similar neural units are stimulated by a cue (either an external, bottom-up, or internal, top-down, cue) and similar processing results. As Craik put it- "Encoding is simply the set of processes involved in the perception and interpretation of the original event and retrieval is the attempted recapitulation of the original pattern of encoding activity."

Supporting research comes from many areas, including current research into the effects of normal aging on memory. Whenever a task requires a process that is initiated by an internally produced cue-regardless of whether the task is episodic, semantic, or whatever- performance will be less successful in the elderly than when the process can use an externally provided cue. Thus the type of processing is more predictive of memory performance than the presumed underlying memory system.

One criticism of the processing approach has been that it is vague about exactly how many processes are involved. The process dissociation framework is one attempt to separate the contribution of different processes. The basic logic is to examine at least two situations. One test, an inclusion test, is designed so that all processes can contribute beneficially to recall; a second test, the exclusion test, is designed so that one response cannot contribute. In essence, the effect of one process can be subtracted out and its contribution assessed.

Several other areas of research highlight the view that memory is cue driven, dynamic, and reconstructive. The reality monitoring paradigm examines the ability of people to remember the source of an event. Subjects may be asked to imagine an episode, or may actually experience the episode. During the test phase, the question of interest is whether the subjects can determine the source. The data show that people are more likely to say that an imagined event was real than a real event was imagined. The study of eyewitness memory reinforces these findings. Unless there is objective evidence available, there is no way of assessing the accuracy of recollection of an eyewitness: They may be very accurate, very inaccurate, or somewhere in the middle. Among the factors that do not predict subsequent accuracy are the duration of the event; the emotional intensity of the event; the unusualness of the event; the number of details that can be recalled; the confidence expressed about the memory; and the delay between the event and the subsequent questioning.

Current interest focuses on what is unfortunately called false memory, recalling information that was not presented. The term is unfortunate because it implies a dichotomy between "true" and "false" memories; if these really were the only options, then all memories would have to be labeled false. The far more interesting and important question is the degree to which the current recollection departs from the original episode. With subsequent tests, the recollection may become more or less accurate, but it always contains some distortion and thus some false elements on the part of the rememberer.

Current formal models of memory are also reflective of the fourth phase, the emphasis on both encoding and retrieval. Indeed, a large number of models are termed global memory models because they address memory performance in a wide variety of paradigms. The four most influential are ACT* (pronounced act star), SAM (search of associative memory), TODAM (theory of distributed associative memory), and MINERVA2 (after the Greek goddess of wisdom). Connectionist models of memory have not fared well and have had less impact on the field.

Memory, then, is a dynamic, fundamentally reconstructive set of processes that enable previously encoded information to affect current and future performance. The effects of memory need not be consciously available to the rememberer and each successive recollection may further distort or reconstruct the memory.

Metacognition

John Flavell originally coined the word "metacognition." He defined the word as "cognition about cognitive phenomenon", or basically thinking about thinking. Subsequent studies on metacognition described the term comparative to Flavell's meaning. Cross and Paris defined it as "the knowledge and control children have over their own thinking and learning activities." For Hennessey, it is the "awareness of one's own thinking, awareness of the content of one's conception, as active monitoring of one's cognitive processes, an attempt to regulate one's cognitive processes in relationship to further learning, and an application of a set of heuristics as an effective device for helping people organize their methods of attacks in general."

Metacognition denotes in-depth thinking in which cognitive processes involved in learning are actively controlled. This includes planning how to accomplish a given learning task, monitoring understanding, and estimating progress toward the completion of a task. It was said that students can have greater ability to control goals, dispositions, and attention when they are more aware of their thinking processes as they learn. This means that self-regulation is a result of self-awareness. If a student is aware of how dedicated he is to reaching his goals, of how strong his trait of perseverance is, and of how focused his attention is to a task that involves thinking or writing, he can regulate his dedication, disposition, and attention. For instance, when a student is aware of his lack of commitment to write his thesis, and bears the knowledge that he is procrastinating, delaying, and allowing himself to be distracted by other less important things, then he could take action to get started on doing the task. This is possible only if the student becomes aware of his procrastination and takes control in planning on how to approach his thesis completion.

Although the term has been known for a long time, especially in the field of educational psychology, defining metacognition can be difficult. Until now, there are still debates as to what the term exactly means. This confusion can be rooted from the idea that there are terms presently used to characterize the same basic phenomenon, such as self-regulation, executive control, or an aspect of that phenomenon such as meta-memory. These terms are commonly used interchangeably in literature. While there are some differences between explanations of the term, the role of executive processes in monitoring and regulation of cognitive methods is emphasized.

Components of Metacognition

Metacognition is classified as having three components – (1) Metacognitive knowledge, (2) Metacognitive regulation, and (3) Metacognitive experiences. Metacognitive knowledge refers to the awareness individuals possess about themselves and other people as cognitive processors. Metacognitive regulation, on the other hand, has to do with people's control over cognition and learning experiences through a set of methods that help people regulate their learning while metacognitive experiences involve cognitive efforts that are currently taking place.

Types of Metacognitive Knowledge

Aside from these three components, metacognition also has three different types of metacognitive knowledge – (1) Declarative knowledge, (2) Procedural knowledge, and (3) Conditional knowledge. Declarative knowledge refers to the factual information that one knows, and can both be spoken or written. This is also the knowledge about oneself as a learner and about what factors can influence one's performance. Procedural knowledge comprises information on how to do something or how to perform the procedural steps that make up a task. A high degree of procedural knowledge allows individuals to perform tasks more automatically through a variety of strategies. Conditional knowledge, on the other hand, refers to the knowledge about when to use a procedure, skill, or strategy or when not to, information as to why a procedure works and under what conditions it works, in addition to why one procedure is better than another. Such knowledge affords the individual a chance to assign resources when using strategies.

Skills in Metacognitive Regulation

There are three important skills in metacognitive regulation – (1) Planning, (2) Monitoring, and (3) Evaluating. Planning involves suitable selection of strategies and the right assignment of resources. Monitoring includes awareness of understanding and task performance, while evaluating refers to the assessment of the final result of a task and the efficiency carried out during task performance.

Metacognitive Strategies

Research has shown that teaching students metacognitive strategies can improve learning. Studies reveal, however, that there are only a few instructors who explicitly teach study strategies because most instructors assume that students have already acquired these skills in high school. Among the different learning strategies that are commonly used when studying or doing homework are rote memorization, goal setting, monitoring, self-assessing, and regulating during thinking and writing processes.

Dual Coding Theory

The dual coding theory proposed by Paivio attempts to give equal weight to verbal and non-verbal processing. Paivio states: "Human cognition is unique in that it has become specialized for dealing simultaneously with language and with nonverbal objects and events. Moreover, the language system is peculiar in that it deals directly with linguistic input and output (in the form of speech or writing) while at the same time serving a symbolic function with respect to nonverbal objects, events, and behaviors. Any representational theory must accommodate this dual functionality."

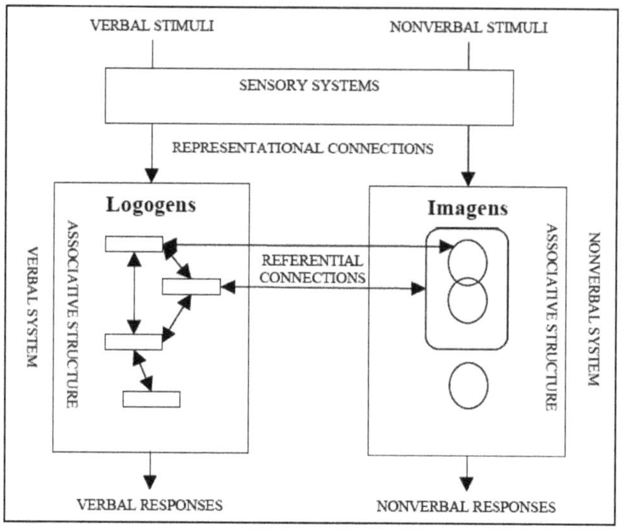

The theory assumes that there are two cognitive subsystems, one specialized for the representation and processing of nonverbal objects/events (i.e., imagery), and the other specialized for dealing with language.

Paivio also postulates two different types of representational units:

- "Imagens" for mental images and "logogens" for verbal entities which he describes as being similar to "chunks" as described by Miller. Logogens are organized in terms of associations and hierarchies while imagens are organized in terms of part-whole relationships.
- Dual Coding theory identified three types of processing: (1) representational, the direct activation of verbal or non-verbal representations, (2) referential, the activation of the verbal system by the nonverbal system or vice-versa, and (3) associative processing, the activation of representations within the same verbal or nonverbal system. A given task may require any or all of the three kinds of processing.

Scope/Application

Dual coding theory has been applied to many cognitive phenomena including: mnemonics, problem-solving, concept learning and language. Dual coding theory accounts for the significance of spatial abilities in theories of intelligence (e.g., Guilford). Paivio provides a dual coding explanation of bilingual processing. Clark & Paivio presents dual coding theory as a general framework for educational psychology.

Theory

"Dual coding" implies that verbal and non-verbal systems are alternative internal representations of events. For example, one can think of a house by thinking of the word "house", or by forming a mental image of a house The verbal and image systems are connected and related, for one can think of the mental image of the house and then describe it in words, or read or listen to words and then form a mental image.

Verbal system units are called logogens; these units contain information that underlie our use of the word. Non-Verbal system units are called imagens. Imagens contain information that generates mental images such as natural objects, holistic parts of objects, and natural grouping of objects. Imagens operate synchronously or in parallel; thus all parts of an image are available at once.

Logogens operate sequentially, words come one at a time in a syntactically appropriate sequence in a sentence. The two codes may overlap in the processing of information but greater emphasis is on one or the other. The verbal and non-verbal systems are further divided into subsystems that process information from different modalities.

Experiment:

- Give students a long list of pictures or words to remember.
- Later test memory with either a recall or recognition test.
- Students recall more pictures than words.
- The Imagen system has superior memory.
- Representing ideas in both systems is superior to representing ideas in only one system.
- Paivio claimed that picture memory was superior because whenever we see a picture we also represent that picture verbally.
- However when we see a word we do not always form a mental image of the word.

References

- Cognitive-Development: healthofchildren.com, Retrieved 2 January, 2019
- Piaget: simplypsychology.org, Retrieved 13 May, 2019
- Major-stages-of-intellectual-development-in-children: momjunction.com, Retrieved 11 April, 2019
- Vygotsky: simplypsychology.org, Retrieved 20 February, 2019
- Causal-reasoning: explorable.com, Retrieved 29 July, 2019
- Learning-and-memory, developmental-psychology: psychology.iresearchnet.com, Retrieved 3 March, 2019
- Metacognition: psychologynoteshq.com, Retrieved 30 August, 2019

5

Concepts and Theories of Intelligence

The mental quality through which human beings are able to learn from experience as well as adapt to new situations is termed as intelligence. There are a number of theories which deal with the conceptions of intelligence such as Sternberg's Triarchic theory intelligence, Spearman theory and Gardner's frames of mind. This chapter discusses in detail these theories and concepts related to intelligence.

Human Intelligence

Human intelligence is a mental quality that consists of the abilities to learn from experience, adapt to new situations, understand and handle abstract concepts, and use knowledge to manipulate one's environment.

Much of the excitement among investigators in the field of intelligence derives from their attempts to determine exactly what intelligence is. Different investigators have emphasized different aspects of intelligence in their definitions. For example, in a 1921 symposium the American psychologists Lewis M. Terman and Edward L. Thorndike differed over the definition of intelligence, Terman stressing the ability to think abstractly and Thorndike emphasizing learning and the ability to give good responses to questions. More recently, however, psychologists have generally agreed that adaptation to the environment is the key to understanding both what intelligence is and what it does. Such adaptation may occur in a variety of settings: a student in school learns the material he needs to know in order to do well in a course; a physician treating a patient with unfamiliar symptoms learns about the underlying disease; or an artist reworks a painting to convey a more coherent impression. For the most part, adaptation involves making a change in oneself in order to cope more effectively with the environment, but it can also mean changing the environment or finding an entirely new one.

Effective adaptation draws upon a number of cognitive processes, such as perception, learning, memory, reasoning, and problem solving. The main emphasis in a definition of intelligence, then, is that it is not a cognitive or mental process per se but rather a selective combination of these processes that is purposively directed toward effective adaptation. Thus, the physician who learns about a new disease adapts by perceiving material on the disease in medical literature, learning what the material contains, remembering the crucial aspects that are needed to treat the patient, and then utilizing reason to solve the problem of applying the information to the needs of the patient. Intelligence, in total, has come to be regarded not as a single ability but as an effective drawing together of many abilities. This has not always been obvious to investigators of the subject, however; indeed, much of the history of the field revolves around arguments regarding the nature and abilities that constitute intelligence.

Development of Intelligence

There have been a number of approaches to the study of the development of intelligence. Psychometric theorists, for instance, have sought to understand how intelligence develops in terms of changes in intelligence factors and in various abilities in childhood. For example, the concept of mental age was popular during the first half of the 20th century. A given mental age was held to represent an average child's level of mental functioning for a given chronological age. Thus, an average 12-year-old would have a mental age of 12, but an above-average 10-year-old or a below-average 14-year-old might also have a mental age of 12 years. The concept of mental age fell into disfavour, however, for two apparent reasons. First, the concept does not seem to work after about the age of 16. The mental test performance of, say, a 25-year-old is generally no better than that of a 24- or 23-year-old, and in later adulthood some test scores seem to start declining. Second, many psychologists believe that intellectual development does not exhibit the kind of smooth continuity that the concept of mental age appears to imply. Rather, development seems to come in intermittent bursts, whose timing can differ from one child to another.

The Work of Jean Piaget

The landmark work in intellectual development in the 20th century derived not from psychometrics but from the tradition established by the Swiss psychologist Jean Piaget. His theory was concerned with the mechanisms by which intellectual development takes place and the periods through which children develop. Piaget believed that the child explores the world and observes regularities and makes generalizations—much as a scientist does. Intellectual development, he argued, derives from two cognitive processes that work in somewhat reciprocal fashion. The first, which he called assimilation, incorporates new information into an already existing cognitive structure. The second, which he called accommodation, forms a new cognitive structure into which new information can be incorporated.

The process of assimilation is illustrated in simple problem-solving tasks. Suppose that a child knows how to solve problems that require calculating a percentage of a given number. The child then learns how to solve problems that ask what percentage of a number another number is. The child already has a cognitive structure, or what Piaget called a "schema," for percentage problems and can incorporate the new knowledge into the existing structure.

Suppose that the child is then asked to learn how to solve time-rate-distance problems, having never before dealt with this type of problem. This would involve accommodation—the formation of a new cognitive structure. Cognitive development, according to Piaget, represents a dynamic equilibrium between the two processes of assimilation and accommodation.

As a second part of his theory, Piaget postulated four major periods in individual intellectual development. The first, the sensorimotor period, extends from birth through roughly age two. During this period, a child learns how to modify reflexes to make them more adaptive, to coordinate actions, to retrieve hidden objects, and, eventually, to begin representing information mentally. The second period, known as preoperational, runs approximately from age two to age seven. In this period a child develops language and mental imagery and learns to focus on single perceptual dimensions, such as colour and size. The third, the concrete-operational period, ranges from about age 7 to age 12. During this time a child develops so-called conservation skills, which enable him to recognize that things that may appear to be different are actually the same—that is, that their fundamental properties are "conserved." For example, suppose that water is poured from a wide short beaker into a tall narrow one. A preoperational child, asked which beaker has more water, will say that the second beaker does (the tall thin one); a concrete-operational child, however, will recognize that the amount of water in the beakers must be the same. Finally, children emerge into the fourth, formal-operational period, which begins at about age 12 and continues throughout life. The formal-operational child develops thinking skills in all logical combinations and learns to think with abstract concepts. For example, a child in the concrete-operational period will have great difficulty determining all the possible orderings of four digits, such as 3-7-5-8. The child who has reached the formal-operational stage, however, will adopt a strategy of systematically varying alternations of digits, starting perhaps with the last digit and working toward the first. This systematic way of thinking is not normally possible for those in the concrete-operational period.

Piaget's theory had a major impact on the views of intellectual development, but it is not as widely accepted today as it was in the mid-20th century. One shortcoming is that the theory deals primarily with scientific and logical modes of thought, thereby neglecting aesthetic, intuitive, and other modes. In addition, Piaget erred in that children were for the most part capable of performing mental operations earlier than the ages at which he estimated they could perform them.

Post-Piaget Theories

Despite its diminished influence, Piaget's theory continues to serve as a basis for other views. One theory has expanded on Piaget's work by suggesting a possible fifth, adult, period of development, such as "problem finding." Problem finding comes before problem solving; it is the process of identifying problems that are worth solving in the first place. A second course has identified periods of development that are quite different from those suggested by Piaget. A third course has been to accept the periods of development Piaget proposed but to hold that they have different cognitive bases. Some of the theories in the third group emphasize the importance of memory capacity. For example, it has been shown that children's difficulties in solving transitive inference problems such as If A is greater than B, B is greater than C, and D is less than C, which is the greatest.

result primarily from memory limitations rather than reasoning limitations (as Piaget had argued). A fourth course has been to focus on the role of knowledge in development. Some investigators argue that much of what has been attributed to reasoning and problem-solving ability in intellectual development is actually better attributed to the extent of the child's knowledge.

Environmental Viewpoint

The views of intellectual development described above all emphasize the importance of the individual in intellectual development. But an alternative viewpoint emphasizes the importance of the individual's environment, particularly his social environment. This view is related to the cognitive-contextual theories discussed above. Championed originally by the Russian psychologist L.S. Vygotsky, this viewpoint suggests that intellectual development may be largely influenced by a child's interactions with others: a child sees others thinking and acting in certain ways and then internalizes and models what is seen. An elaboration of this view is the suggestion by the Israeli psychologist Reuven Feuerstein that the key to intellectual development is what he called "mediated learning experience." The parent mediates, or interprets, the environment for the child, and it is largely through this mediation that the child learns to understand and interpret the world.

The role of environment is particularly evident in studies across cultures. In her research on the cultural contexts of intelligence, Greenfield, while studying indigenous Mayan people, found that the Mayan conception of intelligence is much more collective than the conception of intelligence in European or North American cultures. To the Maya, much of being intelligent involves being able to work with others effectively. In addition, the psychologist Elena Grigorenko and her colleagues, in "The Organization of Luo Conceptions of Intelligence: A Study of Implicit Theories in a Kenyan Village", found that rural Kenyans have a broad conception of intelligence that emphasizes moral behaviour, particularly duty to others.

Children who grow up in environments that do not stress Western principles of education may not be able to demonstrate their abilities on conventional Western intelligence tests. Sternberg and others have found that rural Tanzanian children performed much better on skills tests when they were given extended instruction beyond the normal test instructions. Without this additional instruction, however, the children did not always understand what they were supposed to do, and, because of this, they underperformed on the tests. Similarly, a study in Kenya measured children's knowledge of natural remedies used to combat parasites and other common illnesses. Tests for this type of knowledge were combined with conventional Western tests of intelligence and academic achievement. Results showed a negative correlation between practical intelligence (knowledge of medical remedies) and academic achievement. These findings suggested that in some cultures, academic skills may not be particularly valued; as a result, the brighter children invest more effort in acquiring practical skills.

Measuring Intelligence

Almost all of the theories discussed above employ complex tasks for gauging intelligence in both children and adults. Over time, theorists chose particular tasks for analyzing human intelligence, some of which have been explicitly discussed here—e.g., recognition of analogies, classification of similar terms, extrapolation of number series, performance of transitive inferences, and the like. Although the kinds of complex tasks discussed so far belong to a single tradition for the measurement of intelligence, the field actually has two major traditions. The tradition that has been discussed most prominently and has been most influential is that of the French psychologist Alfred Binet.

Sir Francis Galton, detail of an oil painting by G. Graef, 1882; in the National Portrait Gallery, London.

An earlier tradition, and one that still shows some influence upon the field, is that of the English scientist Sir Francis Galton. Building on ideas put forth by his uncle Charles Darwin in On the Origin of Species, Galton believed that human capabilities could be understood through scientific investigation. From 1884 to 1890 Galton maintained a laboratory in London where visitors could have themselves measured on a variety of psychophysical tasks, such as weight discrimination and sensitivity to musical pitch. Galton believed that psychophysical abilities were the basis of intelligence and, hence, that these tests were measures of intelligence. The earliest formal intelligence tests, therefore, required a person to perform such simple tasks as deciding which of two weights was heavier or showing how forcefully one could squeeze one's hand.

The Galtonian tradition was taken to the United States by the American psychologist James McKeen Cattell. Later, one of Cattell's students, the American anthropologist Clark Wissler, collected data showing that scores on Galtonian types of tasks were not good predictors of grades in college or even of scores on other tasks. Catell nonetheless continued to develop his Galtonian approach in psychometric research and, with Edward Thorndike, helped to establish a centre for mental testing and measurement.

James McKeen Cattell

Clark Wissler

The IQ Test

The more influential tradition of mental testing was developed by Binet and his collaborator, Theodore Simon, in France. In 1904 the minister of public instruction in Paris named a commission to study or create tests that would ensure that mentally retarded children received an adequate education. The minister was also concerned that children of normal intelligence were being placed in classes for mentally retarded children because of behaviour problems. Even before Wissler's research, Binet, who was charged with developing the new test, had flatly rejected the Galtonian tradition, believing that Galton's tests measured trivial abilities. He proposed instead that tests of intelligence should measure skills such as judgment, comprehension, and reasoning—the same kinds of skills measured by most intelligence tests today. Binet's early test was taken to Stanford University by Lewis Terman, whose version came to be called the Stanford-Binet test. This test has been revised frequently and continues to be used in countries all over the world.

The Stanford-Binet test, and others like it, have yielded at the very least an overall score referred to as an intelligence quotient, or IQ. Some tests, such as the Wechsler Adult Intelligence Scale (Revised) and the Wechsler Intelligence Scale for Children (Revised), yield an overall IQ as well as separate IQs for verbal and performance subtests. An example of a verbal subtest would be vocabulary, whereas an example of a performance subtest would be picture arrangement, the latter requiring an examinee to arrange a set of pictures into a sequence so that they tell a comprehensible story.

Later developments in intelligence testing expanded the range of abilities tested. For example, in 1997 the psychologists J.P. Das and Jack A. Naglieri published the Cognitive Assessment System, a test based on a theory of intelligence first proposed by the Russian psychologist Alexander Luria. The test measured planning abilities, attentional abilities, and simultaneous and successive processing abilities. Simultaneous processing abilities are used to solve tasks such as figural matrix problems, in which the test taker must fill in a matrix with a missing geometric form. Successive processing abilities are used in tests such as digit span, in which one must repeat back a string of memorized digits.

IQ was originally computed as the ratio of mental age to chronological (physical) age, multiplied by 100. Thus, if a child of age 10 had a mental age of 12 (that is, performed on the test at the level of an average 12-year-old), the child was assigned an IQ of $^{12}/_{10} \times 100$, or 120. If the 10-year-old had a mental age of 8, the child's IQ would be $^{8}/_{10} \times 100$, or 80. A score of 100, where the mental age equals the chronological age, is average.

The concept of mental age has fallen into disrepute. Many tests still yield an IQ, but they are most often computed on the basis of statistical distributions. The scores are assigned on the basis of what percentage of people of a given group would be expected to have a certain IQ.

The Distribution of IQ scores

Intelligence test scores follow an approximately normal distribution, meaning that most people score near the middle of the distribution of scores and that scores drop off fairly rapidly in frequency as one moves in either direction from the centre. For example, on the IQ scale, about 2 out of 3 scores fall between 85 and 115, and about 19 out of 20 scores fall between 70 and 130. Put another way, only 1 out of 20 scores differs from the average IQ (100) by more than 30 points.

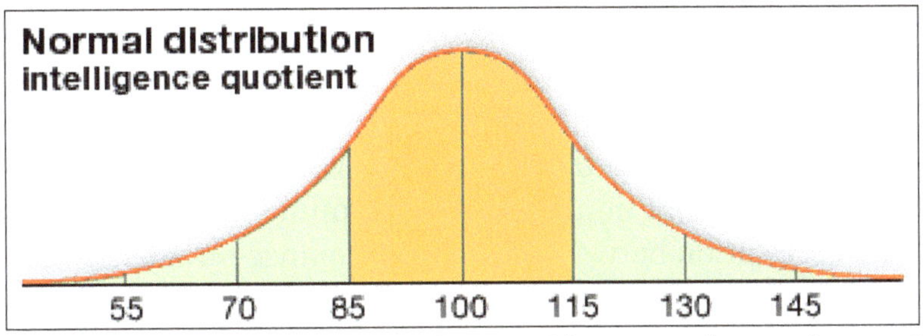

Graph of intelligence quotient (IQ) as a normal distribution with a mean of 100 and a standard deviation of 15. The shaded region between 85 and 115 (within one standard deviation of the mean) accounts for about 68 percent of the total area, hence 68 percent of all IQ scores.

It has been common to attach labels to certain levels of IQ. At the upper end, the label gifted is sometimes assigned to people with IQs of 130 or higher. Scores at the lower end have been given the labels borderline retarded (70 to 84) and severely retarded (25 to 39). All such terms, however, have pitfalls and can be counterproductive. First, their use assumes that conventional intelligence tests provide sufficient information to classify someone as gifted or mentally retarded, but most authorities would reject this assumption. In fact, the information yielded by conventional intelligence tests represents only a fairly narrow range of abilities. To label someone as mentally retarded solely on the basis of a single test score, therefore, is to risk doing a disservice and an injustice to that person. Most psychologists and other authorities recognize that social as well as strictly intellectual skills must be considered in any classification of mental retardation.

Second, giftedness is generally recognized as more than just a degree of intelligence, even broadly defined. Most psychologists who have studied gifted persons agree that a variety of aspects make up giftedness. Howard E. Gruber, a Swiss psychologist, and Mihaly Csikszentmihalyi, an American psychologist, were among those who doubted that giftedness in childhood is the sole predictor of adult abilities. Gruber held that giftedness unfolds over the course of a lifetime and involves achievement at least as much as intelligence. Gifted people, he contended, have life plans that they seek to realize, and these plans develop over the course of many years. As was true in the discussion of mental retardation, the concept of giftedness is trivialized if it is understood only in terms of a single test score.

Third, the significance of a given test score can be different for different people. A certain IQ score may indicate a higher level of intelligence for a person who grew up in poverty and attended an inadequate school than it would for a person who grew up in an upper-middle-class environment and was schooled in a productive learning environment. An IQ score on a test given in English also may indicate a higher level of intelligence for a person whose first language is not English than it would for a native English speaker. Another aspect that affects the significance of test scores is that some people are "test-anxious" and may do poorly on almost any standardized test. Because of these and similar drawbacks, it has come to be believed that scores should be interpreted carefully, on an individual basis.

Heritability and Malleability of Intelligence

Intelligence has historically been conceptualized as a more or less fixed trait. Whereas a minority of investigators believe either that it is highly heritable or that it is minimally heritable, most take an intermediate position.

Among the most fruitful methods that have been used to assess the heritability of intelligence is the study of identical twins who were separated at an early age and reared apart. If the twins were raised in separate environments, and if it is assumed that when twins are separated they are randomly distributed across environments (often a dubious assumption), then the twins would have in common all of their genes but none of their environment, except for chance environmental overlap. As a result, the correlation between their performance on intelligence tests could identify any possible link between test scores and heredity. Another method compares the relationship between intelligence-test scores of identical twins and those of fraternal twins. Because these results are computed on the basis of intelligence-test scores, however, they represent only those aspects of intelligence that are measured by the tests.

Studies of twins do in fact provide strong evidence for the heritability of intelligence; the scores of identical twins reared apart are highly correlated. In addition, adopted children's scores are highly correlated with their birth parents and not with their adoptive parents. Also significant are findings that heritability can differ between ethnic and racial groups, as well as across time within a single group; that is, the extent to which genes versus environment matter in IQ depends on many factors, including socioeconomic class. Moreover, the psychologist Robert Plomin and others have found that evidence of the heritability of intelligence increases with age; this suggests that, as a person grows older, genetic factors become a more important determinant of intelligence, while environmental factors become less important.

Whatever the heritability factor of IQ may be, it is a separate issue whether intelligence can be increased. Evidence that it can was provided by the American-born New Zealand political scientist James Flynn, who showed that intelligence test scores around the world rose steadily in the late 20th century. The reasons for the increase are not fully understood, however, and the phenomenon thus requires additional careful investigation. Among many possible causes of the increase, for example, are environmental changes such as the addition of vitamin C to prenatal and postnatal diet and, more generally, the improved nutrition of mothers and infants as compared with earlier in the century. In their book The Bell Curve, Richard Herrnstein and Charles Murray argued that IQ is important for life success and that differences between racial groups in life success can be attributed in part to differences in IQ. They speculated that these differences might be genetic. As noted above, such claims remain speculative".

Despite the general increase in scores, average IQs continue to vary both across countries and across different socioeconomic groups. For example, many researchers have found a positive correlation between socioeconomic status and IQ, although they disagree about the reasons for the relationship. Most investigators also agree that differences in educational opportunities play an important role, though some believe that the main basis of the difference is hereditary. There is no broad agreement about why such differences exist. Most important, it should be noted that these differences are based on IQ alone and not on intelligence as it is more broadly defined. Even less is known about group differences in intelligence as it is broadly defined than is known about differences in IQ. Nevertheless, theories of inherited differences in IQ between racial groups have been found to be without basis. There is more variability within groups than between groups.

Finally, no matter how heritable intelligence may be, some aspects of it are still malleable. With intervention, even a highly heritable trait can be modified. A program of training in intellectual skills can increase some aspects of a person's intelligence; however, no training program—no environmental condition of any sort—can make a genius of a person with low measured intelligence. But some gains are possible, and programs have been developed for increasing intellectual skills. Intelligence, in the view of many authorities, is not a foregone conclusion the day a person is born. A main trend for psychologists in the intelligence field has been to combine testing and training functions to help people make the most of their intelligence.

Theories of Intelligence

Intelligence is a complex thing to define. But it can be broadly thought of as the measure of a person's ability to master a specific cognitive function, such as problem-solving, logical reasoning, and self-awareness. We're going to explore three competing theories of intelligence to help you understand the different cognitive strengths you may possess:

- Spearman's Two-factor theory of intelligence.
- Sternberg's Triarchic Theory of Intelligence.
- Gardner's Theory of Multiple Intelligence.

What is Spearman's Theory of Intelligence?

Charles Spearman, an English psychologist, noticed that students who did well in one subject area tended to do well in corresponding subjects. He concluded that human beings possess a generalized form of intelligence, known as a g-factor, which can lead to other specialized forms of intelligence, measured by s-factor.

G-factor is a sum of s-factor scores that measure a person's abilities in one particular area. Generally excepted s-factors of intelligence include memory, attention, verbal comprehension, spatial skills, and abstract reasoning. The g-factor and the s-factor are two parts of Spearman's Two-factor theory of intelligence.

IQ tests, which measure general cognitive ability, are derived from his theory of general intelligence.

Triarchic Theory of Intelligence

American psychologist, Robert Sternberg, made his name by proposing the triarchic theory of intelligence. This theory asserts that human intelligence can be divided into three types: analytical, creative, and practical intelligence.

- Analytical intelligence refers to a person's ability to assess information and use deductive reasoning to arrive at plausible solutions.
- Creative intelligence draws on a person's ability to create something from nothing or to do something in a unique and novel way.
- Practical intelligence is the intelligence of common sense reasoning, commonly referred to as "street smarts".

Sternberg believed that a balanced measure of all three forms of intelligence would result in the greatest life success.

Gardner's Theory of Multiple Intelligence

In contrast to the two theories of intelligence we've just examined, Gardner's theory proposes nine different types of intelligence. Howard Gardner is an American psychologist who first proposed his theory in the 1980s. He counters the standard psychological view of generalized intelligence by suggesting nine unique forms of intelligence:

Naturalistic Intelligence

Naturalistic intelligence is the intelligence of the natural world. People who possess naturalistic intelligence to have keen outdoor sensibilities, are born way finders, and have a strong connection with Mother Nature.

Musical Intelligence

People who are musically intelligent have a natural draw to all things acoustic and musical. They have a talent for identifying sound, pitch, rhythm, and timbre.

Logical-mathematical Intelligence

We're all familiar with this form of intelligence. If you are logically intelligent, you're able to use deductive analysis, logical reasoning, and executive planning to your advantage. Those with this form of intelligence work well with numbers and are skilled problem solvers.

Existential Intelligence

Those with existential intelligence have a knack for tackling the big questions of life. What is life? Where does it come from? Who am I? What should I do with my life? If you possess existential intelligence, you have a philosophical mind and have no trouble grappling with abstract concept and theory.

Interpersonal Intelligence

If you possess great interpersonal abilities, you possess emotional intelligence. People with this intelligence have a natural ability to understand the thoughts, actions, and motives of others.

Bodily-kinesthetic Intelligence

This type of intelligence is displayed by those with great control over their physical bodies. Many dancers, athletes, and physical therapists possess kinesthetic intelligence. These people have mastered control over the physical form and are effective physical communicators.

Linguistic Intelligence

People with linguistic intelligence are skilled wordsmiths. They're able to use words to convey different feelings, ideas, and theories with ease. They also have a predisposition for visual learning, so they can quickly master new languages.

Intrapersonal Intelligence

Intrapersonal intelligence is the intelligence of the self. True self-awareness is rare in today's world, and those with intrapersonal intelligence know themselves more intimately than any other. This is the intelligence of introspection and self-knowing.

Visual-spatial Intelligence

Those with visual-spatial intelligence relate well to the world around them. They are natural born navigators and possess a keen understanding of the visual world. They often pick up on fine details others are unaware of and can manipulate three-dimensional images in their mind's eye.

Sternberg's Triarchic Theory Intelligence

The triarchic theory of intelligence was formulated by Robert Sternberg in the 1980s. The theory attempts to understand the human intelligence in terms of distinct components rather than a single ability.

The triarchic theory by Sternberg categorized intelligence into three different aspects:

- Componential – Analytic skills
- Experiential – Creativity
- Practical – Contextual skills

Before Sternberg, general intelligence was the idea that dominated most of the intelligence theories. However, Sternberg believed intelligence to be a much more complex subject matter, which leads him to propose a theory dealing with the cognitive approach to intelligence theory rather than a behavioristic view point. He believed that a person's adaptation to the changing environment and his contribution of knowledge in shaping the world around them had a significant importance in determining their intelligence.

Sternberg also argued that intelligent tests were wrong to ignore creativity, and there are always other important characteristics like cognitive processes, performance components, planning and decision making skills, and so on.

Key functions in different aspects of Tri-archic theory of Intelligence. Key functions in each aspects of intelligence:

Componential	Experiential	Practical
Analyze	Create	Apply
Critique	Invent	Use
Judge	Discover	Put into practice
Compare/Contrast	Imagine if	Implement
Evaluate	Suppose that	Employ
Assess	Predict	Render Practical

Componential – Analytical Intelligence

Analytical Intelligence can also be referred to as being book smart. This form of intelligence is more in terms with the traditional definitions of IQ and academic achievement. It's also called componential intelligence. Because of its analytical nature, the person with high analytical intelligence is good at problem solving. These people are generally more able to see the solutions not normally seen, because of their abstract thinking and evaluation skills. Analyzing someone's analytical intelligence can be done by few general questions like:

- How good are you at analyzing technical problems?
- What's your history of scoring in standardized tests?

Example: Emma always scores high on standardized tests. It's because of her ability to evaluate and analyze materials using abstract thinking in order to achieve solutions.

Experiential – Creative Intelligence

The ability to invent new ideas and solutions when dealing with new situations is regarded as creative intelligence. It's also referred as experiential intelligence. This form of intelligence is associated with using existing knowledge and skills in order to deal with new problems or situations. Analyzing someone's creative intelligence level can be done by few general questions like:

- How quickly can they solve a new problem?

- Will they automatically resort to applying new skill in order to deal with the situation?

Creative intelligence can be further divided into two categories:

- Novelty: This concerns the ability of a person to deal with the problem for the first time.
- Automation: This concerns the ability of a person to automatically perform the repeated tasks.

Example: James Bond is a person high in creative intelligence because of his ability to use his knowledge and skills to deal with new problems every time.

Practical – Contextual Intelligence

In simple words, practical intelligence can be defined as street-smart. The ability of a person to adapt in an environment or change it accordingly to best suit the personal needs is dubbed as practical intelligence. Another way to understand such type of intelligence is as common sense. Dealing with the everyday tasks in the best possible manner shows the person's intelligence. Analyzing someone's practical intelligence level can be done by few general questions like:

- Would the person be taken advantage of easily?
- Do they adjust well to the world around them?
- Are they comfortable with the daily adventures?

A person, who is street-smart, or high on practical intelligence, is more able to cope with concrete situations.

Example: Johnny is considering buying a second hand motorbike. A salesman, being salesman, would obviously try to con the buyer, but Johnny is already prepared with price comparisons and has made up his mind to say no to unnecessary extras.

Critical Evaluation

The major criticism about the Triarchic theory of intelligence has been regarding its unempirical nature. Psychologist Linda Gottfredson argued that it's not accurate to assume traditional IQ tests do not measure practical intelligences. Researches have shown people with high IQ to have reached higher in their career, have higher income. Also, traditional analytical intelligence also showed correlation with staying alive and out of jail, which is generally categorized as practical intelligence or street smarts.

Spearman Theory

Spearman and General Intelligence

Charles Spearman was one of the researchers who helped develop a statistical technique known as factor analysis. Factor analysis allows researchers to a number of different test items that can measure common abilities. For example, researchers might find that people who score well on questions that measure vocabulary also perform better on questions related to reading comprehension.

Spearman believed that general intelligence represented an intelligence factor underlying specific mental abilities. All tasks on intelligence tests, whether they related to verbal or mathematical abilities, were influenced by this underlying g-factor.

Many modern intelligence tests, including the Stanford-Binet, measure some of the cognitive factors that are thought to make up general intelligence. These include visual-spatial processing, quantitative reasoning, knowledge, fluid reasoning, and working memory:

- Visual-spatial processing involves such abilities as putting together puzzles and copying complex shapes.
- Quantitative reasoning involves the capacity to solve problems that involve numbers.
- Knowledge involves a person's understanding of a wide range of topics.
- Fluid reasoning involves the ability to think flexibly and solve problems.
- Working memory involves the use of short-term memory such as being able to repeat a list of items.

Challenges to the Concept of General Intelligence

The notion that intelligence could be measured and summarized by a single number on an IQ test was controversial during Spearman's time and has remained so over the decades since. Some psychologists, including L.L. Thurstone, challenged the concept of a g-factor. Thurstone instead identified a number of what he referred to as "primary mental abilities."

More recently, psychologists such as Howard Gardner have challenged the notion that a single general intelligence can accurately capture all of human mental ability. Gardner instead proposed that different multiple intelligences exist. Each intelligence represents abilities in a certain domain such as visual-spatial intelligence, verbal-linguistic intelligence, and logical-mathematical intelligence.

Research today points to an underlying mental ability that contributes to performance on many cognitive tasks. IQ scores, which are designed to measure this general intelligence, are also thought to influence an individual's overall success in life. However, while IQ can play a role in academic and life success, other factors such as childhood experiences, educational experiences, socioeconomic status, motivation, maturity, and personality also play a critical role in determining overall success.

Gardner's Frames of Mind

When you hear the word intelligence, the concept of IQ testing may immediately come to mind. Intelligence is often defined as our intellectual potential; something we are born with, something that can be measured, and a capacity that is difficult to change. In recent years, however, other views of intelligence have emerged. One such conception is the theory of multiple intelligences proposed by Harvard psychologist Howard Gardner.

Theory of Multiple Intelligences

This theory suggests that traditional psychometric views of intelligence are too limited. Gardner first outlined his theory in his 1983 book "Frames of Mind: The Theory of Multiple Intelligences," where he suggested that all people have different kinds of "intelligences." Gardner proposed that there are eight intelligences, and has suggested the possible addition of a ninth known as "existentialist intelligence.

In order to capture the full range of abilities and talents that people possess, Gardner theorizes that people do not have just an intellectual capacity, but have many kinds of intelligence, including musical, interpersonal, spatial-visual, and linguistic intelligences. While a person might be particularly strong in a specific area, such as musical intelligence, he or she most likely possesses a range of abilities. For example, an individual might be strong in verbal, musical, and naturalistic intelligence.

Criticism

Gardner's theory has come under criticism from both psychologists and educators. These critics argue that Gardner's definition of intelligence is too broad and that his eight different "intelligences" simply represent talents, personality traits, and abilities. Gardner's theory also suffers from a lack of supporting empirical research.

Despite this, the theory of multiple intelligences enjoys considerable popularity with educators. Many teachers utilize multiple intelligences in their teaching philosophies and work to integrate Gardner's theory into the classroom.

Visual-Spatial Intelligence

Strengths: Visual and spatial judgment-People who are strong in visual-spatial intelligence are good at visualizing things. These individuals are often good with directions as well as maps, charts, videos, and pictures.

Characteristics

Characteristics of visual-spatial intelligence include:

- Enjoys reading and writing.
- Good at putting puzzles together.
- Good at interpreting pictures, graphs, and charts.
- Enjoys drawing, painting, and the visual arts.
- Recognizes patterns easily.

Potential Career Choices

If you're strong in visual-spatial intelligence, good career choices for you are:

- Architect
- Artist
- Engineer.

Linguistic-Verbal Intelligence

Strengths: Words, language, and writing-People who are strong in linguistic-verbal intelligence are able to use words well, both when writing and speaking. These individuals are typically very good at writing stories, memorizing information, and reading.

Characteristics

Characteristics of linguistic-verbal intelligence include:

- Good at remembering written and spoken information.
- Enjoys reading and writing.
- Good at debating or giving persuasive speeches.
- Able to explain things well.
- Often uses humor when telling stories.

Potential Career Choices

If you're strong in linguistic-verbal intelligence, good career choices for you are:

- Writer/journalist
- Lawyer
- Teacher.

Logical-Mathematical Intelligence

Strengths: Analyzing problems and mathematical operations-People who are strong in logical-mathematical intelligence are good at reasoning, recognizing patterns, and logically analyzing problems. These individuals tend to think conceptually about numbers, relationships, and patterns.

Characteristics

Characteristics of logical-mathematical intelligence include:

- Excellent problem-solving skills.
- Enjoys thinking about abstract ideas.

- Likes conducting scientific experiments.
- Good at solving complex computations.

Potential Career Choices

If you're strong in logical-mathematical intelligence, good career choices for you are:

- Scientist
- Mathematician
- Computer programmer
- Engineer
- Accountant.

Bodily-Kinesthetic Intelligence

Strengths: Physical movement, motor control-Those who have high bodily-kinesthetic intelligence are said to be good at body movement, performing actions, and physical control. People who are strong in this area tend to have excellent hand-eye coordination and dexterity.

Characteristics

Characteristics of bodily-kinesthetic intelligence include:

- Good at dancing and sports.
- Enjoys creating things with his or her hands.
- Excellent physical coordination.
- Tends to remember by doing, rather than hearing or seeing.

Potential Career Choices

If you're strong in bodily-kinesthetic intelligence, good career choices for you are:

- Dancer
- Builder
- Sculptor
- Actor.

Musical Intelligence

Strengths: Rhythm and music-People who have strong musical intelligence are good at thinking in patterns, rhythms, and sounds. They have a strong appreciation for music and are often good at musical composition and performance.

Characteristics

Characteristics of musical intelligence include:

- Enjoys singing and playing musical instruments.
- Recognizes musical patterns and tones easily.
- Good at remembering songs and melodies.
- Rich understanding of musical structure, rhythm, and notes.

Potential Career Choices

If you're strong in musical intelligence, good career choices for you are:

- Musician
- Composer
- Singer
- Music teacher
- Conductor.

Interpersonal Intelligence

Strengths: Understanding and relating to other people-Those who have strong interpersonal intelligence are good at understanding and interacting with other people. These individuals are skilled at assessing the emotions, motivations, desires, and intentions of those around them.

Characteristics

Characteristics of interpersonal intelligence include:

- Good at communicating verbally.
- Skilled at nonverbal communication.
- Sees situations from different perspectives.
- Creates positive relationships with others.
- Good at resolving conflict in groups.

Potential Career Choices

If you're strong in interpersonal intelligence, good career choices for you are:

- Psychologist
- Philosopher

- Counselor
- Salesperson
- Politician.

Intrapersonal Intelligence

Strengths: Introspection and self-reflection-Individuals who are strong in intrapersonal intelligence are good at being aware of their own emotional states, feelings, and motivations. They tend to enjoy self-reflection and analysis, including daydreaming, exploring relationships with others, and assessing their personal strengths.

Characteristics

Characteristics of intrapersonal intelligence include:

- Good at analyzing his or her strengths and weaknesses.
- Enjoys analyzing theories and ideas.
- Excellent self-awareness.
- Clearly understands the basis for his or her own motivations and feelings.

Potential Career Choices

If you're strong in intrapersonal intelligence, good career choices for you are:

- Philosopher
- Writer
- Theorist
- Scientist.

Naturalistic Intelligence

Strengths: Finding patterns and relationships to nature-Naturalistic is the most recent addition to Gardner's theory and has been met with more resistance than his original seven intelligences. According to Gardner, individuals who are high in this type of intelligence are more in tune with nature and are often interested in nurturing, exploring the environment, and learning about other species. These individuals are said to be highly aware of even subtle changes to their environments.

Characteristics

Characteristics of naturalistic intelligence include:

- Interested in subjects such as botany, biology, and zoology.
- Good at categorizing and cataloging information easily.

- May enjoy camping, gardening, hiking, and exploring the outdoors.
- Doesn't enjoy learning unfamiliar topics that have no connection to nature.

Potential Career Choices

If you're strong in naturalistic intelligence, good career choices for you are:

- Biologist
- Conservationist
- Gardener
- Farmer.

Psychometrics Intelligence

Despite the variety of concepts of intelligence, the most influential approach to understanding intelligence (i.e., with the most supporters and the most published research over the longest period of time) is based on psychometric testing, which regards intelligence as cognitive ability.

Intelligence, narrowly defined, can be measured by intelligence tests, also called IQ (intelligence quotient) tests. Such intelligence tests take many forms, but the common tests (Stanford-Binet, Raven's Progressive Matrices, Wechsler Adult Intelligence Scale, Wechsler-Bellevue I, and others) all measure the same dominant form of intelligence, g or "general intelligence factor". The abstraction of g stems from the observation that scores on all forms of cognitive tests correlate positively with one another. g can be derived as the principal factor from cognitive test scores using the method of factor analysis.

In the psychometric view, the concept of intelligence is most closely identified with g, or Gf ("fluid g"). However, psychometricians can measure a wide range of abilities, which are distinct yet correlated. One common view is that these abilities are hierarchically arranged with g at the vertex (or top, overlaying all other cognitive abilities). However, this is by no means universally accepted.

References

- Human-intelligence-psychology, science: britannica.com, Retrieved 4 July, 2019
- Theories-of-intelligence: mindvalley.com, Retrieved 24 March, 2019
- Triarchic, intelligence, cognitive: psychestudy.com, Retrieved 14 January, 2019
- What-is-general-intelligence: verywellmind.com, Retrieved 29 May, 2019
- Gardners-theory-of-multiple-intelligences: verywellmind.com, Retrieved 2 August, 2019
- Psychometric-intelligence, intelligence, educational-psychology: k12academics.com, Retrieved 9 June, 2019

6

Personal and Social Development

The activities which are aimed at improving awareness and identity, build human capital, and develop talents and potential are known as personal development. There are renowned philosophers who have developed theories related to this field such as Sigmund Freud and Erik Erikson. The topics elaborated in this chapter will help in gaining a better perspective about personal and social development as well as the theories related to it.

The personal and social development domain includes the skills necessary for emotional and social competence in young children. Teachers learn about children's sense of responsibility to themselves and others and how they feel about themselves and view themselves as learners—their emotional development—through ongoing observation, conversations with children, and information from family members. Teachers acquire information about children's social competence and approaches to learning by interacting with them, observing their interactions with other adults and peers, and reflecting on how they make decisions and solve academic and social problems.

Self-concept

Demonstrates Self-confidence

Self-confidence is an important contribution to young children's accomplishments in early education and their achievement in the primary grades. During the early years, self-confidence is built on children's actual accomplishments, how these accomplishments are valued by important adults (such as parents and teachers), and later, how these accomplishments are valued by their peers. As children move through the early primary grades, self-confidence is also built on children's evaluations of their own achievements and their ability to achieve the expectations they set for themselves.

In light of this, it is important to recognize that preschoolers tend to have an unrealistically optimistic view of their capabilities which causes them, at times, to expect that they can accomplish far more difficult tasks than they are really capable of doing. This arises, in part, because of young children's belief that increased effort can yield better achievement regardless of differences in ability. As children proceed through the primary grades, they develop a more mature understanding of differences in achievement and their self-evaluations become more realistic. This can cause, however, a decrease in self-confidence as children realize that some things will be difficult for them no matter how hard they try. Adult support is important, especially in helping children appreciate how important their own efforts are to academic success.

Shows some Independence and Self-direction

Owing to their natural curiosity and enthusiasm for mastery, children of all ages show initiative in learning situations. However, there are developmental changes in children's initiative and self-direction that occur from preschool through early primary grades. Within this developmental period, younger children approach new learning situations with enthusiasm and self-confidence but not necessarily with persistence, especially when they confront difficult problem-solving situations. Older children, by contrast, are more persistent, but are also more creative problem-solvers, proposing their own ideas, and approaching new learning opportunities with initiative and involvement.

Developmental differences in self-direction also derive from changes in the growth of self-regulation. The growth of self-regulation is viewed by developmental scientists as consisting of development in three interrelated areas: inhibition (i.e., resisting a strong inclination to enact a primary response and instead acting in an alternative manner), working memory (i.e., holding information in mind while mentally working on it), and cognitive flexibility (i.e., being able to switch perspective, attention, or mental focus). Together, these three developing competencies are called executive functions. The development of executive functions is based on sophisticated brain systems that mature very slowly, with some not becoming fully mature until early adulthood. As a result, limitations in self-regulation and self-direction in young children derive from the immature brain, with developing competencies slowly emerging as these areas of the brain develop and enable greater self-control of behavior, attention, and emotion. Similar brain maturity-compentencies development relationships occur in personal and social development and related areas.

Self-control

Follows Simple Classroom Rules and Routines with Guidance

Research on early school achievement has found that children's cooperation with classroom rules and procedures is directly associated with early academic success. McClelland, Morrison, and Holmes found, for example, that "work-related skills" (e.g., compliance with instructions; completion of work) in kindergarten predicted children's academic achievement three years later, even after controlling for earlier academic achievement.

The preceding discussion of the growth of self-regulation—consisting of the specific competencies known as executive functions—helps to explain the slow progress of young children in their abilities to follow classroom rules and routines. More specifically, in the early years children have difficulty following rules and complying with routines on their own not because they are egocentric, but rather because their immature brains support only limited capacities for self-regulation. In fact, it is easy to see how each of the components of self-regulation—or executive functions—accounts for young children's limited ability to follow rules without reminders. First, limited capacities for inhibition mean that young children are likely to act impulsively rather than in a rule-governed manner (e.g., may speak out of turn instead of raising his or her hand). Second, limited working memory means that young children are unlikely to keep a relevant rule in mind as they are engaged in activity (e.g., cleaning up food items after snack time). Third, limited cognitive flexibility means that young children are likely to be cognitively focused on a preferred activity (e.g., playing with sand in the sand table) rather than on a relevant rule (e.g., keeping all the sand in the sand table and off the floor).

The slow growth of self-regulation, or executive functions, has been described by the Center for the Developing Child at Harvard University as metaphorically similar to the slow emergence of the child's internal "air traffic controller" that manages competing demands for the child's attention, thinking, and behavioral regulation. Until that internal air traffic controller has fully matured (which takes many years), children will struggle to manage these demands in a competent and flexible manner. In young children, this can sometimes make them appear egocentric. This explanation for their behavior is incorrect, however, because in other respects young children's behavior is very non-egocentric (e.g., in their sensitivity to others' feelings). By contrast, understanding the slow growth rate of children's capacity to follow rules and routines (with regard to the development of executive functions) offers a much more precise and appropriate description of the growth of these abilities. In addition, research has shown that carefully designed classroom environments and routines for young children can assist them in self-regulation by aiding in the exercise of these executive functions.

Manages Transitions

One of the important accomplishments of early childhood is the development of event knowledge: the ability to understand and predict routine events in which the child participates. As a consequence, young children become increasingly competent at understanding how activities in the daily schedule are sequenced and conducted, and this enables them to prepare themselves for what comes next.

Classroom transitions are thus one of the most significant self-regulatory challenges faced by young children, especially if they are provided little preparation for transitions or little warning of changes in routines, locations, or procedures. One reason is their limited cognitive flexibility discussed earlier. Once they have achieved enough understanding of the daily schedule to predict the day's events, for example, it can be difficult for young children to flexibly adapt their expectations to a different schedule in order to accommodate a new activity. Limitations in working memory are also relevant, especially if young children are required to remember, during a transition, to enact a sequence of activities (e.g., stop a desired activity, clean up, go to another location, prepare for the next activity, and await further instructions). As a consequence, children may proceed through part of the sequence before forgetting the next steps and doing something else. Transitions thus become easier as children mature cognitively and neurobiologically. As the internal "air traffic controller" becomes more competent at remembering transitional events and understanding the standard routine in relation to occasional changes to the routine, the child can become more adaptable.

It is important to note that even as children are maturing in their self-regulatory capacities, limitations in these executive functions can still be seen. For example, one of the characteristics of children in early primary grades is their inflexibility with rules and routines: they insist that everyone adhere to the rules (even when they themselves sometimes forget), and they can be rigid in their insistence on a predictable schedule. This also derives from limits in cognitive flexibility, especially in the child's difficulty in distinguishing the broader purpose of the rule from apparent violations in its application, or understanding the difference between the predictable schedule and one day's exception to it. This illustrates the slow maturation of the higher brain regions underlying executive functions, and the fact that even as children are making progress on many aspects of self-regulation, other developmental challenges remain.

For these reasons, teachers and caregivers can be helpful to children throughout this developmental period by providing advance notice of changes in locations, routines, and events, and managing transitions by guiding children through the altered sequences of activities required. They can also be helpful in providing patient support when young children feel anxious in the face of unexpected changes to which they are having difficulty adjusting.

Approaches to Learning

Shows Eagerness and Curiosity as a Learner

There is considerable evidence that curiosity and eagerness to learn are early-developing, possibly intrinsic characteristics in infants and young children. Besides developing instructional methods to enlist children's natural curiosity, classroom teachers must ensure that children's self-confidence as learners (discussed earlier) is supported and strengthened through their achievements in the classroom. In addition, helping to provide multiple avenues for the expression of their natural curiosity is important to children. This can mean the exploration of interests through art, movement, construction, emergent writing activities, conversation, and other approaches.

Attends Briefly and Seeks Help when Encountering a Problem

Although children of all ages sustain attention to tasks that capture their interest, there are developmental changes in children's persistence in academic work. Generally, children devote more sustained attention to tasks with increasing age. There are several reasons for this. First, children become capable of more focused and sustained attention with age owing to growth in the self-regulatory competencies discussed earlier. In particular, growth in inhibition enables children to be less distractable and better capable of focusing their attention and thinking on relevant task-related matters. Second, when faced with difficult cognitive challenges, older children are more likely to persist at the task than younger children owing, in part, to the cognitive flexibility that enables them to devise more creative, novel problem-solving approaches. By contrast, younger children are more likely to give up when conventional problem-solving strategies fail. Third, developmental changes in attention and task persistence also emerge because of older children's greater experience and self-confidence in tackling cognitive challenges. Taken together, the abilities to become cognitively engaged in a task with focused attention, to persist in the face of challenges and frustrations, and to generate new ideas and work on them are collectively described as "approaches to learning." These develop significantly during early and middle childhood, and are critical to success in kindergarten and throughout elementary school.

There are also individual differences in children's sustained attention and persistence in academic work that derive from their learning orientation. Some children with a "mastery orientation" tend to persist when faced with difficult challenges because of a belief that enhanced effort will be rewarded with eventual success. Other children tend not to persist because they believe that their initial failures are due to poor ability that they do not believe can be improved through increased effort; this can contribute to learned helplessness in academic situations. These differences in learning orientation emerge early, and thus are apparent by the time that children are in primary grades.

Approaches Tasks with Flexibility and Inventiveness

With increasing age, young children approach tasks with greater inventiveness and flexibility that can contribute to more effective problem-solving approaches. To be sure, very young children can be creative in their use of materials, but this creativity typically does not transfer to creating better solutions to problem tasks. As children proceed through early primary grades, they are able to approach cognitive challenges with new ideas after their initial solutions have failed, and are often capable of devising new solutions on this basis. This makes their creativity more problem-focused and useful. Indeed, children's inventiveness contributes to their experimental and systematic strategies to problem-solving.

Interaction with Others

Interacts with One or More Children

An important contributor to children's classroom achievement is their capacity to interact comfortably with others, including peers. Research has shown that children who are accepted by their peers look forward more to coming to school, participate more in classroom activities, and achieve more in the classroom compared to children who are low in peer acceptance. By contrast, peer rejection causes children to withdraw from involvement with peers in the classroom, express a desire to avoid school, and perform more poorly on academic achievement measures.

The preschool years and early primary grades are a period of rapid growth in peer interaction skills and the development of friendship. Young children advance from simple activities with one or two classmates to more complex interactions with several other children in play or cooperative tasks. Older preschoolers and kindergarteners also become more adept at the skills that make for smoother peer interaction, including communication, emotional understanding, cooperative strategies (e.g., turn-taking), and conflict resolution. These are important foundational elements for peer relationships in the primary grades, where classroom group size is typically larger and where children are expected to participate actively in group learning tasks. Throughout early primary grades, children enhance their social repertoire with a growing comprehension of fairness in peer interactions, an expanding range of social problem-solving skills, and greater emotional understanding and sensitivity to others.

The sophistication and significance of children's friendships also grows during this period. During the preschool years, friendships become increasingly stable, exclusive, and reciprocal, involving mutual assistance. Older children are also more psychologically aware of the friendships they share, including the mutual obligations that friendship entails. Children typically engage in more sophisticated forms of play with their friends, exhibit greater prosocial behavior, and also experience greater conflict (owing primarily to the frequency of interaction between friends). With increasing age, children become more capable of both maintaining friendships and recovering from conflict.

Interacts with Familiar Adults

Classroom learning requires the ability to interact comfortably with familiar adults as well as with peers. The adults with whom a child interacts can vary in familiarity, of course, ranging from a lead teacher who is present daily to occasional encounters with a custodian, school secretary, or volunteer staff. Not surprisingly, young children interact most comfortably with the adults with whom they are most familiar, and the adults with whom the child interacts most frequently are likely to have the greatest influence on classroom performance. These interactions with nonparental familiar adults contribute to developing social skills as well as to children's learning in the classroom.

Several studies have found that the security and warmth of a preschooler's relationship with the teacher predicts the child's classroom behavior, attention, and social competence in kindergarten and primary grade classrooms. In a similar manner, the quality of the teacher–child relationship in kindergarten and primary grades is important to children's school adjustment and success in the classroom, while conflict in the child–teacher relationship predicts poorer academic performance and greater behavioral problems. Children who develop warm, positive relationships with their teachers are more excited about learning, more positive about coming to school, more self-confident, and achieve more in the classroom. A positive teacher–child relationship may be especially important for young children who are otherwise at risk of academic difficulty because of the support it can provide for their classroom participation and self-confidence.

Developmental changes in young children's interactions with familiar adults are consistent with their developing social and emotional understanding, and also their growing social skills. A preschooler shows growing ease in interacting with familiar adults. Children of this age may show off their accomplishments, seek the adult's assistance, and respond to the adult's initiatives or requests with increasing self-confidence. Older preschoolers are capable of taking greater initiative and they engage in more sustained interactions with an adult, such as participating in an extended conversation about the morning's events in which the child contributes new and relevant information. By primary school, children better understand the roles of the various adults they encounter at school, and they engage these adults in appropriate ways. Interactions with adults are also important sources of approval and affirmation.

Participates in the Group Life of the Class

Beginning in preschool and continuing through primary grades, children are expected to participate in classroom activities in developmentally appropriate ways. This includes understanding and cooperating with the roles and responsibilities of group membership, such as helping to prepare for and clean up after tasks, participating in group activities and projects, knowing what to do during daily routines (such as circle time or recess), managing transitions in classroom activities, complying with teacher requests, and cooperating with other children. Most of these skills require children to take other people's interests into consideration, and this is an important foundation for the social skills required of the classroom. Participating in the group life of the class is an essential component of school success and an integral part of classroom dynamics.

Young children are beginners in these aspects of classroom learning not because they are egocentric, but rather because they are just starting to acquire the component skills required for successful group participation. Fortunately, the preschool years and early primary grades are periods when these component skills develop significantly, as earlier noted. First, developing working memory and event knowledge increasingly enable children to remember the daily routines and the behavior that is expected of them. This allows children to anticipate transitions, know what they must do during daily activities, and plan for later events. Second, growth in self-regulation and, more specifically, in executive functions increasingly enables children to stay on task, apply behavioral expectations to their own conduct, and spontaneously self-correct to maintain compliance. In particular, the growth of inhibition slowly enables children to better focus their attention and thinking on the task at hand (ignoring distractions), manage impulses and emotions, sit still for longer periods without fidgeting, and participate in classroom activities that may require quitting a more preferred activity. Third, developing social and emotional understanding better enables children to comprehend others' perspectives and needs and coordinate them with their own desires, especially as cognitive flexibility develops. This provides the basis for cooperation and compromise when disagreements arise. Fourth, children are also developing morally, which means that their desire to comply with adult requests and obtain adult approval is complemented by the motivation to comply in order to behave consistently with the self-image of a good person who seeks to do the right thing. These internal motivators of responsible conduct are important foundations for group participation.

As these component skills of group participation develop during the preschool years and early primary grades, children become increasingly capable of responsible conduct in the classroom. Moreover, their positive relationships with teachers and other adults throughout this period provide further motivation to cooperate with classroom routines and comply with adult requests.

Begins to Identify Feelings and Responds to those of others

Two of the important social skills relevant to children's interactions in the classroom are the abilities to empathize and to show caring for others. It is important to distinguish these abilities, especially when young children are concerned. Empathy concerns a person's resonant emotional response to another's distress, and it can be observed even in infants and toddlers. Caring concerns a person's efforts to help another person, which may (but not always) derive from empathy. Distinguishing empathy and caring is important because a young child may feel empathy for another's distress but may not be capable or competent enough to respond in a helpful, caring manner. Knowing how to assist a distressed adult or peer is a challenging task for a young child, and thus a helpful response may not necessarily occur, even when the child empathizes with the distressed person. In such a situation, a young child may pay close attention to a distressed peer, for example, but their failure to help may cause an adult observer to regard them as egocentric. They are not necessarily egocentric, but may be constrained by their limited understanding of how to help. With increasing age, children become more reliable helpers when others are distressed.

Developing emotional understanding and empathy are important to children of all ages. Young children who are more competent in understanding others' feelings have been found, for example, to achieve more in elementary school, perhaps because of their more successful peer and adult relationships. Children who are more socially and emotionally perceptive are better playmates and get along better with adults, and this extends from preschool into primary grades. Emotional understanding emerges early in life and develops rapidly in early childhood as young children become capable of accurately identifying others' feelings, understanding the causes and consequences of those feelings, and linking emotions to people's desires, needs, goals, and thoughts. This provides a basis for understanding how to provide assistance to another who is distressed, and this understanding continues to expand as children proceed through primary grades.

Begins to use Simple Strategies to Resolve Conflict

When conflict inevitably arises between children and others (especially peers), social and emotional growth is reflected in their increasing skill at solving social problems flexibly and competently. Doing so requires many of the abilities discussed earlier, including self-regulation (especially executive functions of inhibition and cognitive flexibility), social and emotional understanding, and knowledge of alternative strategies that are likely to be helpful. Each of these abilities grows significantly during the preschool years and the early primary grades. As a consequence, while young preschoolers may not be readily capable of solving peer conflict on their own, but instead require adult assistance, children in the primary grades show greater skill in negotiating, bargaining, compromising, and enlisting other simple problem-solving strategies on their own.

Although the self-regulatory limitations of young children (not egocentrism) help explain their difficulties in resolving social conflict, it is important to recognize also that the complexity of social problem-solving is also challenging to young children. As described by Crick and Dodge, competent solutions to social problems involve several steps, including (a) interpreting social cues from other children or adults (is the person hostile? upset?), (b) formulating social goals for the situation (e.g., escaping a difficult conflict? defending self?), (c) generating alternative problem-solving strategies (e.g., compromise? aggression?), and (d) evaluating the likely consequences of each alternative strategy. When the heightened emotion involved in social conflict is also considered, social problem-solving becomes even more challenging. There is considerable research to indicate that children in the primary grades who have difficulties with peers are often deficient in one or more of these social problem-solving steps, sometimes interpreting social cues in a hostile manner, sometimes formulating limited or inappropriate goals for the situation (e.g., defeating the other person), and often considering an impoverished number of alternative strategies for resolving the conflict. In light of this, the slow growth in social problem-solving skills can be appropriately understood as reflecting the complexity of the process and the knowledge systems that are required to make successful social decisions in situations involving conflict with another person.

Sigmund Freud

According to Freud's psychoanalytic theory, personality develops through a series of stages, each characterized by a certain internal psychological conflict.

Sigmund Freud: Freud developed the psychoanalytic theory of personality development, which argued that personality is formed through conflicts among three fundamental structures of the human mind: the id, ego, and superego.

Sigmund Freud's psychoanalytic theory of personality argues that human behavior is the result of the interactions among three component parts of the mind: the id, ego, and superego. This theory, known as Freud's structural theory of personality, places great emphasis on the role of unconscious psychological conflicts in shaping behavior and personality. Dynamic interactions among these fundamental parts of the mind are thought to progress through five distinct psychosexual stages of development. Over the last century, however, Freud's ideas have since been met with criticism, in part because of his singular focus on sexuality as the main driver of human personality development.

Freud's Structure of the Human Mind

According to Freud, our personality develops from the interactions among what he proposed as the three fundamental structures of the human mind: the id, ego, and superego. Conflicts among these three structures, and our efforts to find balance among what each of them "desires," determines how we behave and approach the world. What balance we strike in any given situation determines how we will resolve the conflict between two overarching behavioral tendencies: our biological aggressive and pleasure-seeking drives vs. our socialized internal control over those drives.

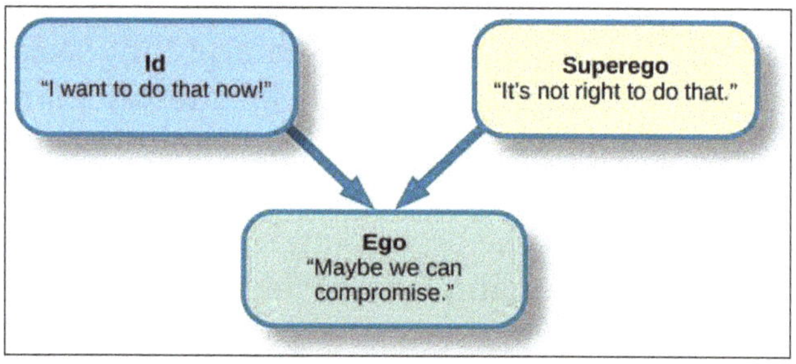

Conflict within the mind: According to Freud, the job of the ego is to balance the aggressive/pleasure-seeking drives of the id with the moral control of the superego.

The Id

The id, the most primitive of the three structures, is concerned with instant gratification of basic physical needs and urges. It operates entirely unconsciously (outside of conscious thought). For example, if your id walked past a stranger eating ice cream, it would most likely take the ice cream for itself. It doesn't know, or care, that it is rude to take something belonging to someone else; it would care only that you wanted the ice cream.

The Superego

The superego is concerned with social rules and morals—similar to what many people call their "conscience" or their "moral compass." It develops as a child learns what their culture considers right and wrong. If your superego walked past the same stranger, it would not take their ice cream because it would know that that would be rude. However, if both your id and your superego were involved, and your id was strong enough to override your superego's concern, you would still take the ice cream, but afterward you would most likely feel guilt and shame over your actions.

The Ego

In contrast to the instinctual id and the moral superego, the ego is the rational, pragmatic part of our personality. It is less primitive than the id and is partly conscious and partly unconscious. It's what Freud considered to be the "self," and its job is to balance the demands of the id and superego in the practical context of reality. So, if you walked past the stranger with ice cream one more time, your ego would mediate the conflict between your id ("I want that ice cream right now") and superego ("It's wrong to take someone else's ice cream") and decide to go buy your own ice cream. While this may mean you have to wait 10 more minutes, which would frustrate your id, your ego decides to make that sacrifice as part of the compromise– satisfying your desire for ice cream while also avoiding an unpleasant social situation and potential feelings of shame.

Freud believed that the id, ego, and superego are in constant conflict and that adult personality and behavior are rooted in the results of these internal struggles throughout childhood. He believed that a person who has a strong ego has a healthy personality and that imbalances in this system can lead to neurosis (what we now think of as anxiety and depression) and unhealthy behaviors.

Psychosexual Stages of Development

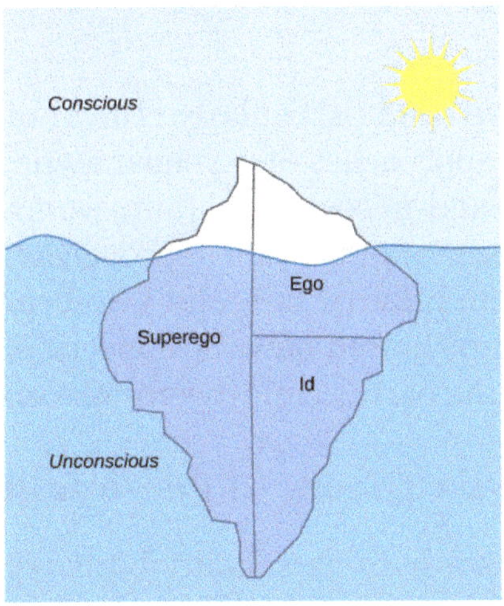

The id, ego, and superego: According to Freud's structural model, the personality is divided into the id, ego, and superego. On this diagram, the smaller portion above the water signifies the conscious mind, while the much larger portion below the water illustrates the unconscious mind.

Freud believed that the nature of the conflicts among the id, ego, and superego change over time as a person grows from child to adult. Specifically, he maintained that these conflicts progress through a series of five basic stages, each with a different focus: oral, anal, phallic, latency, and genital. He called his idea the psychosexual theory of development, with each psychosexual stage directly related to a different physical center of pleasure.

Across these five stages, the child is presented with different conflicts between their biological drives (id) and their social and moral conscience (superego) because their biological pleasure-seeking urges focus on different areas of the body (what Freud called "erogenous zones"). The child's ability to resolve these internal conflicts determines their future ability to cope and function as an adult. Failure to resolve a stage can lead one to become fixated in that stage, leading to unhealthy personality traits; successful resolution of the stages leads to a healthy adult.

Criticism of Freud's Theories

Although Freud's theories have many advantages that helped to expand our psychological understanding of personality, they are not without limits.

Narrow Focus

In his singular emphasis on the structure of the human mind, Freud paid little to no attention to the impact of environment, sociology, or culture. His theories were highly focused on pathology and largely ignored "normal," healthy functioning. He has also been criticized for his myopic view of human sexuality to the exclusion of other important factors.

No Scientific Basis

Many critics point out that Freud's theories are not supported by any empirical (experimental) data. In fact, as researchers began to take a more scientific look at his ideas, they found that several were unable to be supported: in order for a theory to be scientifically valid, it must be possible to disprove ("falsify") it with experimental evidence and many of Freud's notions are not falsifiable.

Misogyny

Feminists and modern critics have been particularly critical of many of Freud's theories, pointing out that the assumptions and approaches of psychoanalytic theory are profoundly patriarchal (male-dominated), anti-feminist, and misogynistic (anti-woman). Karen Horney, a psychologist who followed Freud, saw the mainstream Freudian approach as having a foundation of "masculine narcissism." Feminist Betty Friedan referred to Freud's concept of "penis envy" as a purely social bias typical of the Victorian era and showed how the concept played a key role in discrediting alternative notions of femininity in the early to mid-twentieth century.

Neo-Freudian Psychoanalytic Theory of Personality

Neo-Freudian approaches to the study of personality both expanded on and countered Freud's original theories.

Neo-Freudian Approaches to Personality

Freud and his followers: Several of the psychologists who studied Freud's theories worked directly with Freud himself at Clark University. This photograph shows Carl Jung (front row, right) with Freud (front row, left) and other colleagues.

Although Sigmund Freud contributed a great deal to the field of psychology through his psychoanalytic theory of personality, his work did not go without scrutiny. Many criticized his theories for being overly focused on sexuality; over the years since his work, many other theorists have adapted and built on his ideas to form new theories of personality. These theorists, referred to as Neo-Freudians, generally agreed with Freud that childhood experiences are important, but they lessened his emphasis on sex and sexuality. Instead of taking a strictly biological approach to the development of personality (as Freud did in his focus on individual evolutionary drive), they focused more holistically on how the social environment and culture influence personality development.

Notable Neo-Freudians

Many psychologists, scientists, and philosophers have made meaningful additions to the psychoanalytic study of personality. Four particularly notable Neo-Freudians are Alfred Adler, Erik Erikson, Carl Jung, and Karen Horney.

Alfred Adler

Alfred Adler was the first to explore and develop a comprehensive social theory of the psychodynamic person. He founded a school of psychology called individual psychology, which focuses on our drive to compensate for feelings of inferiority. Adler proposed the concept of the inferiority complex, which describes a person's feelings that they lack worth and don't measure up to the standards of others or of society. He also believed in the importance of social connections, seeing childhood development as emerging through social development rather than via the sexual stages outlined by Freud. From these ideas, Adler identified three fundamental social tasks that all of us must experience: occupational tasks (careers), societal tasks (friendship), and love tasks (finding an intimate partner for a long-term relationship).

Erik Erikson

Erik Erikson is influential for having proposed the psychosocial theory of development, which suggests that an individual's personality develops throughout the lifespan based on a series of social relationships—a departure from Freud's more biology-oriented view. In his psychosocial theory, Erikson emphasized the social relationships that are important at each stage of personality development, in contrast to Freud's emphasis on sex. Erikson identified eight stages, each of which represents a conflict or developmental task. The development of a healthy personality and a sense of competence depend on the successful completion of each task.

Carl Jung

Carl Jung followed in Adler's footsteps by developing a theory of personality called analytical psychology. One of Jung's major contributions was his idea of the collective unconscious, which he deemed a "universal" version of Freud's personal unconscious, holding mental patterns, or memory traces, that are common to all of us (Jung, 1928). These ancestral memories, which Jung called archetypes, are represented by universal themes as expressed through various cultures' literature and art, as well as people's dreams. Jung also proposed the concept of the persona, referring to a kind of "mask" that we adopt based on both our conscious experiences and our collective unconscious. Jung believed this persona served as a compromise between who we really are (our true self) and what society expects us to be; we hide those parts of ourselves that are not aligned with society's expectations behind this mask.

Karen Horney

Karen Horney was one of the first women trained as a Freudian psychoanalyst. Horney's theories focused on "unconscious anxiety," which she believed stemmed from early childhood experiences of unmet needs, loneliness, and isolation. She theorized three styles of coping that children adopt in relation to anxiety: moving toward people, moving away from people, and moving against people.

Horney was also influential in the advancement of feminism within the field of psychodynamics. Freud has been widely critiqued for his almost exclusive focus on men and for what some perceive as a condescension toward women; for example, Horney disagreed with the Freudian idea that girls have "penis envy" and are jealous of male biological features. According to Horney, any jealousy is most likely due to the greater privileges that males are often given, meaning that the differences between men's and women's personalities are due to the dynamics of culture rather than biology. She further suggested that men have "womb envy" because they cannot give birth.

Erik Erikson

Erikson maintained that personality develops in a predetermined order through eight stages of psychosocial development, from infancy to adulthood. During each stage, the person experiences a psychosocial crisis which could have a positive or negative outcome for personality development. For Erikson, these crises are of a psychosocial nature because they involve psychological needs of the individual (i.e., psycho) conflicting with the needs of society (i.e., social).

According to the theory, successful completion of each stage results in a healthy personality and the acquisition of basic virtues. Basic virtues are characteristic strengths which the ego can use to resolve subsequent crises. Failure to successfully complete a stage can result in a reduced ability to complete further stages and therefore a more unhealthy personality and sense of self. These stages, however, can be resolved successfully at a later time.

Stage	Psychosocial Crisis	Basic Virtue	Age
1.	Trust vs. Mistrust	Hope	0 - 1½
2.	Autonomy vs. Shame	Will	1½ - 3
3.	Initiative vs. Guilt	Purpose	3 - 5
4.	Industry vs. Inferiority	Competency	5 - 12
5.	Identity vs. Role Confusion	Fidelity	12 - 18
6.	Intimacy vs. Isolation	Love	18 - 40
7.	Generativity vs. Stagnation	Care	40 - 65
8.	Ego Integrity vs. Despair	Wisdom	65+

Trust vs. Mistrust

Trust vs. mistrust is the first stage in Erik Erikson's theory of psychosocial development. This stage begins at birth continues to approximately 18 months of age. During this stage, the infant is uncertain about the world in which they live, and looks towards their primary caregiver for stability and consistency of care.

If the care the infant receives is consistent, predictable and reliable, they will develop a sense of trust which will carry with them to other relationships, and they will be able to feel secure even when threatened. If these needs are not consistently met, mistrust, suspicion, and anxiety may develop.

If the care has been inconsistent, unpredictable and unreliable, then the infant may develop a sense of mistrust, suspicion, and anxiety. In this situation the infant will not have confidence in the world around them or in their abilities to influence events.

Success in this stage will lead to the virtue of hope. By developing a sense of trust, the infant can have hope that as new crises arise, there is a real possibility that other people will be there as a source of support. Failing to acquire the virtue of hope will lead to the development of fear.This infant will carry the basic sense of mistrust with them to other relationships. It may result in anxiety, heightened insecurities, and an over feeling of mistrust in the world around them.

Consistent with Erikson's views on the importance of trust, research by Bowlby and Ainsworth has outlined how the quality of the early experience of attachment can affect relationships with others in later life.

Autonomy vs. Shame and Doubt

Autonomy versus shame and doubt is the second stage of Erik Erikson's stages of psychosocial development. This stage occurs between the ages of 18 months to approximately 3 years. According to Erikson, children at this stage are focused on developing a sense of personal control over physical skills and a sense of independence. Success in this stage will lead to the virtue of will. If children in this stage are encouraged and supported in their increased independence, they become more confident and secure in their own ability to survive in the world.

If children are criticized, overly controlled, or not given the opportunity to assert themselves, they begin to feel inadequate in their ability to survive, and may then become overly dependent upon others, lack self-esteem, and feel a sense of shame or doubt in their abilities.

What Happens during this Stage?

The child is developing physically and becoming more mobile, and discovering that he or she has many skills and abilities, such as putting on clothes and shoes, playing with toys, etc. Such skills illustrate the child's growing sense of independence and autonomy.

For example, during this stage children begin to assert their independence, by walking away from their mother, picking which toy to play with, and making choices about what they like to wear, to eat, etc.

What can Parents do to Encourage a Sense of Control?

Erikson states it is critical that parents allow their children to explore the limits of their abilities within an encouraging environment which is tolerant of failure.

For example, rather than put on a child's clothes a supportive parent should have the patience to allow the child to try until they succeed or ask for assistance. So, the parents need to encourage the child to become more independent while at the same time protecting the child so that constant failure is avoided.

A delicate balance is required from the parent. They must try not to do everything for the child, but if the child fails at a particular task they must not criticize the child for failures and accidents (particularly when toilet training). The aim has to be "self-control without a loss of self-esteem".

Initiative vs. Guilt

Initiative versus guilt is the third stage of Erik Erikson's theory of psychosocial development. During the initiative versus guilt stage, children assert themselves more frequently.

These are particularly lively, rapid-developing years in a child's life. According to Bee, it is a "time of vigor of action and of behaviors that the parents may see as aggressive."

During this period the primary feature involves the child regularly interacting with other children at school. Central to this stage is play, as it provides children with the opportunity to explore their interpersonal skills through initiating activities. Children begin to plan activities, make up games, and initiate activities with others. If given this opportunity, children develop a sense of initiative and feel secure in their ability to lead others and make decisions.

Conversely, if this tendency is squelched, either through criticism or control, children develop a sense of guilt. The child will often overstep the mark in his forcefulness, and the danger is that the parents will tend to punish the child and restrict his initiatives too much.

It is at this stage that the child will begin to ask many questions as his thirst for knowledge grows. If the parents treat the child's questions as trivial, a nuisance or embarrassing or other aspects of their behavior as threatening then the child may have feelings of guilt for "being a nuisance".

Too much guilt can make the child slow to interact with others and may inhibit their creativity. Some guilt is, of course, necessary; otherwise the child would not know how to exercise self-control or have a conscience.

A healthy balance between initiative and guilt is important. Success in this stage will lead to the virtue of purpose, while failure results in a sense of guilt.

Industry vs. Inferiority

Erikson's fourth psychosocial crisis, involving industry (competence) vs. inferiority occurs during childhood between the ages of five and twelve.

Children are at the stage where they will be learning to read and write, to do sums, to do things on their own. Teachers begin to take an important role in the child's life as they teach the child specific skills. It is at this stage that the child's peer group will gain greater significance and will become a major source of the child's self-esteem. The child now feels the need to win approval by demonstrating specific competencies that are valued by society and begin to develop a sense of pride in their accomplishments.

If children are encouraged and reinforced for their initiative, they begin to feel industrious (competent) and feel confident in their ability to achieve goals. If this initiative is not encouraged, if it is restricted by parents or teacher, then the child begins to feel inferior, doubting his own abilities and therefore may not reach his or her potential.

If the child cannot develop the specific skill they feel society is demanding (e.g., being athletic) then they may develop a sense of inferiority.

Some failure may be necessary so that the child can develop some modesty. Again, a balance between competence and modesty is necessary. Success in this stage will lead to the virtue of competence.

Identity vs. Role Confusion

The fifth stage of Erik Erikson's theory of psychosocial development is identity vs. role confusion, and it occurs during adolescence, from about 12-18 years. During this stage, adolescents search for a sense of self and personal identity, through an intense exploration of personal values, beliefs, and goals. During adolescence, the transition from childhood to adulthood is most important. Children are becoming more independent, and begin to look at the future in terms of career, relationships, families, housing, etc. The individual wants to belong to a society and fit in.

The adolescent mind is essentially a mind or moratorium, a psychosocial stage between childhood and adulthood, and between the morality learned by the child, and the ethics to be developed by the adult.

This is a major stage of development where the child has to learn the roles he will occupy as an adult. It is during this stage that the adolescent will re-examine his identity and try to find out exactly who he or she is. Erikson suggests that two identities are involved: the sexual and the occupational.

According to Bee, what should happen at the end of this stage is "a reintegrated sense of self, of what one wants to do or be, and of one's appropriate sex role". During this stage the body image of the adolescent changes.

Erikson claims that the adolescent may feel uncomfortable about their body for a while until they can adapt and "grow into" the changes. Success in this stage will lead to the virtue of fidelity. Fidelity involves being able to commit one's self to others on the basis of accepting others, even when there may be ideological differences. During this period, they explore possibilities and begin to form their own identity based upon the outcome of their explorations. Failure to establish a sense of identity within society ("I don't know what I want to be when I grow up") can lead to role confusion. Role confusion involves the individual not being sure about themselves or their place in society.

In response to role confusion or identity crisis, an adolescent may begin to experiment with different lifestyles (e.g., work, education or political activities). Also pressuring someone into an identity can result in rebellion in the form of establishing a negative identity, and in addition to this feeling of unhappiness.

Intimacy vs. Isolation

Intimacy versus isolation is the sixth stage of Erik Erikson's theory of psychosocial development. This stage takes place during young adulthood between the ages of approximately 18 to 40 yrs.

During this period, the major conflict centers on forming intimate, loving relationships with other people. During this period, we begin to share ourselves more intimately with others. We explore relationships leading toward longer-term commitments with someone other than a family member.

Successful completion of this stage can result in happy relationships and a sense of commitment, safety, and care within a relationship. Avoiding intimacy, fearing commitment and relationships can lead to isolation, loneliness, and sometimes depression. Success in this stage will lead to the virtue of love.

Generativity vs. Stagnation

Generativity versus stagnation is the seventh of eight stages of Erik Erikson's theory of psychosocial development. This stage takes place during during middle adulthood (ages 40 to 65 yrs). Generativity refers to "making your mark" on the world through creating or nurturing things that will outlast an individual.

People experience a need to create or nurture things that will outlast them, often having mentees or creating positive changes that will benefit other people. We give back to society through raising our children, being productive at work, and becoming involved in community activities and organizations. Through generativity we develop a sense of being a part of the bigger picture.

Success leads to feelings of usefulness and accomplishment, while failure results in shallow involvement in the world.

By failing to find a way to contribute, we become stagnant and feel unproductive. These individuals may feel disconnected or uninvolved with their community and with society as a whole. Success in this stage will lead to the virtue of care.

Ego Integrity vs. Despair

Ego integrity versus despair is the eighth and final stage of Erik Erikson's stage theory of psychosocial development. This stage begins at approximately age 65 and ends at death. It is during this time that we contemplate our accomplishments and can develop integrity if we see ourselves as leading a successful life.

Erikson described ego integrity as "the acceptance of one's one and only life cycle as something that had to be" and later as "a sense of coherence and wholeness".

As we grow older (65+ yrs) and become senior citizens, we tend to slow down our productivity and explore life as a retired person.

Erik Erikson believed if we see our lives as unproductive, feel guilt about our past, or feel that we did not accomplish our life goals, we become dissatisfied with life and develop despair, often leading to depression and hopelessness. Success in this stage will lead to the virtue of wisdom. Wisdom enables a person to look back on their life with a sense of closure and completeness, and also accept death without fear. Wise people are not characterized by a continuous state of ego integrity, but they experience both ego integrity and despair. Thus, late life is characterized by both integrity and despair as alternating states that need to be balanced.

Critical Evaluation

By extending the notion of personality development across the lifespan, Erikson outlines a more realistic perspective of personality development. Based on Erikson's ideas, psychology has reconceptualized the way the later periods of life are viewed. Middle and late adulthood are no longer viewed as irrelevant, because of Erikson, they are now considered active and significant times of personal growth.

Erikson's theory has good face validity. Many people find that they can relate to his theories about various stages of the life cycle through their own experiences. However, Erikson is rather vague about the causes of development. What kinds of experiences must people have to successfully resolve various psychosocial conflicts and move from one stage to another? The theory does not have a universal mechanism for crisis resolution.

Indeed, Erikson acknowledges his theory is more a descriptive overview of human social and emotional development that does not adequately explain how or why this development occurs. For example, Erikson does not explicitly explain how the outcome of one psychosocial stage influences personality at a later stage.

However, Erikson stressed his work was a 'tool to think with rather than a factual analysis.' Its purpose then is to provide a framework within which development can be considered rather than testable theory. One of the strengths of Erikson's theory is its ability to tie together important psychosocial development across the entire lifespan.

Emotional Development

Emotional development is an emergence of the experience, expression, understanding, and regulation of emotions from birth and the growth and change in these capacities throughout childhood, adolescence, and adulthood. The development of emotions occurs in conjunction with neural, cognitive, and behavioral development and emerges within a particular social and cultural context.

Infancy

The expression of emotions during infancy promotes the transition from complete dependency to autonomy. The expression of interest promotes exploration and cognitive development. Social (intentional) smiles and other expressions of joy promote social interaction and healthy attachment relationships with primary caregivers. The expression of sadness encourages empathy and helping behaviour, and the expression of anger signals protest and discomfort. Infants' unique tendency to experience and express particular emotions and the threshold for expressing those emotions is usually referred to as their temperament or characteristic emotionality.

Researchers generally agree that neonatal (non-intentional) smiles are present at birth and that social smiling and emotional expressions of interest appear as early as six weeks of age. By four to five months of age, infants selectively smile at familiar faces and at other infants, and their caregivers begin to share positive emotional exchanges with them.

Researchers disagree in their explanations of the development and time of emergence of discrete negative emotional expressions. Consistently with the view that infant express negative emotions in early infancy, scientists have shown that infants perceive and respond differentially to the negative emotional expressions (e.g., sadness, anger) of others by the age of four months.

During the second six months of life, as infants gain rudimentary cognitive and memory capacities, they begin to express particular emotions based on context. Emotions begin to emerge dynamically as the infant begins to take a more direct role in emotional exchanges with caregivers. The emotional bond with the caregiver is increasingly important, as infants seek support for exploration and look for signals of danger.

Toddlerhood and Early Childhood

During the toddler period, in conjunction with rapid maturation of the frontal lobes and the limbic circuit in the brain, recognition of the self emerges. As a result, the toddler strives to become more independent, and the expression of anger and defiance increases in that struggle for autonomy. The ability to differentiate the self from others also promotes basic empathetic behaviour and moral understanding. By the end of the second year of life, toddlers respond to negative signals from others, and they have specific emotional responses to their own negative actions. The emotions that emerge with a rudimentary conception of the self are often called self-conscious emotions and include shame, embarrassment, guilt, and pride. Some self-conscious emotions, such as pride and guilt, do not emerge until toddlers and young children have learned to conceptualize internalized standards of behaviour.

As children enter preschool, they begin to label their own emotions and rely on discourse about emotions within the family to facilitate their understanding of basic emotions. Young children first distinguish happiness from negative emotions and then begin to distinguish negative emotions such as sadness, anger, and fear from each other. They begin to recognize these emotions in facial expressions, and then, as they enter middle childhood, they begin to understand situational determinants of emotions. An understanding of emotional subjectivity also develops as children learn that what makes one child happy may not make another child feel the same way.

The emergence of emotional self-regulation is particularly important during early childhood and occurs in the context of family and peer relationships. Open expression of positive emotions and warm, supportive relationships between parents and children promote effective emotional self-regulation. On the other hand, frequent expression of negative emotions in the family and harsh, punitive disciplinary responses increase the experience of distressing and dysregulated emotions that may lead to psychopathology. Appropriate peer relationships characterized by shared play activities are also important for the development of emotional regulation during early childhood. Children gain emotional understanding and the capacity for empathetic and helping behaviour from well-regulated emotional exchanges with peers.

Middle and Late Childhood

During middle and late childhood, stable self-concepts based on the child's typical emotional experiences emerge. With the increased capacity for self-reflection, children gain an understanding of their self-conscious emotions. As a result, the consistent experience of patterns of self-conscious emotions has an impact on the child's self-concept. For example, the tendency to experience shame rather than guilt in response to negative transgressions affects the child's emergent self-esteem and may encourage a tendency to respond with aggression or violence.

Also during middle and late childhood, children begin to understand that a single situation or event can lead to the experience of multiple, mixed emotions. For example, older children understand that a goodbye party for a sibling who will leave for college is likely to be both a happy and a sad event for the child and his sibling. This capacity likely emerges with the cognitive capacity to understand multiple aspects of a situation, called decentration.

Children also learn emotional display rules as they progress through middle and late childhood. For example, a child learns to look happy even though she feels upset when a friend or family member gives her an undesirable gift. The use of display rules tends to increase as children begin to consider what consequences their actions may have for others. Display rules are used judiciously, and the likelihood of suppressing negative emotion depends on a number of factors, including the child's gender, the likely recipients of the expression, the specific context, and the child's cultural milieu.

Adolescence

With adolescence comes an additional struggle for autonomy and increased time spent with peers and less time spent with the family. Adolescents become less emotionally dependent on their parents, but this emotional autonomy often emerges after a period of conflict and increased experience of negative emotions. Young adolescents often experience more negative affect than younger children, but the negative affect often decreases during the high school years. However, girls often experience a longer period of elevated negative affect than boys. Adolescents tend to experience more extreme emotions, both negative and positive, than their parents even in response to the same event.

The rise in negative emotional experiences during early adolescence emerges in conjunction with the capacity for abstract thinking. Adolescents often experience emotional distress in response to ambiguous and imagined romantic exchanges, and their capacity to experience complex and diverse emotions further promotes the development of abstract thinking. As adolescents grapple with increasingly abstract and complex social problems, they often seek a stable peer group as the context for emotional management. Positive peer relationships emerge from the recognition of equality and the tendency to offer emotional support. Adolescents who are not accepted by their peers face numerous risks, including school dropout and delinquency. Even adolescents who are accepted by peers and have close friends often show an increase in negative emotions such as anger and anxiety in the peer context during adolescence. Overall, positive and supportive peer relations during adolescence promote healthy emotional development and mental health as the adolescent enters adulthood.

Dating relationships also become prominent during adolescence, but young adolescents may still have difficulty understanding that one person can evoke different and conflicting emotional responses. Therefore, dating during adolescence is often characterized by extreme emotional variability. Dating partners are also prone to experiencing jealousy, particularly when they make errors in determining the intent of their partner's actions.

Identity development is important for adolescents as they approach adulthood. When adolescents or young adults are exploring many identity options, they often have high levels of anxiety but show interest in exploring those options. Adolescents who make an early commitment to a particular identity, usually an identity promoted by their family, have low levels of anxiety and do not experience much conflict in their family relationships. Adolescents who are not exploring identity options tend to have low levels of motivation and often appear bored or apathetic. They have poorer peer relationships and are at greatest risk for mental-health problems during adulthood. Finally, young adults who have achieved a stable sense of identity tend to be more empathetic and are more successful at managing their emotions.

Classroom Applications of Erikson's Theory

According to Erik Erikson's theory of psychosocial development, each individual's psyche is shaped through a series of conflicts called developmental crises. Three of these crises occur during childhood and adolescence, which means that teachers who believe in Erikson's theory should focus on these crises to ensure that students develop healthy, fully realized identities. According to Erikson, the key crisis for children between the ages of three and six is "initiative vs. guilt." From six to twelve, the crisis is "industry vs. inferiority," and for teenagers, "identity vs. role confusion."

Initiative vs. Guilt

Give children the opportunity to make choices and act upon those choices. Because the crisis of initiative vs. guilt determines whether a child learns to plan activities on her own or comes to associate self-directed behavior with punishment, she must have the opportunity to make decisions. Provide a portion of the day when children can choose their own activities. Have a classroom library where children can pick their own books during reading time. This allows children the opportunity to learn how to make decisions for themselves.

Break instruction and activities down into small steps. This makes it easier for children to succeed and encourages them to take risks. Without this framework, children may become frustrated by activities and sense that they are doomed to complete them poorly.

Ensure that any competitive games or activities have well-balanced teams. If children consistently lose at math games, they may believe they are bad at math. Conversely, even a struggling student may feel confident in her mathematical abilities if her team performs well overall.

Accept mistakes that result from students attempting activities on their own. If a student damages something or makes a serious error, show him how to fix, clean or redo it instead of simply punishing him. This will make students feel more confident in their abilities to attempt activities on their own.

Industry vs. Inferiority

Allow students the opportunity to set realistic goals. Have them create academic and personal goals for each quarter and revisit those goals every few weeks to monitor their own progress. Break down each assignment into parts so the students can learn how to set time management goals. For instance, instead of collecting all parts of a project at once, collect a brainstorming worksheet on a certain date, a rough draft two weeks later and a final draft the next week. If a child successfully navigates the crisis of industry vs. inferiority, he will enter adolescence with a sense that hard work and perseverance will pay off. If not, he will feel that he is a helpless observer of his life.

- Assign jobs to the students: Let them stack chairs, feed class pets, hand out and collect papers, take attendance sheets to the office and so on. Rotate these jobs regularly so all students have a chance to participate. This will give the students a sense of accomplishment.
- Teach children study skills: Explain how to budget time and keep notebooks, binders and folders organized. If students fail at these organizational skills, their grades will suffer and they may feel that they are stupid or doomed to failure.

Provide regular feedback to students, particularly those who seem discouraged. Praise them for what they are doing right and give constructive criticism of what they are doing wrong. If your school has a program such as Student of the Month, choose students who have academic or behavioral issues but are making strong efforts at improvement as well as high achievers. This will show them that their efforts are paying off even if they are not making straight A's.

Identity vs. Role Confusion

Provide a variety of positive role models for students. Adolescence is a time of discovering one's own identity. A teenager who successfully navigates the crisis of identity vs. role confusion will be able to answer the question, "Who am I?" with confidence. Provide a series of role models to give students a potential identity model. Teach students about women and minorities who succeeded at a variety of careers, so all students have a role model to whom they can relate. Mention individuals who made lesser-known contributions to your academic discipline. A budding poet may feel more kinship with Eavan Boland than Emily Dickinson.

Provide models of exemplary work so students know what an excellent project looks like and can compare their own work to the model. This will show them how to incorporate academic success into their identities, essentially providing role models for their work instead of their career goals.

Provide opportunities for students to bring their own interests into projects and assessments, as they may feel these interests are vital parts of their identities. Allow students to choose between a variety of final projects -- skits, essays, art projects, music compositions, etc. -- so they can either choose a project that appeals to their interests or explore new aspects of their identities. Criticize behaviors rather than making personal condemnations of the students themselves. Students are "trying on" roles at this point, and negative feedback for a behavior may encourage them to drop it and try another.

Explain the long-term consequences of misbehavior or poor performance so students will know how it affects themselves and others. This may encourage them to adopt a more responsible identity. Encourage and support student interests. Attend school plays, concerts and games to affirm students' identities as actors, musicians and athletes.

Identity Crisis

You have probably heard the term "identity crisis" before and you probably have a fairly good idea of what it means. But where did this idea originate? Why do people experience this kind of personal crisis? Is it something confined to the teenage years? The concept originates in the work of developmental psychologist Erik Erikson, who believed that the formation of identity was one of the most important parts of a person's life. While developing a sense of identity is an important part of the teenage years, Erikson did not believe that the formation and growth of identity were just confined to adolescence. Instead, identity is something that shifts and grows throughout life as people confront new challenges and tackle different experiences.

Are you unsure of your role in life? Do you feel like you don't know the 'real you'? If you answer yes to the previous questions, you may be experiencing an identity crisis. Theorist Erikson coined the term identity crisis and believed that it was one of the most important conflicts people face in development. According to Erikson, an identity crisis is a time of intensive analysis and exploration of different ways of looking at oneself.

Erikson's own interest in identity began in childhood. Raised Jewish, Erikson appeared very Scandinavian and often felt that he was an outsider of both groups. His later studies of cultural life among the Yurok of northern California and the Sioux of South Dakota helped formalize Erikson's ideas about identity development and identity crisis. Erikson described identity as "a subjective sense as well as an observable quality of personal sameness and continuity, paired with some belief in the sameness and continuity of some shared world image. As a quality of unself-conscious living, this can be gloriously obvious in a young person who has found himself as he has found his communality."

Identity Status Theory

Researcher James Marcia has expanded upon Erikson's initial theory. According to Marcia and his colleagues, the balance between identity and confusion lies in making a commitment to an identity.

Marcia also developed an interview method to measure identity as well as four different identity statuses. This method looks at three different areas of functioning: occupational role, beliefs and values, and sexuality.

- Identity achievement occurs when an individual has gone through an exploration of different identities and made a commitment to one.
- Moratorium is the status of a person who is actively involved in exploring different identities but has not made a commitment.
- Foreclosure status is when a person has made a commitment without attempting identity exploration.
- Identity diffusion occurs when there is neither an identity crisis or commitment. Those with a status of identity diffusion tend to feel out of place in the world and don't pursue a sense of identity.

Causes

In Erikson's stages of psychosocial development, the emergence of an identity crisis occurs during the teenage years in which people struggle with feelings of identity versus role confusion.

In today's rapidly changing world, identity crises are more common today than in Erikson's day. These conflicts are certainly not confined to the teenage years.

People tend to experience them at various points throughout life, particularly at points of great change, including:

- Losing or starting a job.
- Beginning a new relationship.
- Ending a marriage or partnership.
- Having a child.
- Losing a loved one.
- Moving.
- Experiencing a traumatic event.
- Learning about a health condition.

Identity crises are also common among people with mental illness, including depression, codependence, bipolar disorder, and borderline personality disorder.

Symptoms

How can you tell if you're having an identity crisis? While we all question who we are from time to time, you may be having an identity crisis if you are going through a big change or stressful time in life and the following questions begin to interfere with your daily life:

- Who am I? This question may be in general, or in regards to your relationships, age, and/or career.
- What are my values?
- What is my role in society or purpose in life?
- What are my spiritual beliefs?
- What am I passionate about?

There's a good reason to overcome an identity crisis. Researchers have found that those who have made a strong commitment to an identity tend to be happier and healthier than those who have not.

Exploring different aspects of yourself in the different areas of life, including your role at work, within the family, and in romantic relationships, can help strengthen your personal identity. Consider looking within to figure out the qualities and characteristics that define you and make you feel grounded and happy as well as your values, interests, passions, and hobbies.

Alienation

Alienation occurs when a person withdraws or becomes isolated from their environment or from other people. People who show symptoms of alienation will often reject loved ones or society. They may also show feelings of distance and estrangement, including from their own emotions.

Alienation is a complex, yet common condition. It's both sociological and psychological, and can affect your health and aggravate existing medical conditions. Treatment involves diagnosing the cause of alienation, and following through with treatment.

Symptoms of Alienation

Feeling distanced from work, family, and friends is a common symptom of alienation. Other symptoms include:

- Feeling helpless.
- Feeling that the world is empty or meaningless.
- Feeling left out of conversations or events.
- Feeling different or separate from everyone else.
- Having difficulty approaching and speaking with others, especially parents.
- Feeling unsafe when interacting with others.
- Refusing to obey rules.

There can also be symptoms of depression that include:

- Having a poor appetite or overeating.
- Sleeping excessively or having insomnia.
- Being fatigued.
- Lacking self-worth.
- Having feelings of hopelessness.

Types of Alienation

Alienation is a complex condition that affects many people. There are six common types.

Type	Definition
Cultural estrangement	Feeling removed from established values
Isolation	Having a sense of loneliness or exclusion, such as being a minority in a group

Meaninglessness	Being unable to see meaning in actions, relationships, or world affairs, or having a sense that life has no purpose
Normlessness	Feeling disconnected from social conventions, or engaging in deviant behavior
Powerlessness	Believing that actions have no effect on outcomes, or that you have no control over your life
Self-estrangement	Being out of touch with yourself in different ways, mostly being unable to form your own identity

Causes of Alienation

Alienation can have many causes, from psychological disorders to social situations.

Health-related Causes

Alienation can be the result of a mental or physical condition. Possible health-related causes of alienation include:

- Mental health disorders, such as anxiety, obsessive compulsive disorder, and schizophrenia.
- Post-traumatic stress disorder (ptsd).
- Self-stigma as a result of mental illness.
- Conditions that cause chronic pain.
- Any conditions that may cause a person to feel singled out or disconnected.

When alienation has health-related causes, there will typically be other symptoms that persist for more than a few days. Talk to a doctor if you're concerned about any symptoms.

Social Causes

Social causes are typically defined by how you, or someone you know, feels disconnected from other people, their environment, or themselves. For example, a change in your environment, like changing jobs or schools, can cause alienation.

Job-related Causes

Work alienation occurs when a person feels estranged from what they produce in the workplace. This disconnection may cause dissatisfaction and a feeling of alienation from:

- The work they do
- Their coworkers
- The environment
- Themselves.

Causes in Adolescents

Alienation is common among teenagers. It can also be a side effect of:

- Attachment to a parent or caregiver in early childhood,
- Big changes in their comfort zone,
- Bullying or peer victimization,
- Growing up.

As children grow, they may begin to distrust adults or the values they were raised with. Teens can often feel isolated from their parents, teachers, and peers. They may feel anxious about their social skills or physical appearance. Teens can even feel isolated from their own identity. This can happen as they discover themselves and think about their future.

Adolescent alienation is only considered a symptom if it accompanies other disorders, such as a phobia or a personality disorder.

Parental Causes

Parental alienation is a term that broadly describes negative, alienating behaviors displayed by a parent, like not being present. Parental alienation syndrome describes a psychiatric disorder in children, particularly in the context of divorce. Sometimes it can be an explanation for a child's refusal to visit a parent.

Rejection of a parent has multiple factors. These can include interactions from both parents and feelings of vulnerability from the child. This is not the same alienation that a child may feel toward a parent who is abusive, particularly if the child severs ties with that parent as an adult.

How is Alienation Treated?

To treat alienation, the cause must be identified. People who experience psychological pain because of alienation may benefit from seeing a mental health professional. Gaining a feeling of empowerment may also help a persons' battle alienation. For adolescents, a sense of purpose is an asset. But searching for that purpose can induce stress. Researchers suggest that parental support can help teens who experience alienation due to feelings of purposelessness.

Research also shows that a strong parent-child relationship can help a child cope with bullying. This is another possible cause of alienation during childhood.

What are the Complications of Alienation?

Feeling alienated can lead to many different social problems that include:

- Drug or alcohol abuse,
- Truancy,
- Criminal activity,

- Poor school or work performance.

Alienation may also increase symptoms of mental and physical disorders that can include:

- Psychological pain, including anger and depression,
- Health effects from drug or alcohol abuse,
- Eating disorders,
- Attempted suicide.

While alienation can increase feelings of powerlessness and estrangement, it's important talk to someone, especially if you've recently had thoughts of suicide. Seek help or advice from a mental healthcare professional if you're concerned about alienation. Alienation may be a symptom of an underlying cause. Sometimes it can be a side effect of a new experience or environment and will pass with time.

It may also help to open up other avenues of support. Talk to your friends and family. You can also show support for someone you know by reaching out and spending time with them. In cases of parental alienation, your next steps may involve counselling sessions.

References

- Psychodynamic-perspectives-on-personality, boundless-psychology: courses.lumenlearning.com, Retrieved 1 February, 2019
- Erik-Erikson: simplypsychology.org, Retrieved 24 June, 2019
- Emotional-development, science: britannica.com, Retrieved 28 August, 2019
- Apply-eriksons-theory-instruction: theclassroom.com, Retrieved 8 April, 2019
- What-is-an-identity-crisis: verywellmind.com, Retrieved 21 January, 2019
- Alienation, health: healthline.com, Retrieved 19 May, 2019

7

Heredity and Learning Needs

The entirety of all biological processes through which particular characteristics are transmitted from parents to their offspring is called heredity, or inheritance. The topics elaborated in this chapter will help in gaining a better perspective about heredity as well as the factors which affect growth and development in children.

Heredity

Behavior is not only influenced by biology through the mechanisms of anatomy and physiology. Heredity also plays a major role in the emergence and control of behavior. The study of heredity, genetics, particularly its subfield behavioural genetics, is crucial in understanding the relationship between heredity and behavior.

Genetics and Psychology

Heredity is defined as the manner in which characteristics and traits are passed on from parents to their offsprings. These traits may include hair color, eye color, height, facial structure and others. Genetic information containing these traits are stored in the nuclei of cells called genes. These genes are found in strands of DNA referred to as chromosomes. Forty-six of these chromosomes are found in each human cell, with the exception of sex cells, which contain only 23 chromosomes each.

Studies under behavioural genetics focus on the genetic factors that influence behavioural traits. These studies mostly have families and twins as subjects. In twin studies, fraternal twins and identical twins are compared to see which traits and behaviors are influenced by their genetic makeup. In family studies, the investigation is centered on the similarities in one or more traits among blood relatives. For instance, there are studies that try to find out the similarities on the occurrence of bipolar disorder among the members of the family.

Genetic Defects

Studies of genetic defects (for example, certain types of developmental disabilities) also provide pertinent information on the effects of heredity/environment upon behavior. Relevant information on the influence of heredity versus behavior on behavior are being gathered from the studies concerning genetic defects. Some genetic defects include phenyketonuria (PKU), Down syndrome and Canavan disease.

Phenylketonuria

PKU is a metabolic disorder that can be inherited. A person with PKU has a gene that makes him unable to process phenylalanine, an essential amino acid. When phenylalanine is left unprocessed, excessive phenylalanine causes interference in the myelin formation in the brain. This results to one or more developmental disabilities.

Down Syndrome

A condition that results from an excess 21st chromosome, Down syndrome is a defect that can be passed on from parent to offspring. People who has Down syndrome experience on or more developmental disabilities, and also have characteristic physical features.

Canavan Disease

Another genetic disorder is Canavan disease, which results from the gradual degeneration of nerve cells in the brain. There is damage to the myelin, a layer that serves as insulators of neural axons. Symptoms of Canavan disease include mental retardation from infancy, feeding problems and loss of motor skills that were acquired from infancy to childhood.

Genes Influence Child Development

What determines how a child develops? While it is impossible to account for each and every influence that contributes to who a child eventually becomes, what researchers can do is look at some of the most apparent factors. These include things such as genetics, parenting, experiences, friends, family, education, and relationships. By understanding the role that these factors play, researchers are better able to identify how such influences contribute to development.

Think of these influences as building blocks. While most people tend to have the same basic building blocks, these components can be put together in an infinite number of ways. Consider your own overall personality. How much of whom you are today was shaped by your genetic background, and how much is a result of your lifetime of experiences?

This question has puzzled philosophers, psychologists, and educators for hundreds of years and is frequently referred to as the nature versus nurture debate. Are we the result of nature (our genetic background) or nurture (our environment)? Today, most researchers agree that child development involves a complex interaction of both nature and nurture.

While some aspects of development may be strongly influenced by biology, environmental influences may also play a role. For example, the timing of when the onset of puberty occurs is largely the results of heredity, but environmental factors such as nutrition can also have an effect.

From the earliest moments of life, the interaction of heredity and the environment works to shape who children are and who they will become. While the genetic instructions a child inherits from his parents may set out a road map for development, the environment can impact how these directions are expressed, shaped or event silenced. The complex interaction of nature and nurture does not just occur at certain moments or at certain periods of time; it is persistent and lifelong.

Earliest Period of Child Development

At its very beginning, the development of a child starts when the male reproductive cell, or sperm, penetrates the protective outer membrane of the female reproductive cell, or ovum. The sperm and ovum each contain chromosomes that act as a blueprint for human life.

The genes contained in these chromosomes are made up of a chemical structure known as DNA (deoxyribonucleic acid) that contains the genetic code, or instructions, that make up all life. Except for the sperm and ova, all cells in the body contain 46 chromosomes. As you might guess, the sperm and ova each contains only contain 23 chromosomes. This ensures that when the two cells meet, the resulting new organism has the correct 46 chromosomes.

Environment Influences Gene Expression

So how exactly do the genetic instructions passed down from both parent influence how a child develops and the traits they will have? In order to fully understand this, it is important to first distinguish between a child's genetic inheritance and the actual expression of those genes.

A genotype refers to all of the genes that a person has inherited. A phenotype is how these genes are actually expressed. The phenotype can include physical traits, such as height and color or the eyes, as well as nonphysical traits such as shyness and extroversion.

While your genotype may represent a blueprint for how children grow up, the way that these building blocks are put together determines how these genes will be expressed. Think of it as a bit like building a house. The same blueprint can result in a range of different homes that look quite similar but have important differences based on the material and color choices used during construction.

Factors that Influence how Genes are Expressed

Whether or not a gene is expressed depends on two different things: the interaction of the gene with other genes and the continual interaction between the genotype and the environment.

- Genetic Interactions: Genes can sometimes contain conflicting information, and in most cases, one gene will win the battle for dominance. Some genes act in an additive way. For example, if a child has one tall parent and one short parent, the child may end up splitting the difference by being of average height. In other cases, some genes follow a dominant-recessive pattern. Eye color is one example of dominant-recessive genes at work. The gene for brown eyes is dominant and the gene for blue eyes is recessive. If one parent hands down a dominant brown eye gene while the other parent hands down a recessive blue eye gene, the dominant gene will win out and the child will have brown eyes.
- Gene-Environment Interactions: The environment a child is exposed to both in utero and throughout the rest of his or her life can also impact how genes are expressed. For example, exposure to harmful drugs while in utero can have a dramatic impact on later child development. Height is a good example of a genetic trait that can be influenced by environmental factors. While a child's genetic code may provide instructions for tallness, the expression of this height might be suppressed if the child has poor nutrition or chronic illness.

Genetic Abnormalities

Genetic instructions are not infallible and can go off track at times. Sometimes when a sperm or ovum is formed, the number of chromosomes may divide unevenly, causing the organism to have more or less than the normal 23 chromosomes. When one of these abnormal cells joins with a normal cell, the resulting zygote will have an uneven number of chromosomes.

Researchers suggest that as many as half of all zygotes that form have more or less than 23 chromosomes, but most of these are spontaneously aborted and never develop into a full-term baby. In some cases, babies are born with an abnormal number of chromosomes. In every case, the result is some type of syndrome with a set of distinguishing characteristics.

Abnormalities of the Sex Chromosomes

The vast majority of newborns, both boys and girls, have at least one X chromosome. In some cases, about 1 in every 500 births, children are born with either a missing X chromosome or an additional sex chromosome. Klinefelter syndrome, Fragile X syndrome, and Turner syndrome are all examples of abnormalities involving the sex chromosomes.

Kleinfelter's syndrome is caused by an extra X chromosome and is characterized by a lack of development of the secondary sex characteristics and as well as learning disabilities. Fragile X syndrome is caused when part of the X chromosome is attached to the other chromosomes by such a thin string of molecules that it seems in danger of breaking off. It can affect both males and females, but the impact can vary. Some with Fragile X show few if any signs, while others develop mild to severe mental retardation.

Turner syndrome occurs when only one sex chromosome (the X chromosome) is present. It affects only females and can result in short stature, a "webbed" neck and a lack of secondary sex characteristics. Psychological impairments associated with Turner syndrome include learning disabilities and difficulty recognizing emotions conveyed through facial expressions.

Down Syndrome

The most common type of chromosomal disorder is known as trisomy 21, or Down syndrome. In this case, the child has three chromosomes at the site of the 21st chromosomes instead of the normal two.

Down syndrome is characterized by facial characteristics including a round face, slanted eyes, and a thick tongue. Individuals with Down syndrome may also face other physical problems including heart defects and hearing problems. Nearly all individuals with Down syndrome experience some type of intellectual impairment, but the exact severity can vary dramatically.

Effects of Heredity and Environment

Every individual on this earth is different from the other. No one person is fully like other person. Every person differs from the other, either physically or psychologically. Even the twins are no exception to this. They differ in some aspects or other. Particularly when we look at people from psychological point of view these differences are quite obvious. In many instances even the children differ from their parents.

They will have some similarities with some forefathers or grandparents instead of their parents.

What makes these differences to exist? What are the causes? The answer to these queries can be traced from two factors, viz. heredity and environment.

The basic sources of personality development are heredity and environment.

Heredity

Heredity refers to the genetic inheritance received by every individual at the time of conception. The origin of every human life can be traced to a single cell called zygote. It is formed by the union of sperm and ovum.

The sperm and ovum will contain 23 pairs of chromosomes out of which one will be sex determining chromosome. Female will have 23 pairs of XX chromosomes. Male will have 22 pairs of XX and 2 single, represented as XY. X chromosome from mother and Y chromosome from father will lead to male offspring, XX from both parents give rise to female. In each chromosome there are innumerable genes.

These genes are the real determiners of hereditary characteristics—which pass on from one generation to the other. At the time of conception, the genes from chromosomes of both the father and the mother fuse together and determine the traits of the offspring to be born.

The physical characteristics such as height, weight, colour of eye and skin, social and intellectual behaviour are determined by heredity. Differences in these characteristics are due to the change in the genes transmitted. Fraternal twins also differ from each other, because they are born out of different genes. However, we find more resemblances in identical twins because they are born out of monozygotic.

Environment

In simple terms environment means the society, the fields of society and even the whole world. But here, the word environment is restricted to mean the environment within mother's womb and just born, as well as the environment around the individual. Like heredity, environment also has been found to play a very important role in determining the behaviour and personality development of an individual. The environmental influences are those which act upon the organism at the earlier stages of development, i.e., before and also after birth.

Environment includes all the extrinsic forces, influences and conditions which affect the life, nature, behaviour, the growth, development and maturation of living organism (Douglass and Holland).

Hence, we can say that environment means all that is found around the individual. The zygote is surrounded by a jelly like substance known as 'cytoplasm'. The cytoplasm is an intracellular environment which influences the development. Though the life begins with single cell, in the process of cell division several new cells are formed and a new internal environment comes into existence.

As the fetus develops the endocrine glands are formed. The hormonal secretion by these glands gives rise to another intracellular environment. Hormones are necessary for normal development, but defects in hormone secretion like over or under secretion may lead to congenital deformities.

The growing embryo is surrounded by amniotic fluid in the uterus which creates another environment. This fluid will provide the necessary warmth and protection against the dangers due to organisms and other chemical effects on fetus.

The fetus is also connected to the mother by the umbilical cord, through which the nourishment is supplied. Sufficient nourishment is necessary from the mother. Otherwise the child will suffer from malnutrition. The defects in mother like drug or alcohol addiction, smoking, malnutrition, diabetes, endocrinal disturbances, small uterus and such other problems cause many problems in child. The psychological state of mother like over excitement, depression also may cause damaging effect on the child.

After nine months, the child is born and enters a new environment which is entirely different. A new life begins in a new environment. This new environment will have a different culture, ideology, values, etc. The home atmosphere, parental love and affection, association with sibling, neighbours, peers, teachers, etc. will create an entirely different and new atmosphere. This is called social environment. All the social factors stated above shape the personality of the child.

There is a long standing controversy regarding the importance of heredity and environment. Supporters of heredity say that the environment cannot change a dog into a goat. On the other hand, the environmentalists are of the opinion that for the development of a plant only seed is not important but also environment like sunlight, manure, water, etc.

Innumerable studies have been conducted on both sides. However, the results indicate that heredity and environment are interdependent forces. Whatever the heredity supplies, the favourable environment brings it out. Personality characteristics attained by heredity are shaped by environment.

Factors that affect Growth and Development in Children

Although the terms growth and development are used synonymously, they have different meanings biologically. Growth refers to the incremental changes in physical characteristics such as height, weight, size, etc., while development refers to qualitative changes to growth in an orderly and meaningful fashion which results in maturity. Growth and development contribute to each other, are inseparable, and occur simultaneously. For example, most babies, by the time they grow up to be 8 months old, can weigh around 8 to 10 kilograms and can sit up.

10 Factors that Influence the Growth and Development of a Child

Nature and nurture both contribute to the growth and development of children. Although what's endowed by nature is constant, nurture tends to make a big difference too. Here are a few factors affecting children's growth and development.

Heredity

Heredity is the transmission of physical characteristics from parents to children through their genes. It influences all aspects of physical appearance such as height, weight, body structure, the colour of the eye, the texture of the hair, and even intelligence and aptitudes. Diseases and conditions such as heart disease, diabetes, obesity, etc., can also be passed through genes, thereby affecting the growth and development of the child adversely. However, environmental factors and nurturing can bring the best out of the already present qualities in the genes.

Environment

The environment plays a critical role in the development of children and it represents the sum total of physical and psychological stimulation the child receives. Some of the environmental factors influencing early childhood development involve the physical surroundings and geographical conditions of the place the child lives in, as well his social environment and relationships with family and peers. It is easy to understand that a well-nurtured child does better than a deprived one; the environment children are constantly immersed in contributes to this. A good school and a loving family builds in children strong social and interpersonal skills, which will enable them to excel in other areas such as academics and extracurricular activities. This will, of course, be different for children who are raised in stressful environments.

Sex

The sex of the child is another major factor affecting the physical growth and development of a child. Boys and girls grow in different ways, especially nearing puberty. Boys tend to be taller and physically stronger than girls. However, girls tend to mature faster during adolescence, while boys mature over a longer period of time. The physical structure of their bodies also has differences which make boys more athletic and suited for activities that require physical rigour. Their temperaments also vary, making them show interest in different things.

Exercise and Health

The word exercise here does not mean physical exercise as a discipline or children deliberately engaging in physical activities knowing it would help them grow. Exercise here refers to the normal play time and sports activities which help the body gain an increase in muscular strength and put on bone mass. Proper exercise helps children grow well and reach milestones on time or sooner. Exercise also keeps them healthy and fights off diseases by strengthening the immune system, especially if they play outside. This is because outdoor play exposes them to microbes that help them build resistance and prevent allergies.

Hormones

Hormones belong to the endocrine system and influence the various functions of our bodies. They are produced by different glands that are situated in specific parts of the body to secrete hormones that control body functions. Their timely functioning is critical for normal physical growth and development in children. Imbalances in the functioning of hormone-secreting glands can result in growth defects, obesity, behavioural problems and other diseases. During puberty, the gonads produce sex hormones which control the development of the sex organs and the appearance of secondary sexual characteristics in boys and girls.

Nutrition

Nutrition is a critical factor in growth as everything the body needs to build and repair itself comes from the food we eat. Malnutrition can cause deficiency diseases that adversely affect the growth and development of children. On the other hand, overeating can lead to obesity and health problems in the long run, such as diabetes and heart disease. A balanced diet that is rich in vitamins, minerals, proteins, carbohydrates and fats is essential for the development of the brain and body.

Familial Influence

Families have the most profound impact in nurturing a child and determining the ways in which they develop psychologically and socially. Whether they are raised by their parents, grandparents or foster care, they need basic love, care and courtesy to develop as healthy functional individuals. The most positive growth is seen when families invest time, energy and love in the development of the child through activities, such as reading to them, playing with them and having deep meaningful conversations. Families that abuse or neglect children would affect their positive development. These children may end up as individuals who have poor social skills and difficulty bonding with other people as adults. Helicopter parenting also has negative effects as they render children dependent on the parent even as young adults and unable to deal with difficulties in life on their own.

Geographical Influences

Where you live also has a great influence on how your children turn out to be. The schools they attend, the neighbourhood they live in, the opportunities offered by the community and their peer circles are some of the social factors affecting a child's development. Living in an enriching community that has parks, libraries and community centres for group activities and sports all play a role in developing the child's skills, talents, and behaviour. Uninteresting communities can push some children to not go outside often but play video games at home instead. Even the weather of a place influences children in the form of bodily rhythms, allergies and other health conditions.

Socio-Economic Status

The socio-economic status of a family determines the quality of the opportunity a child gets. Studying in better schools that are more expensive definitely has benefits in the long run. Well-off families can also offer better learning resources for their children and they afford special aid if the kids need it. Children from poorer families may not have access to educational resources and good nutrition to reach their full potential. They may also have working parents who work too many hours and cannot invest enough quality time in their development.

Learning and Reinforcement

Learning involves much more than schooling. It is also concerned with building the child up mentally, intellectually, emotionally, and socially so they operate as healthy functional individuals in the society. This is where the development of the mind takes place and the child can gain some maturity. Reinforcement is a component of learning where an activity or exercise is repeated and refined to solidify the lessons learned. An example is playing a musical instrument; they get better at playing it as they practice playing the instrument. Therefore, any lesson that is taught has to be repeated until the right results are obtained.

Although nature contributes much to the growth and development of children, nurture contributes much more. As mentioned earlier, some of these factors may not be controllable, and you'll have to make do with what you have. But there are certain things you can definitely ensure for your child. This includes ensuring that your child gets enough rest every day, because his development is heavily dependent on the amount of sleep he gets. Pay close attention to your child's nutritional and exercise levels, as these too play an important role in promoting your child's timely and healthy growth and development.

References

- Heredity: explorable.com, Retrieved 2 March, 2019
- Genes-and-development: verywellmind.com, Retrieved 14 June, 2019
- Effects-of-heredity-and-environment-on-our-personality: psychologydiscussion.net, Retrieved 8 February, 2019
- Factors-that-affect-growth-and-development-in-children: parenting.firstcry.com, Retrieved 18 April, 2019

Permissions

All chapters in this book are published with permission under the Creative Commons Attribution Share Alike License or equivalent. Every chapter published in this book has been scrutinized by our experts. Their significance has been extensively debated. The topics covered herein carry significant information for a comprehensive understanding. They may even be implemented as practical applications or may be referred to as a beginning point for further studies.

We would like to thank the editorial team for lending their expertise to make the book truly unique. They have played a crucial role in the development of this book. Without their invaluable contributions this book wouldn't have been possible. They have made vital efforts to compile up to date information on the varied aspects of this subject to make this book a valuable addition to the collection of many professionals and students.

This book was conceptualized with the vision of imparting up-to-date and integrated information in this field. To ensure the same, a matchless editorial board was set up. Every individual on the board went through rigorous rounds of assessment to prove their worth. After which they invested a large part of their time researching and compiling the most relevant data for our readers.

The editorial board has been involved in producing this book since its inception. They have spent rigorous hours researching and exploring the diverse topics which have resulted in the successful publishing of this book. They have passed on their knowledge of decades through this book. To expedite this challenging task, the publisher supported the team at every step. A small team of assistant editors was also appointed to further simplify the editing procedure and attain best results for the readers.

Apart from the editorial board, the designing team has also invested a significant amount of their time in understanding the subject and creating the most relevant covers. They scrutinized every image to scout for the most suitable representation of the subject and create an appropriate cover for the book.

The publishing team has been an ardent support to the editorial, designing and production team. Their endless efforts to recruit the best for this project, has resulted in the accomplishment of this book. They are a veteran in the field of academics and their pool of knowledge is as vast as their experience in printing. Their expertise and guidance has proved useful at every step. Their uncompromising quality standards have made this book an exceptional effort. Their encouragement from time to time has been an inspiration for everyone.

The publisher and the editorial board hope that this book will prove to be a valuable piece of knowledge for students, practitioners and scholars across the globe.

Index

CPSIA information can be obtained
at www.ICGtesting.com
Printed in the USA
LVHW062016100122
708212LV00002B/267